I0025128

Staging Nationalism

Staging Nationalism

Essays on Theatre and National Identity

Edited by KIKI GOUNARIDOU

McFarland & Company, Inc., Publishers

Jefferson, North Carolina, and London

Library of Congress Cataloguing-in-Publication Data

Staging nationalism : essays on theatre and national identity / edited
by Kiki Gounaridou.
    p.   cm.
    Includes bibliographical references and index.

    ISBN 0-7864-2204-1 (softcover : 50# alkaline paper) ∞

    1. Theater and state.   2. Nationalism.
I. Gounaridou, Kiki.
PN2042.S72   2005
792 — dc22   2005007322

British Library cataloguing data are available

©2005 Kiki Gounaridou. All rights reserved

*No part of this book may be reproduced or transmitted in any form
or by any means, electronic or mechanical, including photocopying
or recording, or by any information storage and retrieval system,
without permission in writing from the publisher.*

Cover photograph: ©2005 Rubberball Productions.

Manufactured in the United States of America

*McFarland & Company, Inc., Publishers
  Box 611, Jefferson, North Carolina 28640
  www.mcfarlandpub.com*

For Joel

Table of Contents

Theatre and Nationalism: Introductory Remarks and Acknowledgments

Kiki Gounaridou

When a nation seeks to be reconnected with a sense of national identity, its cultural celebrations often express nostalgia for a past that defines a cultural high point in its history. This was the premise on which the seminar on "Composing National Identity Through the (Re)construction of National Culture" was based, during the 2002 American Society for Theatre Research (ASTR) Conference in Philadelphia. The seminar essays mainly addressed the use of theatre in the construction of national cultural identity. The participants discussed the relationship between political power and the construction or subversion of cultural identity, and explored the ways in which nations create a "neo-classical" culture in order to construct a new version of their national cultural identity. Moreover, as the description of the seminar topic suggested, "While this cultural 'neo-classicism' seeks to create an overall feeling of ... national identity, rarely is the classical culture presented in all its complexities."[1]

My own interest in the relationship between theatre and nationalism dates back to 1997, when Matthias Langhoff's direction of Euripides' *The Bacchae* for the National Theatre of Northern Greece was followed by serious critical controversy. My ASTR seminar essay, which I am not including in this volume, discussed this example of both construction and subversion of national cultural identity through the performance of *The Bacchae*.[2] A brief account of this production, because of its controversial nature, will provide a useful point of departure for these introductory remarks.

The National Theatre of Northern Greece and several other state-subsidized theatre companies understand the continuing connection of contemporary audiences to ancient Greek plays, both tragedies and comedies, as part of their cultural mission. Every summer there are performances of plays by Aeschylus, Sophocles, Euripides, and Aristophanes in the Hellenistic open theatre of Epidaurus, as well as in several other open-air venues. *The Bacchae* was performed in Epidaurus in the summer of 1997 and then again in the fall of 1997, during the Sixth Festival of the Union of the Theatres of Europe. The production caused a remarkable controversy among theatre audiences and critics on the subject of Greek national cultural identity, on the role of tragic performance in the formation of this identity, and on the ways in which Langhoff's production of *The Bacchae* exposed the relationship between performance and identity in contemporary Greek culture.

After the premiere of *The Bacchae*, the newspaper reviewers and the audiences, as well as the general public, became part of the controversy, one of the most noteworthy in recent Greek theatre history. First and foremost, it reflected the dramatic changes in contemporary Greek society during the last decade, as different ethnic and racial groups, mainly from Africa, Eastern Europe, and the Middle East, penetrated a relatively homogeneous population, both culturally and linguistically. Similar issues of immigration have been haunting most of the European countries in the last ten years. In Greece, the results of this penetration manifested themselves not only in terms of the social changes that they precipitated, but also in terms of the changes in the unspoken regulations that governed the production of art, including theatre, in Greek society. The work of a few directors, actors, and designers started exploring the implications of the new interculturalism, as well as the cultural differences that already existed in Greek society before the "invasion" of the last ten years.

In *The Bacchae*, Matthias Langhoff's directorial reversals took up several of the above issues and worked on three different levels:

(a) First, as cultural critique of contemporary Greek society through the questioning of the ancient myth; this was mainly manifested in the chorus of women, all dressed in bright-colored inexpensive dresses and shoes, and occupied with everyday housekeeping activities and with reading popular magazines and singing pop tunes. Later on, the women took their places on the swings stage left which were part of a slaughterhouse — in fact, raw meat hung from them in the previous scene — thus pointing out the social, economic, and cultural space that they occupy as women. To complete this picture were a huge bulletin board advertising bottled water, a television antenna on top of a roof, a telephone, halogen lamps, a radio broadcasting a soccer game, and Cadmus singing popular tunes and drinking the traditional Greek coffee. Last, but not least, Langhoff included in this eclectic mix elements of European and American popular culture: Hollywood movies, television (and more specifically *Star Trek* "Klingon"–looking characters), and apocalyptic images were strikingly evident during Dionysus' last speech. Dionysus delivered the speech from high up, behind the bulletin board that advertised bottled water, while a bright light shined from his direction toward the actors on stage. In turn, the actors looked up toward the light, shading their eyes with their hands, a familiar movie and television image for people's "encounters" with UFOs.

(b) On a second level of reversals, the production was a linguistic comment on a racially mixed society in which communication is not a given anymore. For example, some of the characters spoke in dialect; the Servant spoke his monologue in the Pontiaki dialect. (Pontiaki, interestingly enough, has common features with the syntactical and grammatical constructions of Ancient Greek. It was the dialect spoken by the Greeks of the South Black Sea, who lived there for about 25 centuries, before they had to leave in the 1920s, in accordance with the international treaties after World War One.) But the most shocking moment of the play, in terms of linguistic commentary, was Agave's entrance. The French actress Evelyne Didi, blond and tall in a short, shiny red dress and red high-heel shoes, entered the stage and started to speak Greek with a thick French accent. This was also the moment when the contemporary Greek audiences started to loudly register their disagreement with Langhoff's choices. Reportedly, Evelyne Didi, after the opening performance, cried for hours because of the audience's yelling and booing during her monologue.

(c) Lastly, on a third level of reversals, the production functioned as a self-conscious theatrical construct, which not only mirrored cultural and linguistic attitudes but also mirrored itself. Among the many devices that furthered this direction, the most captivating one was the use of animals and small children on stage. The unpredictability of their moves, especially those of the animals, made it a fascinating experience to watch, as a big white horse came out of a red velvet room, furnished with armchairs and chandeliers, and paraded across the stage with Pentheus in a white dress, riding to his doom, or as the Messenger fed a live baby lamb, while he delivered his emotional speech describing the destruction and death of Pentheus. During the earthquake scene, the chorus walked down to the orchestra, among the audience, and tried to communicate with the audience, while the world of the play, as well as the play itself, were becoming more and more unstable. Small objects were occasionally and unpredictably falling off the stage and into the pit for the duration of the performance, underlining the instability and unpredictability of the theatrical event. Another self-conscious moment, immersed in its own theatricality, was the final dialogue between Cadmus and Agave, which was sung by the actors in the style of light opera or operetta. The performance ended with African drummers playing a loud, fast, ecstatic, and, by all accounts, Dionysiac tune.

The main argument in the controversy that followed the performance of Langhoff's *The Bacchae* was "We [Greeks] don't need any Germans [Matthias Langhoff was born in Zurich of German parents] to tell us who we are and what we are about." This was countered with "This is the clearest picture of our cultural identity as Greeks that we've ever seen on the stage of a theatre." Here is a brief selective sample of the critics' reactions, both pro and con: "...not only a laughing tragedy but a musical tragedy as well ... the ridiculous swallowed the tragic"; "If Langhoff intended to shake up conventional theatre and the theatrical establishment, he certainly succeeded"; "Langhoff's production was a slap in the face of Greek society. Half of the audience, nervous at first, shocked later, started booing the performance, while the other half were cheering enthusiastically"; "Langhoff showed a shameful disrespect toward Euripides"; and lastly, Eleni Varopoulou, one of the most respected Greek theatre critics, wrote in the newspaper *To Vima*, "Ancient drama is a cultural treasure without ownership titles. It belongs to the whole world in order to be studied and used by all people, who, depending on their needs, will demolish it and rebuild it, will confront it and clash with it."[3] Thus Langhoff, a foreigner in Greece, became a participant in this experience, as both the director and the scapegoat, both Dionysus and Pentheus, and significantly directed *The Bacchae* against the myth of unified national cultural identity in contemporary Greek society.

This example of Langhoff's *The Bacchae* is the most recent viv-à-vis the ten essays in this volume, which represent a wide global and historical perspective. They cover a large geographical range, from Western and Eastern Europe to North and Central America to North Africa and East Asia, and their chronological range, according to which they have been roughly arranged here, is also varied. Recent bibliography on theatre and nationalism includes, among several others, *Performing America: Cultural Nationalism in American Theater*, edited by Jeffrey Mason and J. Ellen Gainor. *Performing America* suggests that the boundaries of the cultures and communities that constitute the United States are unstable and under constant renegotiation in American theatre and drama. The May 1996 issue of the *Performing Arts Journal* is also dedicated to nationalism, with special emphasis on theatre in the disintegrating former Yugoslavia. S.E. Wilmer's (one of the contributors to this volume) book *Theatre, Society, and the Nation: Staging*

American Identities discusses the changing identity of American theatre, from the nation's independence from British rule in the eighteenth century to the multiculturalism of the American stage in the 1990s. In addition, a number of journal articles and books, narrower in scope, focus on specific problems associated with theatre and nationalism in different countries and historical periods, and discuss both the fashioning and questioning of nationhood and national identity.

This volume enhances and intensifies the discourse on theatre and nationalism from the point of view of different countries, distinct historical periods, and diverse cultures. The first essay is Natalya Baldyga's "Reconstructing the Nation: Conflicting Cultural Imaginaries in Eighteenth-Century Poland." Baldyga proposes that, at the end of the eighteenth century, in the case of the Polish-Lithuanian Commonwealth, conflicting efforts to retain or reshape a coherent cultural identity gained paramount importance as the political borders of the state were erased through its three partitions by Austria, Prussia, and Russia. Theatre staged in Poland during the time of the partitions revealed multiple and differing efforts to reconstitute the identity of those among the Polish nobility, known as *szlachta*, who clung to an imagined classical heritage known as Sarmatism. Sarmatism was an ideology that originated in the sixteenth century claiming that the *szlachta* were not actually Slavs, but had descended from the Sarmatians, an eastern warrior tribe that conquered territory around the Black Sea in the fifth century BCE. This ideology became the cornerstone of noble identity and led to the belief that to be a Pole meant to be one of the *szlachta*. The arts were very much a part of this reform campaign. *The Return of the Deputy* by Julian Ursyn Niemcewicz explores the nature of Polish nationality through the representation of new Polish types.

Scott Magelssen's "Celebrating the Revolution While the King Is Still on the Throne: *The Fall of the Bastille* and the Festival of Federation (July 1790)," examines *The Fall of the Bastille* and the Festival of Federation within the context of emergent festival practices during the French Revolution and explores the ways these events operated within the revolutionary discourse. *The Fall of the Bastille* and the subsequent Festival were not intended to be mirror representations of the events they commemorated. They indicated, however, a pivotal threshold of theatre history and the French Revolution, in that these were representations of the events of the revolution while the king was still in power. Thus, the performances were not necessarily intended as propagandistic affirmations of a new regime, as were later festivals celebrating the revolution. Rather, they were careful articulations for specific purposes: (a) to construct a network of symbols designed to give meaning to the recent events of the Revolution; (b) to affirm the moral injunctions of

Jean-Jacques Rousseau in his *Lettre à d'Alembert,* advocating non-representational communal festival-spectacle-entertainment; and (c) to rein in the
citizens' anxieties surrounding split loyalties to the revolution and the
king.

In "Athenian Preamble to an American Theatre," Gary Jay Williams
suggests that, with the building of new theatres, the first generation of Americans to come of age after the American Revolution found an occasion for
representing a vision of a vital American theatre that would rise with the
development of the new nation. For the openings of new theatres in city
after city, public competitions were conducted to which civic-minded citizens were invited to offer poetic prologues. Drawing on over two hundred
prologues, this paper shows how these prologues often offered a construction of the classical past as precedent for the new American theatre. As neo-
classical in poetic style as the theatres they dedicated were in architectural
style, the prologues are in the classical epideictic tradition: oratorical pieces
written to be declaimed. Their classical allusions, poetic language, and decla-
mation signified the high, civic order of these occasions and the consecra-
tion of these new theatres to the formation of America.

In "Herder and European Theatre," S.E. Wilmer presents a view of
eighteenth-century German intellectuals fostering a Romantic belief in the
importance of the cultural traditions of the common people. Johann Gottfried von Herder encouraged German-speaking people to take pride in their
own cultural past, their native languages, and their peasant culture, which,
he argued, had remained untainted. Herder believed in national distinctiveness and encouraged all nations to express themselves in their own individual ways. Herder's ideas impelled intellectuals in countries throughout
Europe to search for unique aspects of cultural expression among their own
peoples that would testify to separate and distinct identities. In seeking to
formulate their own notion of what tied their people together and made
them unique, cultural nationalists to some extent reinvented the past, often
writing ancient national histories that came to justify the creation of separate nation-states. Wilmer examines the development of German Romanticism and nationalism, and their effects on national theatres in Europe.

David Pellegrini's "Historical Avant-Garde Performance and Japanese
Nationalism," the only essay in the volume that was not originally presented
in the 2002 ASTR seminar, suggests that, in contemporary scholarship, more
emphasis is placed on the sociopolitical coordinates of the historical avant-
garde than on its artistic merits. Linked to the reorganization of continental Europe after World War I, the avant-garde movements are often ascribed
national characteristics and/or nationalistic proclivities. The two overarching avant-garde imperatives, the rejection of aesthetic autonomy and the

eradication of the separation between art and life, are perceived to have paved the way for totalitarian cultural production. This was manifest throughout the 1930s in German, Italian, and Russian cultural bureaucracies as a mandated socially-useful art, produced for the masses, with alleged deep ties to an essentialized nationalism, and ultimately deployed at the service of the state. Although comparatively under-examined, Expressionism, Constructivism, Futurism, Dadaism, Surrealism, and such indigenous movements as MAVO and Sanka, all emerged in Japan during the Taisho era (1912–1926). Pellegrini examines Japanese avant-garde performance and its relation to Japanese nationalism prior to and after the Pacific War. He also explores how avant-garde discourse and techniques, particularly those derived from performance, were assimilated into Japanese fascism as a means of regulating cultural production and instilling national solidarity during the war era.

In "Remembering and Forgetting: Greek Tragedy as National History in Postwar Japan," Carol Fisher Sorgenfrei explains that, after Japan's defeat in World War II, historical memory was revised and rewritten at the insistence of the American Occupation Forces. Thus, in the postwar era, the issue of how the past is represented became of paramount importance. The American Occupation Forces set about transforming Japan into an American-style democracy. Sorgenfrei analyzes radical adaptations of Greek tragedies by Japanese theatre artists since the 1960s and offers insights into the troubled relationships between postwar Japan's imposed identity as a Western-style democracy and its pre-war national identity as a *samurai* nation defending Asia from the West. Democracy is seen as a mythical legacy from the exotic past of ancient Greece that has been imposed by the American conquerors. Sorgenfrei also explores a few examples of rebellious theatre artists, who sought to destroy, re-invent, or re-define Japanese traditions. Some aligned themselves with or set themselves against the Western avant-garde, while others searched for totally new modes of expression and identity.

Evan Darwin Winet, in "The Critical Absence of Indonesia in W.S. Rendra's Village," states that President Suharto, who ruled Indonesia from 1966 to 1998, strove above all to authenticate the idea of Indonesia through increasingly authoritarian unification policies. As his "New Order" regime consolidated power in the early 1970s, his willingness to tolerate the "untidiness" of artistic freedom dwindled. At the time, military expansion became a great priority to Indonesia, and the notion of military defense developed into pervasive martial law. W.S Rendra rose to prominence in the 1970s as the foremost poet of the "new tradition," which, for the first time, explicitly accused the post-colonial government of corruption and oppression. Rendra was arrested and his plays were banned from public performance for seven years. His last play before the ban, *Kisah Perjuangan Suku Naga* (Struggle of the Naga Tribe), depicts urban Javanese victimization of the proletarianized rural people, and the abusive, wasteful, bourgeois policies of development undertaken by Suharto and his generals. Rendra revived *Kisah Perjuangan Suku Naga* in November 1998 for the Indonesian Arts Summit, which was Jakarta's first large theatre festival of the post–Suharto era. Twenty years after his youthful notoriety, Rendra had become a mainstream celebrity, and *Kisah Perjuangan Suku Naga* was a "classic" of contemporary Indonesian theatre.

In "Robert Lepage: Product of Québec?" Karen Fricker suggests that it is difficult for governments and power elites to embrace the elusive, changing nature of nationhood, because this is often seen as undermining the nation's legitimacy. Québec's unique culture has in fact been central to the stateless nation's assertion of its legitimacy. While Québec certainly has a rich, distinct culture, the nation's drive toward internationalism is undermined by contradictions in its nationalist project itself. After all, placing the nation in the international arena exposes the inherent elusive and porous character of Québec. The career of Robert Lepage provides a particularly useful view of the problems involved in the international promotion of the Québécois nation. The content of his work and its touring success have earned Lepage a positive reputation, and Québec's government holds him up as a shining example of the international viability of the nation itself. But the international aspect of Lepage's career has always been controversial among both local and international critics, as different points of view emanate from the anxiety about what could be interpreted as disloyalty to the "Québec nation project."

Patricia Ybarra's "Staging the Nation on the Ruins of the Past: An Investigation of Mexican Archeological Performance," explains that, after the Mexican Revolution in 1910, Mexico came to imagine itself as a *mestizo* (mixed race) country that had its roots in a glorious indigenous past. This process was intimately related to sweeping governmental and economic changes, such as the attempt to eradicate Creole control over the nation's resources by redistributing land and instituting a mixed-race, classless nation. Consequently, Mexico's indigenous people were removed from their nineteenth-century roles as racial inferiors without culture, and repositioned as autonomous cultures which contained positive values. Recently uncovered indigenous ruins became hallmarks of national pride during this transformation, because they provided material evidence of these past classical cultures. Soon performances, creating a palpable cultural nationalism by linking the indigenous past and the Mexican present, were staged at these classical sites. Ybarra argues that the juxtaposition of archeology and performance in

Tlaxcala has moved from articulating a specific classical culture to being complicit in the creation of a classical culture, and suggests that performative reconstructions of classical culture in Mexico may have a more successful and varied future than its creators had ever imagined.

The last essay in the volume is Susan Haedicke's "The Corpse of Algerian Identity: Achour Ouamara's *La Défunte* (The Deceased)." Haedicke proposes that, although Algeria won its independence from France in 1962 after a bloody revolution, by 1992 the promise of a new nation all but disappeared, as Islamist insurgents rebelled against the state, thus plunging the country into a violent civil war. Ouamara's play *La Défunte* reacts to the Algerian civil war by acknowledging a time of horror and atrocity, so poorly documented and plagued by government censorship that it is now known as the "invisible war." Prior to independence, Algeria was often presented metaphorically as a beautiful but distant woman. Ouamara's surrealistic *La Défunte*, published in 2001, reworks the metaphor of the enigmatic woman identified with Algeria, as that of a tortured and mutilated corpse, which hides her secrets from the police investigators. In the final scene of the play, the reconstituted spirit of the woman appears on stage to declare that, in spite of the abuse and dismemberment, Algeria will rise and prevail.

My special thanks and gratitude go to all of the authors in this volume for their excellent work. Also many thanks go to Simon Williams, Timothy Scholl, and all the ASTR participants in the 2002 seminar for their insights and ideas, as well as to the anonymous reviewers and referees for their comments. Last, but not least, very special thanks are due to Tihana Bule and Devon Harrison, my editorial assistants from Smith College, who worked very hard and devoted valuable time, thought, and energy to this project.

Notes

1. The November 2002 ASTR Seminar "Composing National Identity Through the (Re)construction of National Culture" was organized and led by Professor Simon Williams and Timothy W. Scholl.

2. My performance review of Langhoff's *The Bacchae* was published in *Western European Stages* 10.3 (Fall 1998): 41–42.

3. This selection of theatre reviews comes from different Greek newspapers between June and November 1997: *To Vima, Makedonia, Ta Nea*, and *Eleutheroptypia*. The translation is mine.

Reconstructing the Nation: Conflicting Cultural Imaginaries in Eighteenth-Century Poland

Natalya Baldyga

The issue of what constitutes nationality, the shared cultural identity of a people, has historically necessitated an attempt to define imaginary boundaries of statehood and selfhood. Simultaneously, theatrical representation, the historical locus of the imaginary, has traditionally provided one of the means by which nationality has been constructed and contested. Using theatrical representation as a site of cultural formation, artists, scholars, and statesmen have used the theatrical imaginary as a legitimizing force to define a real that is itself imagined. At the end of the eighteenth century, this theatrical legitimization of an imagined identity formed a part of a larger program of hotly contested cultural, social, and political reform in the Polish-Lithuanian Republic (or Commonwealth).[1] Conflicting efforts to retain or reshape a coherent cultural identity became increasingly urgent as the political borders of the state were subsumed by a series of partitions in 1772, 1793, and 1795, which divided the territory of the Commonwealth between the neighboring states of Austria, Prussia, and Russia. Ultimately, although political efforts were unable to preserve the sovereign state from annihilation, and Poland would not exist as a politically independent state for more than a century, the Poland of cultural imagination was maintained in art and literature through the great nationalistic works of the nineteenth century, sustaining a belief that the political state would one day be resurrected. At the time of the final partition, "Dabrowski's Mazurka," the future national anthem of twentieth-century Poland, proclaimed that *"Jeszcze Polska nie zginela/Kiedy my zyjemy"* (Poland has not yet perished/While we live).

This essay will discuss the struggle to delegitimize and replace the imaginary cultural heritage known as Sarmatism, which lay at the center of conflicting efforts to reform or maintain the cultural and political contours of the Polish state. Sarmatism began as an enthusiasm for Eastern fashions in the sixteenth century, shifting over time to become a distinct ideology fundamental to the identity of the Polish nobility. This ideology united the multiethnic Polish nobility through their supposed common descent from an ancient warrior tribe, the Sarmatians. What becomes visible through the theatre of the time are multiple efforts to reconstitute the identity of those among the Polish aristocracy who clung to this constructed classical heritage, through which Polish nationality was conflated with nobility rather than with residency within political borders. Sarmatism provided the nobility with a collective ethnic ancestry and allowed them to rationalize the political, economic, and social status quo.[2] Due to the strength of this cultural imaginary, political reform could not be enacted without first detaching Sarmatism from "Polishness," a campaign that was conducted through educational, artistic, and literary channels. In the theatre, this act of deconstruction was accompanied by the concurrent labor to construct an alternate model for Polish identity through the depiction of new social types. In this essay, I explore the necessity for cultural intervention in the political campaign to reconstruct the identity of the Polish nobility, by demonstrating how the late-eighteenth-century political comedy *Powrot Posla* (The Return of the Deputy) reconstitutes national identity by simultaneously deconstructing Sarmatism and offering a new basis for citizenship (service to the state) that extended beyond the artificial ethnic borders previously imposed by the Polish nobility.

To understand Sarmatism as a political as well as cultural ideology, it is necessary to historically contextualize the singular makeup and identity of the Polish nobility in eighteenth-century Poland. The Polish nobility, or *szlachta*,[3] is perhaps better thought of as a noble caste rather than a class per se, as nobility was tied neither to economic factors nor to ownership of land. Almost a full six to ten percent of the population in Poland was nobility, in contrast to other European nations (three percent in England, two percent in Russia, and a mere one percent in France and the German principalities), a fact that made it easier for the *szlachta* to consider "nobility" as synonymous with "Poland," perceiving the state as the *narod szlachecki,* or nation of nobles. Unlike other European nobility, the *szlachta* did not have a range of titles indicating different levels of nobility, which meant that all members of the *szlachta* were equals in theory, with a penchant for addressing each other as *Panie Bracie*, "my lord brother." In reality, the caste was highly striated, with the highest tier belonging to the magnates, families of great wealth and power who owned villages and sometimes entire towns and maintained their own private armies. At the other end of the spectrum was the "naked one," a nobleman who owned a meager piece of land, or none at all, and one whose daily existence was fundamentally that of a peasant. The fact that he was noble, however, accorded him the same legal rights as that of the wealthiest magnate, a status proclaimed by the "naked one's" coat of arms, horse, and sword. Regardless of the quality of these tokens, they were signifiers of the *szlachta*'s greatest pride — his right to vote. Between the two extremes, magnate and pauper, the nobility was divided into many different levels of power, influence, and wealth, preventing its definition as a socioeconomic class.

If the communal identity of the *szlachta* was not based on economic and social standing, neither was it based on common ethnic or linguistic origins. In ethno-linguistic makeup, the *szlachta* included Poles, Lithuanians, Ruthenians (from present-day Ukraine), Prussian and Baltic peoples of German extraction, and even Tatars.[4] In addition, the *szlachta* did not share a common religion. Although historically, the establishment of the Polish nation in 966 CE coincided with its adoption of Christianity, the Polish Commonwealth during the Polish baroque period was the antithesis of *cuius regio, eius religio*, decreeing that the religion of the monarch was the religion of the nation; instead the Commonwealth was a state whose religious heterogeneity and refusal to limit religious freedom earned it the moniker of *Paradisus Hereticorum*, the paradise of heretics.[5] By the end of the sixteenth century, the *szlachta* contained a large number of Protestants in addition to the Roman Catholic and Eastern Orthodox contingents, although many of the Protestant families would return to Catholicism in the following centuries.

Because of the numerous differences between noble families, the *szlachta* were required to define "Polishness" in a way that would allow them to establish a communal identity that encompassed their diverse ethnicities, religions, languages, and socioeconomic standings. Instrumental to the unification of the *szlachta* into the political entity known as the Polish Commonwealth, was their adoption of sixteenth-century theories that the *szlachta* were not actually Slavs but had in fact descended from an ancient Eastern warrior tribe, the Sarmatians, who conquered immense amounts of territory around the Black Sea regions in the fifth century BCE.[6] In the baroque era, the Sarmatian vogue was manifested primarily in codes of behavior, art, dress, and weaponry, which were drawn from Eastern designs and fashions primarily from Turkey and Persia.[7] Later, however, Sarmatian aesthetics would be transformed into the ideology referred to as Sarmatism, under which *szlachta* of all stripes could be united. The primary duty of the Sarmatian *szlachta* was to rise to the defense of the state in times of war.[8] Art and literature characterized the Sarmatian as an epic hero, chosen by God to hold back the infidel. Due to their perceived mission as a "chosen people," the *szlachta* were able to consider themselves superior to other nations — a worldview that helped foster widespread parochialism in the seventeenth century, when the majority of the *szlachta* shut themselves off intellectually and politically from Western Europe, in great contrast to earlier centuries. Sarmatism not only created a schism between Poland and the East, and between Poland and the West, but also firmly divided the *szlachta* from the other inhabitants of the Commonwealth by giving them, as descendants of the Sarmatians, what amounted to a different racial heritage, dating back to the classical era.

This last facet of Sarmatian ideology allowed the *szlachta* to create, in the words of Adam Zamoyski, a "pseudo-ethnic distinction between the political nation and the rest of the population" (31). This "superior" common ancestry would become the cornerstone of noble identity. Regardless of logical fallacies, Sarmatism, as a shared classical heritage, bound the *szlachta* together while simultaneously separating them from the peasant and burgher populace. Andrzej Walicki explains that,

> for the gentry republicans "nation" was a political and legal concept, deprived of linguistic or ethnic connotations: it was conceived as a body politic, embracing all active citizens, i.e. all members of the gentry, irrespective of their native language or ethnic background. In other words, it was possible to be "*gente Ruthenus, natione Polonus.*" But this indifference toward ethnicity should not be presented as anticipating the modern notion of "multi-culturalism." The gentry republicans of the old Commonwealth described themselves as "Sarmatians" and the term "Sarmatism" referred ... to a distinctive culture common to all of them, remarkably homogenous and deliberately created as a unifying bond. The nation of the gentry was still multi-lingual, but not multicultural [Walicki 156–59].

Ultimately, under Sarmatism, all *szlachta* were Poles, regardless of their ethnic origin, while at the same time, a peasant, even if ethnically Polish, was not regarded as a Pole. To be a Pole meant that one was of the *szlachta*; to be a member of the *szlachta* was to be a Pole. By extension, since the *szlachta* had constructed their unified identity through Sarmatism, this meant that to be a Pole was to be a Sarmatian.[9] The constructed heritage of Sarmatism, under which "Polishness" was equated with nobility, would become a means by which the *szlachta* were able to justify a corrupted political system from which they alone profited.

By the eighteenth century, the Polish governmental structure that had originated as a *monarchia mixta* had altered over time, until the magnate families constituted a de facto oligarchy, with nearly all of the country's legislative power in the hands of the *szlachta*, even though the monarch was ostensibly the head of the state. This situation can be traced back to royal concessions to the *szlachta* beginning in the fourteenth century,[10] which created a commonwealth that basically amounted to a democracy of nobles, with the king functioning as a president-for-life of a bicameral parliament, known as the Sejm.[11] However, in the sixteenth century, due to additional concessions, there was a distinct increase in the political power of the *szlachta*—a shift that occurred at the same time that Sarmatism was being adopted as a unifying strategy. As political power was reallocated, the *szlachta* began to impose a number of legislative controls limiting the power of the king. (The position of the monarch in Poland-Lithuania was unique among European nations — from 1573 onward, the king was elected by the *szlachta* from a list of proposed candidates taken from European nobility.) By the end of the century, all kings of Poland would have to abide by the Cardinal Articles, known to the *szlachta* as the "Golden Freedoms," which required the king to uphold the principle of free election to the monarchy and prevented him from unilaterally declaring war or peace. Although the king held executive power through the senate and could invoke constitutional change, the *szlachta* held the right to refuse to obey the king if his actions were considered in violation of the Golden Freedoms.[12] The *szlachta*'s political self-perception that they were equal to the king because they were the electors of kings was easily connected to the Sarmatian depiction of the *szlachta* as defenders of the state, so that these legislative Golden Freedoms became concomitant with Sarmatian ideology.

What started as a means of checking absolutism in the seventeenth century began to transform into a governmental stalemate within which the king was virtually powerless and the introduction of new legislation almost impossible. Within the Sejm, all nobles were in theory equals, and this principle was emphasized by the stipulation that all resolutions of the Sejm be passed unanimously. During the seventeenth century, this principle was redefined into the infamous *liberum veto*, which allowed a single dissenting nobleman to strike down any legislation disapproved of by him or his constituents, or the magnate to whom he answered politically. Not only did this action disrupt the session in progress, but it also dissolved the Sejm and negated any legislation passed earlier in its sitting. Under this deadlocked system, the magnates strengthened their power — ruling their local empires, feuding among themselves, and refusing to come together for the good of the nation as a whole. The guiding principle of the *szlachta* became

"Nierzadem Polski Stoi" (It is by unrule that Poland stands) (Davies 321). The "republic of nobles" had ceased to function.[13]

In the eighteenth century, the ideological underpinnings of the legislative system, with its associations between Sarmatism, nobility, and national identity, hampered the efforts of those seeking political reforms, as governmental structures were intrinsically linked to the Sarmatian ideals that formed such a crucial part of the *szlachta*'s identity. Political reform was perceived or presented as an attack on those Sarmatian ideals, which in turn meant an attack on the nation itself. Thus the task of political reformers became first to separate Sarmatism from national identity, so that legislative changes could be seen as being in accordance with "Polishness." Because the reformers sought to distribute power more equally by strengthening the role of the monarch in the governmental process and by according the townships much greater representation, the political nation could no longer be considered analogous with the *szlachta*. Deconstructing Sarmatism was the first step to delegitimizing the concept that nationality was founded on nobility. Unfortunately for the reformers, the internal difficulties, inherent in instigating this first step, were compounded by external forces that also inhibited the ability to enact political modification.

Upon his election to the throne in 1764, Stanislaw (II) August Poniatowski (1732–1798), the last king of Poland, immediately initiated legislative reforms in the hopes of addressing the political, economic, cultural, and educational decline of the country. The king's ability to institute change was hampered not only by internal resistance to his policies but also by the fact that, earlier in the eighteenth century, Russia had established itself as the "protector" of the Commonwealth, through the use of military force.[14] The king's actions alarmed not only Russia but all three of Poland's more powerful neighbors, the "three black eagles," Prussia, Russia, and Austria, who preferred the Commonwealth to remain weak and in disarray, and feared potential repercussions in their own countries should Poland become a constitutional monarchy along the lines of the English government so admired by Stanislaw August. In 1772, under the pretext of quelling civil war in Poland, Russia and Prussia invaded the Commonwealth, resulting in the First Partition of Poland, in which significant amounts of Polish territory were annexed by Russia, Prussia, and Austria, and Catherine II dispatched a new Russian ambassador to keep the Polish king under constant surveillance.[15] Stanislaw August and his "Camp of the Reform" (also known informally as the Patriot Party), restricted by internal conditions and external forces that made direct political action impossible, diverted their reconstruction efforts from legislation into other channels. Culture and education would be the tools used to attack Sarmatism, which provided the obscurantist ideological justification for a national identity that granted citizenship solely to the *szlachta* and painted the idea of political change as unpatriotic.[16] The reformers instituted a vigorous polemical literary campaign that was well-coordinated with a series of progressive and dramatic new educational initiatives[17] and extended into the realm of dramatic literature as well, with theatre taking a central role in the reform campaign.[18]

The ideological campaign of which playwrights were a part necessitated a two-tiered assault on the Sarmatian ideals that allowed conservative *szlachta* to justify their privileges through their self-constructed classical heritage. To begin with, it was necessary to deconstruct Sarmatism itself, devalorizing its ideals and disassociating them from Polish identity. Comedy was the voice of the "reform playwrights," who satirized extremist Sarmatian principles, illustrating that the patriotic unifying ideology had become the framework for ignorance, intolerance, and indolence.[19] Simultaneously, reformist literature sought to alter the foundation of Polish noble identity by attempting to reconstitute the model of a patriotic citizen for the *szlachta*, shifting the emphasis away from inherited privilege and toward characteristics such as active service to the state. Later, in the final years of the Polish Commonwealth, reformists would further extend their reconstruction of "Polishness" by challenging the connection between national identity and nobility, divorcing the concept of nationality from the imagined classical and racial heritage that had conflated nation and noble caste. These varying efforts to erase an association between "Polishness" and the image of the Sarmatian *szlachta* are immediately apparent in the political comedies of late-eighteenth-century Poland, including those of reform playwright Julian Ursyn Niemcewicz (1757–1841), whose best known play, *Powrot Posla* (The Return of the Deputy), provides an excellent example of how Sarmatism was satirized and delegitimized through the ridicule of its adherents and the offer of an alternative patriotic paradigm for *szlachta* identity.

In *The Return of the Deputy*, Valery,[20] a young deputy to the Sejm, vies with a friend for the hand of Teresa, the daughter of a highly conservative member of the *szlachta*. As Valery and his family are Patriots, and his prospective father-in-law is a staunch supporter of the Golden Freedoms, difficulties ensue. *The Return of the Deputy*, originally written as a political pamphlet in 1790, was staged in Warsaw in 1791 during the tumultuous events of the Four Year Sejm, a protracted legislative battle that produced the Constitution of the Third of May, Europe's first modern constitution.[21] The play's production came at a crucial moment during the proceedings. Having spent a quarter century working through cultural and educational programs to shape the mindset and opinions of an entire generation, the king and his supporters appeared finally to be in a position to effect the sweeping political changes, including the abolition of the crippling *liberum veto*, that had been quashed twenty years earlier. However, to do so, the older, less flexible generation of the *szlachta* would have to be assured that a change in government would not constitute a betrayal of the Commonwealth. Since Sarmatism allowed the conflation of the *liberum veto* and other Golden Freedoms of traditional legislation with Polish national identity, it was essential that "Polishness" be disconnected from Sarmatism and the ossified government it upheld.

In *The Return of the Deputy*, Niemcewicz devalorizes Sarmatism as a desirable prescriptive model for *szlachta* identity by exposing the corruption of traditional Sarmatian values and the republican government to which they were tied. Through the character of the Starosta Gadulski (Mr. Blabbermouth), Valery's prospective father-in-law, Niemcewicz illustrates the degradation of the Sarmatian role as soldier-hero within a fraternity of equals, unique among nations, whose members are worthy of high regard for their responsibilities as defenders and governors of the state. With the Starosta, the playwright creates a parodic figure whose adherence to Sarmatist ideology is revealed first by his nostalgic yearning for simpler days when a noble needed only to be a soldier-landlord, without concerning himself with the world at large.[22] The Starosta is proudly uneducated, boasting that he never reads and complaining about the new educational reforms that teach "useless" topics such as logic and the study of foreign governments, and longing for the past when a youth knew that glory awaited him "*ze go glosna czeka slawa/Gdy umial po lacinie i Volumen prawa*" (as long as he knew Latin and the collection of traditional laws) (27). The only learning necessary in the Starosta's view is that which allows him to understand the legislation upholding his own privileged position within society. Through the Starosta, Niemcewicz demonstrates that the isolationism and sense of superiority inherent in the Sarmatist ideology have provided an excuse for a generation of *szlachta* to remain profoundly ignorant, eschewing higher thought and any knowledge of the world outside the nation's borders. Supremely self-important, the Starosta holds forth on any number of subjects, supporting his uninformed and parochial opinions by a hearkening back to tradition.

Niemcewicz also uses the Starosta to demonstrate how the Golden Freedoms themselves have become corrupted — no longer legislation designed to support a free "democracy of nobles" responsible for the well being of the state, but instead the justification for an anarchic governmental system supporting individual greed. The first time he appears (I, ii), the Starosta responds to Valery's father (after the latter has praised his son's service to the government as a delegate to the Sejm) with one of his typically wordy outbursts, mourning the loss of luxury and financial reward guaranteed the *szlachta* by the old government:

God only knows what this Sejm has done to the State.
Why this government? Why all these changes?
As if it were so bad until now? As if our forefathers
Were unwise and without wits.
We were powerful under their laws
And so the Pole lived happily under [Saxon] Rule.
Such mansions, such sumptuous tribunals
Such grand Sejms...
A man ate, drank, did nothing and pockets were full [17–18].[23]

The "wisdom" of the forefathers, according to the Starosta, consisted in allowing one to be powerful and rich without the expense of any effort, except that of attending judicial or legislative meetings providing an opportunity for sumptuous and grand festivities. Instead of equating power with responsibility, the Starosta associates a position in the government with the opportunity for personal financial gain. Even worse, under the old system mourned by the Starosta, such gain was achieved by selling that which gave the *szlachta* his identity — his right to vote:

Today everything has changed and will keep changing:
They ruined everything, the brutes that dared to strike down
The Liberum Veto, that which gave freedom...
(he is in tears)
One delegate could hold up the Sejm's deliberations
One held the weight of the entire Fatherland in his hand.
He said: "I will not allow" and escaped [to the other side of the river][24]
...Before the vote
He got a promotion, and a couple of villages.
Today, who gets what [18]?[25]

The rights of any noble to vote and to invoke the *liberum veto* were meant to assure that all within the democratic fraternity held equal power and influence, regardless of financial or social circumstances. Despite his invocation of the freedom and responsibility belonging to each noble who "held the weight of the entire Fatherland in his hand," the Starosta reveals that in reality one's power and freedom were up for sale, and a noble's vote became solely a means to obtaining offices and property. From the moment of the Starosta's first appearance, Niemcewicz uses the character to devalorize Sarmatism by showing the degradation of the governmental systems that formed a part of its ideology and revealing that the Golden Freedoms, such as the *liberum veto,* served only the greed of self-interested *szlachta.* (For the spectator, the fun lies, of course, in the fact that the old system's corruption is nostalgically valorized by the Starosta as a portrait of the nation's glory days.)

Niemcewicz continues to satirize Sarmatist ideology through the Starosta's defense of the elected monarchy, which was under fire at the Four Year Sejm by reformers who advocated the stability of a hereditary, constitutional monarchy. The concomitant establishment of an elected monarchy and the adoption of Sarmatism by the *szlachta* meant that the two were historically linked to *szlachta* self-identity within the Nation of Nobles. Again, the Starosta demonstrates that the *szlachta*'s right to self-government and role as caretakers of the nation (as electors of its kings) has devolved into another opportunity for profiting financially from the electoral process. Freedom from dynastic absolutism is conflated with potential for individual profit. This equivalency is revealed in III, v, when the Starosta fondly reminisces about an incident at a tribunal in which he and other *szlachta* drew their swords and attacked a fellow noble who dared speak out against the election of kings. After cheerfully describing the man's injuries and chortling over the fact that he never spoke up again, the Starosta voices his disbelief that anyone could hold such outrageous opinions:[26]

> But how can one have such wild ideas
> And through the succession want to shackle the nation in a yoke!
> In this case, I ask you, what is to be gained by this?
> The King dies...
> And as before, all remains calm,
> Everyone is quiet and no one bows to anyone;
> In the election, each defends his candidate,
> All mount their horses and, according to custom,
> Immediately form parties throughout the country;
> This one talks to me with a coarse, friendly face:
> "Dear Mr. Peter, I implore you, stand together with me!
> Between us, take this small village as a leaseholder"
> Another, in order that I vote for him, gives me a forest,
> That one gives me cash, and in this way a man gets benefits [82–83].[27]

What begins as a defense of the elected monarchy and warning against absolutism quickly turns into nostalgic approbation for a system of succession in which unscrupulous *szlachta* took extensive bribes from representatives of *each* candidate. With this speech of the Starosta's, Niemcewicz argues that the election of kings — the foundation of the Commonwealth and pride of the Sarmatian *szlachta* as the nation's traditional governing caretakers — has degenerated into further occasion for *szlachta* opportunism.

Not only does the election of kings lend itself to *szlachta* opportunism, but, Niemcewicz argues, the electoral process, rather than unifying the nation, has become instead the source of factionalism and the potential for civil war, thereby increasing the possibility of foreign invasion from non–Polish candidates for the throne (as well as giving Russia its historical excuse for an extension of "protection" to the war-torn state). Again, the Starosta cheerfully describes the degradation of the *szlachta*'s national stewardship as a beneficial situation, brushing aside the impact of civil war and foreign invasion as if it were harmless brawling:

> True, from all this one can get into fights;
> And so that's the way it was after the death of King Augustus III
> Whom the Saxons fought for; fought Leszczynski,
> Burned down villages; but whom did this harm?
> As soon as a foreign army invades, [the Szlachta] unite.
> Afterwards amnesty: the men of the mace, the officials
> Will give the Szlachta relief, promises, indulgences,
> And wasn't it good this way [83]?[28]

The Starosta disregards the dysfunctional nature of the political system upheld by the Sarmatian *szlachta* by downplaying the devastating civil wars of the early eighteenth century, claiming that they ultimately united the *szlachta* and provided them with further concessions from those overseeing the succession and the new government. Therefore, according to the Starosta, the conflict harmed no one and was ultimately beneficial. (That the former inhabitants of the razed villages might disagree is a point that fails to register with this prefect of the king's lands.) Niemcewicz depicts the Sarmatian *szlachta* as completely divorced from his role as defender and caretaker of the nation — he who should be guarding the nation's borders and upholding its integrity is instead advocating a system that pitted the *szlachta* against each other, invited foreign invasion, and resulted in the depredation of the countryside and common people. Through the character of the Starosta, Niemcewicz creates a stereotype of the ignorant, grasping, and pugnacious Sarmatian *szlachta*, to demonstrate that values promoted by Sarmatism — military prowess, equality between nobles through the *liberum veto*, the right to self-government through the election of kings — have been thoroughly corrupted. In Niemcewicz's play, the Sarmatian self-perception as member of a chosen people has resulted in pomposity and pontification. The belief in the superiority of his nation and a rustic, martial lifestyle has led the *szlachta* to dismiss the international exchange of ideas and other intellectual pursuits, to the extent that the Starosta could boast that he never read and that he was perfectly content playing checkers by himself or smoking tobacco. The Sarmatian's pride in being an elector of the nation's sovereign has given way to greediness, with the electoral process serving as a grab-bag of lucrative prizes for the *szlachta*, rather than as the serious task of choosing a head of state. Worst of all, the principle of equality for all *szlachta*, the cornerstone of the "republic of nobles," has been obscured by self-interested advancement and profiteering through the abuse of the *liberum veto* and the selling of votes. "Mr. Blabbermouth" weeps for the *liberum veto* and the principle of free elections while invoking the "wisdom of the forefathers" only because they represent a loss of his unlimited power and occasions for extortion. By creating a character who mourns the loss of the great government of the past while simultaneously extolling its corruption, Niemcewicz delegitimates Sarmatism as a worthy model for *szlachta* self-identification, and argues that the current legislative system represents the decline of noble republican values.

Having delegitimized Sarmatism as a desirable national ideology, Niemcewicz reconstitutes the ideal of a Polish citizen using the figures of Valery, the young deputy, and his father, Pan Podkomorzy. Through these characters, the playwright provides a new paradigm for national identity in which patriotic citizenship is no longer associated with blood membership to a noble caste, but is connected instead to an active participation in a central government concerned with the welfare of the general populace. Pan Podkomorzy is a chamberlain, a nobleman serving as an adjudicator of boundary disputes, and is related to the Starosta through the latter's first marriage. Unlike the Starosta, however, Pan Podkomorzy champions the work of the current Sejm and criticizes the old system in which "*myslelismy o sobie, a nigdy o kraju*" (we thought only of ourselves and never about the country) (18). Podkomorzy is the antithesis of the Starosta, providing a mouthpiece for the views of the Camp of the Reform as he describes himself as a patriotic noble who has suffered from seeing Poland under subjugation.[29] But he can now die in peace, Podkomorzy continues, knowing that his son Valery is serving in the Sejm as a deputy, and that the nation is in a better condition (38–39). Valery, however, gives his father the credit for his own patriotism and moral uprightness; any virtues that he may have, he responds, are due entirely to the values that he learned at his father's knee, "*Co z dziecinstwa w serce mi wpajales/Zebym kochal ojczyzne i trzymal sie cnoty*" (From childhood you taught my heart to love my homeland and be virtuous) (39). Whereas Niemcewicz depicts the Sarmatian Starosta as equating his position as a noble with privilege, both Podkomorzy and Valery see their status as implying a responsibility to their nation. For those *szlachta*, patriotism and national pride are synonymous with service to the nation — one's membership in the Sejm represents a duty to maintain or better the nation's welfare, rather than an opportunity to exploit one's situation for financial gain.

Niemcewicz depicts the character of Valery as the embodiment of his alternative paradigm for noble identity, with its shifted emphasis from entitlement to responsibility. This shift is noticeable in the young deputy's interaction with his childhood friend Szarmancki (Mr. Charming). Both young men are of noble birth, but where Valery is well-educated and has a strong sense of his civic duty, the slavishly fashionable and avidly social Szarmancki has managed to avoid any civic, judicial, or military duties of the *szlachta*, all of which he describes as enormously tedious. While Valery has been serving as a deputy to the Sejm, Szarmancki has been traveling in France and England, squandering his inheritance. Szarmancki's lack of interest in the political situation in either of these countries is countered by Valery's excitement as he imagines his friend's opportunity to witness the efforts of the French to "throw off the fetters of tyranny," and to observe the famous parliamentary government of England in action.[30] The boredom that Szarmancki expresses in reaction to all the sights that he has seen serves to highlight Valery's keen desire to observe the conditions of these nations in which the government is (ostensibly) run by and in service to its people. (Szarmancki responds to Valery's inquiries about the state of revolutionary France and the English government by complaining that the events in France have destroyed the social scene on the boulevards, and that England is only good for horse racing and souvenir shopping.)[31] Valery, the prescriptive model for patriotic citizenship, is placed between the Starosta, representing the older Sarmatian *szlachta* wanting to maintain the political status quo, and Szarmancki, representing those of his own generation whose apathy towards and avoidance of politics is as irresponsible as the older *szlachta*'s greed.

The language with which Valery issues his subsequent friendly but firm rebuke to Szarmancki illustrates the manner in which Niemcewicz and others wished to rewrite the definition of "Polish" so that it was no longer automatically contiguous with nobility, as in the Sarmatist model, but with active citizenship instead. Admonishing his friend for shirking his duties and thinking only of his own comfort, Valery tells him, *"Pamietac, zes polakiem, zes obywate lem/Zes najpierwsze twe winien ojczyznie uslugi"* (Remember, you are a Pole, you are a citizen/You owe your services first of all to your homeland) (50). Not only is being a citizen, holding the right to vote, portrayed as a responsibility rather than a privilege, but in Valery's rebuke, "citizen" becomes synonymous with "Pole." This conflation carries radical implications, as citizenship was a condition that the Patriot Party was working to extend to other residents of the Commonwealth outside the confines of the *szlachta* caste. Here the use of the word "Pole" contrasts sharply with the Starosta's use of the phrase "the Pole lived happily," in his nostalgic evocation of the days when "a man ate, drank, did nothing and pockets were full" (17). When used by the Starosta, the word "Pole" applies only to the *szlachta*. Through Valery, Niemcewicz constructs a definition of "Polishness" in opposition to Sarmatism by disregarding caste membership and providing instead an activist model in which respect and honor are earned through political involvement rather than by hereditary entitlement.

Niemcewicz's reconstruction of Polish national identity disconnects it from an inherited blood membership supported by supposed common ancient origins and attaches it instead to stewardship of the nation and of all who live within its borders. Valery, attempting to convince his friend that a nobleman is not a superior being automatically worthy of the people's regard, stresses to Szarmancki that the respect of the general public is only secured by those who work for humanity, cautioning, *"Ale go nie otrzma, kto tylko proznuje"* (But he who only loafs will not receive it) (50). The *szlachta* as national citizen-caretaker must earn the respect of the people by demonstrating its service to the entire human race, not just to its own ruling class. Again, although Valery's words are addressed to a member of the nobility, through his emphasis on Szarmancki's obligation to serve his country by working for *all* of its inhabitants, Niemcewicz succeeds not only in conflating "Polishness" with the figure of a politically active citizen, but also in introducing the revolutionary concept that the general public is as much a part of the nation as the *szlachta*. Niemcewicz's play may not go so far as to suggest political equality for burghers or peasants, but it does include the inhabitants of the state in its definition of countrymen, a concept antithetical to the formulation of national identity under Sarmatism.[32]

In *The Return of the Deputy*, Sarmatism is delegitimized as a prescriptive model for the *szlachta*, first by ridiculing its degeneration into ignorance and opportunism, and then by disassociating it from nationality through the construction of a new paradigm of Polish identity. Within this new paradigm, as embodied by Valery, Pole now equals citizen, specifically a well-educated, active noble, concerned for the common man, eagerly asking not what his country can do for him, but what he can do for his country. The character of Valery, deputy to the ground-breaking Four Year Sejm, represents the new Pole that King Stanislaw August and his supporters had been seeking to construct through their quarter century of cultural and educational reforms — an iconic figure replacing the Sarmatian *szlachta*, upon whom they could bestow the status of exemplary Polish patriot. That which is most radical in Niemcewicz's play, however, is that it also manages, in direct opposition to Sarmatian ideology, to propose the idea of a national identity extending beyond a "nation of nobles," suggesting that the homeland is constituted of all its inhabitants.

The Return of the Deputy provides an illustration of how "reform playwrights" used theatre to re-envision a national identity that had heretofore been constituted upon the imaginary classical heritage of Sarmatism. Skirting racial issues imbedded in the *szlachta's* improbable descent from the ancient Sarmatians, playwrights such as Niemcewicz deconstructed Sarmatism and delegitimated the conservative ideology as a justifiable foundation for national identity, shifting their focus to the actions, responsibilities, and functions of a national citizen, and implying thereby that membership in the nation was not contingent on the nobility of one's blood. In 1773, Felix Oraczewski, deputy to the Sejm from Krakow, proclaimed that "to make people Poles, and make Poles citizens, will be the source of all desired national achievements" (Mrozowska 125). As Sarmatism provided one of the strategies by which the *szlachta* legitimated the political and legal connection between Polishness and nobility, deconstructing Sarmatism provided a first step to reconstituting national identity. Simultaneously, theatre provided a space in which the reconstitution of Polish nationality could be explored, by transforming the shared understanding of "Polishness" through the representation of new Polish types. The views of these reform playwrights were not original; they had been propagated in poems and periodicals and on the floor of the Sejm itself. The power of theatrical representation, however, is that it makes theoretical arguments a material possibility through their embodiment onstage, making visible that which can be conceptualized. To make an idea visible, to represent it, means that it enters the realm of the possible. The threatening nature of such an embodiment, of the reform views made physical reality through actor's bodies, shows itself in the demand made by the arch-conservative deputy Suchorzewski during a meeting of the Sejm that *The Return of the Deputy* be confiscated and Niemcewicz punished.[33]

The power of the new imaginary of Niemcewicz and his contemporaries, embodying the new Polish citizen of the Camp of the Reform, would not manifest itself at the end of the eighteenth century. In 1795, four years after the debut of *The Return of the Deputy*, the Polish state was officially removed from the map of Europe for over one hundred years.[34] The cultural institutions established by Stanislaw August, however, remained, as did the art produced by the contributors to those institutions. Popular re-imaginings of Polish cultural identity, introduced through the characters of the eighteenth-century Polish theatre, would survive to be reworked and restaged by later artists. The re-formed national Polish identity, divorced from Sarmatism, embodied by the new Polish patriot constructed by Niemcewicz and others, would be adopted and elaborated on in the nineteenth century by the great writers of Polish romanticism. These later writers would themselves create a nationalist ideology founded on the idea of a Polish nation that transcended treaties and state boundaries. Through its material representations of Polish national culture, the stage would insist on the existence of a Poland beyond political borders — a Poland that had been partitioned but had not yet perished.

Notes

1. In this essay I use the term "the Commonwealth" or "Poland" to designate the Polish-Lithuanian Commonwealth. The two states, previously a loose confederation, were formally combined in 1569. The dual state, made up of the Crown (Poland) and the Grand Duchy (Lithuania), was referred to as the Polish Commonwealth (*Rzeczpospolita*), with Lithuania functioning sometimes as an equal partner and at other times as a Polish province. The full name of the state was the "Commonwealth of the Two Nations, Polish and Lithuania," and its enormous territory included most of the land between the Baltic and Black Seas, stretching lengthwise from Silesia to Muscovy. The term *Rzeczpospolita* (commonwealth or republic) was taken from the Latin *respublica*, reflecting the nobility's perception of their government as the political successor to the Roman Republic.

2. Sarmatism was not the only origin theory used to unite a noble caste whose foundation remained a mystery. The nobility also saw Poland as linked to classical Rome through the country's unique "republic of nobles," leading some noble families to trace their origins back to the families of ancient Rome. "By the thirteenth and fourteenth centuries," notes historian Norman Davies, "when some awareness of the exclusive nature of the noble estate was felt, the best that chroniclers could do was to trace its origin to Noah, to Julius Caesar, or to Alexander the Great" (207).

3. The name *szlachta* (pronounced shlákh-ta), writes Norman Davies, "has been the subject of considerable dispute" (207). As he explains, the word's etymological roots derive both from the Old Low German *slahta*—associated with *schlagen* (to strike, fight, cleave, breed) and *Geschlecht* (sex, species, family, race)—and the Czech *slehta* (nobility), so that *szlachta* "neatly combines the two senses of 'high birth' and 'military prowess' which together constitute the original ingredients of medieval nobility" (207–8).

4. As foreigners could be admitted to the nobility (rarely, and almost always for military distinction), one could even find *szlachta* of Italian, Magyar, Transylvanian, Swedish, Livonian, Saxon, Irish, Scots, and Russian extraction — as well as converted Jews and one lone American.

5. The greater population of Poland was made up primarily of Roman Catholics and Eastern Orthodox, but also included Uniates, Jews, and even Tatars who remained loyal to Islam. During the Reformation, many of the northern cities embraced Lutheranism and Calvinism. Poland became the refuge for many fleeing religious persecution, including Anabaptists, Mennonites, and the Czech Brethren.

6. This tribe was originally of Central Asian stock but migrated to the Urals between the sixth and fourth centuries BCE, ultimately moving west to conquer most of southern European Russia and part of the eastern Balkans by the second century BCE. The nomadic Sarmatians were highly skilled warriors known for their superior horsemanship. The tribe was overrun by the Goths in the third century CE and the Huns in the fourth century CE. Those who survived were either assimilated or escaped westward. By the sixth century CE, the Sarmatian people are no longer mentioned in historical records.

7. The distinctive "Oriental" costume adopted by the *szlachta* male included wide trousers, a long smock (the *zupan*), over which he would wear a long coat called a *kontusz*, and a wide silk sash of gold and silk thread, from which his saber would hang. When the Sarmatian *szlachta* was not wearing a round fur cap, one could see his high-shaved forehead, another fashion adopted from regions to the east. Female

clothing was less distinct. Beginning in the seventeenth century, women's clothes followed French fashions; in the eighteenth century, the ostentatiously expensive clothing of the Sarmatian males far outstripped that of noble women.

8. Despite the Eastern influence in dress and manners, the Sarmatian saw himself as the defender of Western Christendom against the ever-present pagan threat that manifested itself in the incursions by Tatars and Turks.

9. This association of Polishness with Sarmatism was signified by the politicization of *szlachta* sartorial fashions. Those who chose western European dress over the traditional costume of the Sarmatian *szlachta* were accused by their enemies of renouncing their Polish identity. Even foreign kings who ruled Poland adopted Sarmatian dress and other accoutrements.

10. From the fifteenth century onward, the *szlachta* were guaranteed exemption from all dues or taxes (excepting property tax), and their persons and property were absolutely inviolable. In the sixteenth century, a new law, known as *Nihil novi*, stipulated that no new dues or duties could be imposed on the nobility by the king without the approval of the deputies and senators.

11. The word "Sejm" (often transliterated as Seym) is alternately translated as "diet" and "parliament." By the sixteenth century, the Sejm, which met annually, was made up of three estates, the *senat* (senate), the lower house (or Sejm proper), and the king. The *senat* functioned as an upper house, with offices held for life. These offices were given to bishops and dignitaries, and for the most part were held by the magnate families, whose wealth and influence were often greater than the king's. The lower house, the *izba poselska* (Chamber of Deputies or Chamber of Envoys), was made up of representatives from the nobility who were elected at regional assemblies or dietines (*Sejmiki*). The king constituted, in effect, an estate composed of a single individual.

12. These articles were initially drawn up to protect the religious freedom of the *szlachta* from their king-elect, Henri of Valois (whom the *szlachta* associated with the 1573 massacre of St. Bartholomew), and were therefore also referred to as the Henrican Articles. It would take only a short while for Henri to tire of this kingship-with-conditions, leading him to abandon the Commonwealth after only a few months.

13. By the beginning of the eighteenth century, the Commonwealth, due to the abuse of the *liberum veto* and other disruptive tactics, had no central government to speak of, no army, and a ruling class whose involvement in central government was grudging and sporadic. In 1697, the principle of elected monarchy, one of the foundations of *szlachta* ideology, became a farce as Saxony placed its elector, Friedrich Augustus (Augustus II the Strong), on the throne through armed force. From 1704 to 1733, civil war between Polish and Saxon claimants devastated the country. During the reign of the Saxon kings, the so-called Saxon Night (1697–1763), Poland's sociopolitical system stagnated further under kings who were happy to draw on revenue provided by the Polish lands, without seeing to the government of the country or checking its unstable economic situation. The motto of the kings and the wealthiest *szlachta* according to a popular song of the time was "*Za krola Sasa/Jedz, pij, i popuszczaj pasa!*" (Under the Saxon king, eat, drink and loosen your belt!) (Davies 508).

14. Although Stanislaw August in fact owed his ascension to the throne to Catherine II of Russia, his reform initiatives, meant to strengthen his weakened nation, did not adhere to Catherine's vision of the central European balance of

power. The election of Stanislaw August was accomplished through the political machinations of the magnate Czartoryski clan (known as "The Family"), who were in turn supported by tens of thousands of Catherine's troops. Despite their political alliance to Russia, the Czartoryskis backed Stanislaw August in his reform policies.

15. Stanislaw August repeatedly attempted to gain foreign support, but none was forthcoming. The Commonwealth itself was powerless to resist the annexation of its territory, as it lacked a standing army of any significance. In 1717, Poland's army was limited, by Russian orders, to 24,000 soldiers, although the actual number of professional soldiers was probably less than 20,000, due to lack of financial support. The pitiful size of the army is best understood by the ratio of the Commonwealth's soldiers in relation to those of its neighbors — Prussia 1:11, Austria 1:17, and Russia 1:28 (Davies 504).

16. Stanislaw August and his allies were fortunate in that freedom of expression in spoken and written word constituted one of the traditional Golden Freedoms so zealously protected by the *szlachta*. Political debate flourished in the world of letters in the form of political pamphlets, treatises, and lampoons. These were joined by the journal *Monitor*, founded by Stanislaw August in 1765 and modeled after Addison and Steele's *Spectator*, which became one of the Patriot Party's foremost instruments for cultural and sociopolitical change.

17. Through education reforms, the king and his supporters set out to reshape the mindset of an entire generation of young *szlachta* by restructuring of the curriculum at the University in Krakow, developing new textbooks through textbook-writing competitions, and establishing the King's Cadet School and the Commission for National Education, founded in 1773, a year after the First Partition.

18. Before the king turned his attention to theatre in Poland, there was no public forum for Polish plays about Polish subjects. Stanislaw August founded the National Theatre in Warsaw, established the first professional troupe of Polish actors, and promoted competitions for original plays in the Polish language (rather than translations or adaptations), increasing the accessibility and topicality of Polish theatre. According to Czeslaw Milosz, the dramatic literature that was employed by the king and his party as a means of communicating their political message would prove to be "the most effective weapon of the Camp of the Reform" (169).

19. Another famous parody of the Sarmatian *szlachta* can be found in Franciszek Zablocki's aptly named play *Sarmatyzm*, written in 1784. Zablocki, famous for his lampoons, presents the Sarmatian *szlachta* as boorish, backwards, unbearably prolix, and quarrelsome (willing to debate not only the boundaries of his land but the priority of his wife's seating in church).

20. Spelled "Walery" in Polish and often transliterated as Valery for non–Polish speakers.

21. This convocation, initiated in 1788, bestowed on itself the official status of a Confederation, which by law allowed the members to continue assembling, instead of recessing after six weeks — the normal procedure for a meeting of the Sejm.

22. A *starosta* was a king's official or prefect, a lifelong holder of royal lands. The office was in principle awarded by the king to the worthy and deserving. Some *starostas* had judicial and administrative responsibilities. Others did not, and their holdings were, in the words of Richard Butterwick, "usually more lucrative" (232).

23.   Bog wie, co porobily sejmujace Stany,
       Dlaczego ten rzad? Po co te wszystkie odmiany?
       Alboz zle bylo dotad? A nasi przodkowie
       Nie mieliz to rozumu i oleju w glowie?
       Bylismy poteznymi pod ich ustawami.
       Tak to Polak szczesliwie zy l pod Augustami!
       Co to za dwory, jakie trybunaly huczne,
       Co za paradne sejmy, jakie wojsko juczne!
       Czlek jadl, pil, nic nie robil i suto w kieszeni.
       (Translations of the Starosta's speeches by Leonard Baldyga.)

24. The text actually reads "escaped to Praga." Praga lay across the river from Warsaw and is now a suburb of the city.

25. Dzis sie wszystko zmienilo i bardziej sie zmieni:

       Zepsuli wszystko, tknac sie smieli okrutnicy
       Liberum Veto, tej to wolnosci zrzenicy...
       Jeden posel mogl wstrzmac sejmowe obrady,
       Jeden ojczyzny calej trzymal w reku wage,
       Powiedzial: "nie pozwalam" i uciekl na Prage...
       Jeszcze, ze tak przedni wniosek,
       Mial promocje i dostal czasem kilka wiosek.
       Dzisiaj co kto dostanie?

26. Brawling was actually quite common at local *sejmiki*. As Daniel Stone describes it, "Participants at dietines generally obeyed regulations to leave their firearms at home, but they wore swords and got into fights despite penalties for obstructing debate. In addition to setting personal grudges, belligerent nobles used their numbers and weapons to suppress political opponents in a rough and ready form of majority rule. But they avoided pitched battles, and the number of deaths and serious injuries was small. The marshals bore the responsibility of repairing damage to local property from dietine funds" (185).

27.   Ale jakze tez mozna miec tak dzikie zdania
       I przez sukcesja narod chciec jarzmem uciskac?
       W tym przypadku, pytam sie, co kto moze zyskac?
       Krol dzis umrze...
       Wszystko sie w spokojnosci, jak wprzody, zostaje,
       Wszyscy cicho i nikt sie nikomu nie skloni;
       W elekcji kazdy swego kandydata broni,
       Wszyscy na kon wsiadaja i, podlug zwyczaju,
       Zaraz panowie partie formuja po kraju;
       Ten mowi do mnie z mina rubasznie przyjemna:
       "Kochany panie Pietrze, prosze, badz Wasc ze mn a!
       Miedzy nami, te wioske wez niby w dzierzawe";
       Drugi, zebym byl za nim, puszcza mi zastawe,
       Ten daje sume, i tak czlek sie zapomoze.

28.   Prawda, z tego wszystkiego przyjsc do czubow moze;
       I tak bylo po smierci Augusta wtorego:
       Ci bili Sasow, owi bili Leszczynskiego,
       Palili sobie wioski; no i coz to szkodzi?
       Obce wojsko jak wkroczy, to wszystko pogodzi.
       Potem amnestia: panom bulawy, urzedy,
       Szlachcie dadza wojtostowa, obietnice, wzgledy,
       Nie byloz to tak dobrze?

29. "The function of his character and the way he behaves," writes Anna

Stradomska-Bialic, "demonstrates that we are dealing with a representative of the middle class *szlachta*, mindful of the landed gentry's virtue and chivalry" (Charakter funkcji z wyboru i sposob jej sprawowania ... swiadcza, ze mamy do czynienia z przedstawicielem sredniej szlachty, dbalej o cnoty ziemianskie i rycerskie) (*Powrot Posla*, Editor's notes 8).

30. Valery's admiration of both the French and English governments allows Niemcewicz to condemn absolutism while simultaneously supporting the model of a constitutional monarchy that would allow greater enfranchisement than the current Polish model.

31. Szarmancki's specific complaints about revolutionary France are that one cannot meet any young women, that there is no entertainment to be found, and that the merchants and artisans are serving in the militia (rather than catering to his sartorial needs).

32. At the end of the play, Niemcewicz demonstrates his support for the Patriot initiative to emancipate the peasants. Pan Podkomorzy gives two of his servants permission to marry and, as a wedding present, frees them from serfdom. The issue of peasant emancipation had to be dropped by the Party to get the majority of the *szlachta* to agree to other significant constitutional reforms.

33. Fortunately for the author, this attack only served to highlight the similarities between Suchorzewski and Niemcewicz's blustering Starosta Gadulski. Suchorzewski also called for the desubsidization of the National Theatre in Warsaw, where the play was being staged, which had provided a platform for the king's reform policies since its founding in 1765.

34. After the Second Partition in 1793, émigrés assembled in Dresden to plot an uprising against Russia, choosing as their leader General Tadeusz Kosciuszko, the Polish hero of the American Revolution, and supporting his plan to enlist able-bodied men from all social classes in the manner of the French and American Revolutions. Kosciuszko went on to radically declare an end to serfdom and with the aid of peasants achieved several astonishing victories before he was finally overwhelmed by the substantially larger Russian forces.

Works Cited

Butterwick, Richard, ed. *The Polish-Lithuanian Monarchy in European Context: c.1500–1795.* New York: Palgrave, 2001.

Davies, Norman. *God's Playground: A History of Poland.* Vol. 1. New York: Columbia University Press, 1982.

Milosz, Czeslaw. *The History of Polish Literature.* Berkeley: University of California Press, 1983.

Mrozowska, Kamilla. "Educational Reform in Poland during the Enlightenment." *Constitution and Reform in Eighteenth-Century Poland: The Constitution of 3 May 1791.* Ed. Samuel Fiszman. Bloomington: Indiana University Press, 1997.

Niemcewicz, Julian Ursyn. *Powrot Posla.* Ed. Anna Stradomska-Bialic. Warszawa: Zaklad Narodowy Imienia Ossolinskich-Wydawnictwo, 1950.

Stone, Daniel. *The Polish-Lithuanian State, 1386–1795.* Seattle: University of Washington Press, 2001.

Walicki, Andrzej. "The Idea of Nation in the Main Currents of Political Thought of the Polish Enlightenment." *Constitution and Reform in Eighteenth-Century Poland: The Constitution of 3 May 1791.* Ed. Samuel Fiszman. Bloomington: Indiana University Press, 1997.

Zamoyski, Adam. "History of Poland in the 16th–18th Centuries." *Land of the Winged Horsemen: Art in Poland, 1572–1764.* Ed. Jan K. Ostrowski. Alexandria, VA: Art Services International, 1999.

Celebrating the Revolution While the King Is Still on the Throne: *The Fall of the Bastille* and the Festival of Federation (July 1790)

Scott Magelssen

JULIE: You know me, Danton...
DANTON: What we call knowing. You have dark eyes, curly hair, fine skin, and you call me "Dear Georges." But! (*Indicates her forehead and her eyes.*) What lies behind here? Ha! Our senses are crude. We'd have to crack open the tops of our skulls to really know each other, tear out each other's thoughts from the fibre of the brain.

Danton's Death (I, i), 1835

Danton's line to Julie in Georg Büchner's *Danton's Death,* written forty years after its title's event, indicates that there is a fundamental disparity between truth and what is represented by physical appearance. The line alludes to the idea that the truth of the French Revolution becomes relative to the viewer, and, to extend the allusion, whatever means one uses to represent it will already separate it from its initial reality. In Büchner's cosmology, life, liberty, and history become manipulable and are produced by those in power. "Life is a whore," Danton tells Camille, his fellow prisoner in IV, iii, "she fornicates with the whole world." And, in the next scene, "Liberty and whores are the most cosmopolitan things under the sun. Liberty will prostitute herself honorably now in the marriage bed of the lawyer from

Arras [Robespierre]. But I think she'll play Clytemnestra on him. I give him less than six months before he follows me."

Büchner has certainly not been the only, nor the first author to represent the French Revolution in this manner. Even in the earliest enunciations, the truth and history of the Revolution were in flux and varied greatly from one another depending on the disposition of the creator(s) and the political state of affairs. In 1789, a military spectacle took place in England with the fall of the Bastille as its subject. Coleridge wrote *The Fall of Robespierre* in 1797. Even in Paris during the years of the French Revolution, plays and spectacles treated the events of the Revolution in order to stabilize particular meanings of those events for the public.[1] Indeed, the first play about the death of Marat was written in the week between the event and Charlotte Corday's execution. The focus of this essay is *The Fall of the Bastille*, a "religious drama," along with the next day's Festival of Federation. These two events fell on the one-year anniversary of the uprising and destruction of the prison. I examine these two commemorative spectacles within the context of emergent festival practices during the Revolution and explore the way these events operated within the Revolutionary discourse.

In *Inventing the French Revolution: Essays on the French Political Culture in the Eighteenth Century*, Keith Michael Baker writes that representation during the French Revolution was a tool used by individuals in power to invent and control public memory. Various writings and other representational practices during and after the Revolution served to challenge and subvert memory, "bringing into contestation what was previously regarded as fixed" (Baker 56). Competition for the control of French history, he writes, took place on the archival level, in documenting events to fix the record as authoritatively authentic on the symbolic level, as well as on the level of direct political action. History, then, was not the domain of discarded memory, but of disputed memory (56). Baker quotes Michel Foucault's passage on memory as an important factor in struggle: "If one controls people's memory, one controls their dynamism [...] It is vital to have possession of this memory, to control it, administer it, tell it what it must contain" (Baker 31).[2] The goal of the archivists and political figures during the Revolution was to select a series of elements from the disparate enunciations of public memory and disengage it from its corresponding social groups, "relocating it in a framework that is external to them [...]. [H]istory fixes fading or fractured memory, substituting discontinuity for continuity, transforming a multiplicity of resemblances into a totality of differences" (Baker 55).

Büchner, in *Danton's Death*, engaged in yet another archival arrangement of the records of the French Revolution. While often giving his characters, Danton and Robespierre, their speeches verbatim, as they were publicly recorded, the playwright did not seek to make his drama an accurate mirror representation of the events he depicted. Büchner takes the historiographic icons of Danton and Robespierre and shows the tensions and negotiations that had been formerly erased by historiographic procedures. Danton's line to Julie echoes the idea that private and public discussion, political rhetoric, or speeches can no longer be depended upon to convey truth and meaning. Neither can one know the person by the words they speak. The only way to get to one's true identity is by cracking open his or her skull and dragging it out. Likewise, history can no longer be regarded as an archive of truth. The representation of the events of the French Revolution do not necessarily correspond to their reality.[3]

Why do I begin an essay on the *Fall of the Bastille* and the Festival of Federation with a discussion of *Danton's Death*, which Büchner wrote a generation later and which, moreover, treats a Revolutionary event, in which the circumstances and power distribution were dramatically different than they were at the time of my main subject four years earlier? Büchner's play describes with style the Festival organizers' modality of representation: these events were meant to produce meaning in the present, not remember meanings of the past. What is striking in both the religious drama and the Festival is the sheer absence of attempts at accurately reconstructing the events depicted. And, indeed, as I will discuss below, Rousseau's advocates sought to reject "representation" altogether. Instead, the spectacles were what Deleuze and Guattari would call fabulations — combinations of allegory, symbols, ancient and modern texts, and political maneuvers (Deleuze and Guattari 71).

In this essay, I hope to bring to light some of the ways in which these two related events made use of, and produced, systems of meaning by which Parisians could access the Revolution, as well as the ways in which these performances helped negotiate a time of upheaval in order to temporarily stabilize a particular notion of national identity. To do so, I will first provide a brief description of *The Fall of the Bastille* and the Festival of Federation, then look at period documents that archived these events through the selection of particular aspects to emphasize and remember. Following this, I will link these events, and the way they have been remembered, to a broader discourse of public performance, especially that articulated by Rousseau earlier in the eighteenth century, always keeping in mind that *The Fall of the Bastille* and the Festival of Federation had a specificity of their own that both aligned with the current discourse and generated its own in the moment of performance. I suggest that the early Revolutionary representational practices depicted in *The Fall of the Bastille* and the Festival of Federation may be understood in terms of what Lynn Hunt refers to as "symbol construction," and what Baker (citing Foucault) describes as tools used by those in power to invent and control public memory. If this is the case, then I argue that *The Fall of the Bastille* and the subsequent Festival indicate a pivotal threshold of theatre history and the French Revolution, in that these were representations of the events of the Revolution while the monarchy was still in power. Thus, the performances were not necessarily intended as propagandistic affirmations of a new regime, as were later festivals celebrating the Revolution. What follows is a brief description of the Bastille drama and the subsequent Festival, the (obscure) former most fully described in English in Marvin Carlson's *Theatre of the French Revolution.*

In Paris, on July 13, 1790, the evening before the first anniversary of the destruction of the Bastille, a solemn ceremony including a representation of that event was conducted at Notre Dame cathedral (the previous day, July 12, 1790, the vote of the Civil Constitution of the Clergy nationalized all Church lands in France, thereby allowing them to be sold). The representation, entitled *The Fall of the Bastille: A religious drama, drawn from the Holy Scriptures*, composed by Marc-Antoine Désaugiers, combined a historical staging with segments of Biblical text. It was performed by actors from various Paris theatres, including the Comédie Française and the Comédie Italienne. The drama began with a series of interchanges referring to the dismissal of Jacque Necker, director general of French Finances:[4]

> CITIZEN: Shall not the land tremble for this, and every one mourn that dwelleth therein?
> THE PEOPLE: Why?
> CITIZEN: Our protector is taken away. [...]
>
> *A citizen announces the exile of "a minister in whom they trust."*
>
> THE PEOPLE: Woe unto us!...
> THE WOMEN: Oh Lord, have mercy upon us and our children.
> ALL: Help us, O Lord [Carlson 45].[5]

After the dialogue, soloists from the Opéra sang a military phrase, an orchestra played a march,

> cannons fired, trumpets sounded a charge, a huge explosion came from the orchestra, and the chorus burst forth with a passage from the Book of Judith: "Woe be unto the nation that riseth up against my people; for the Lord almighty will take revenge on them. In the day of judgment he will visit them." This was followed by a universal Te Deum [Carlson 45].

The next morning, the Festival of Federation began. It included an immense procession of military forces from the site of the Bastille to the Tuileries, where it was joined by the Assembly and municipal officers. From there the procession marched over the Seine, across a bridge built especially for the event, to an amphitheatre on the Champ de Mars filled with four hundred thousand spectators and Louis XVI. The amphitheatre had taken weeks to prepare. Thousands of citizens were enlisted to help move the earth into enormous mounds for spectators on the sides of the field. The King himself pitched in (if only with a handful of symbolic shovel scoops). At the amphitheatre, three hundred priests held a mass on a twenty-five foot high altar in the middle of the field. The King swore to uphold the Constitution. At noon, all over France, soldiers, the National Guard, and officials took an oath, administered by master of ceremonies Lafayette, which included the promise to protect people and property, and to insure the free circulation of grain and collection of taxes. Men, women, and children swore loyalty to Nation, Law, and King. Following the ceremony were several days of festival and celebration.

Visual depictions of the Festival of Federation differ notably in the artists' choice of emphasis and the arrangement and order of the spectacle's participants. "*Le XIV Juillet MVCCLXXXX Fédération des Français*," an engraving by Girard the Younger, shows the Champ de Mars from the perspective of the École Militaire, teaming with crowds of soldiers, holding their swords aloft as they break from organized ranks and rush to join the growing mass surrounding the center dais. The individual soldiers in the foreground rapidly blend into a featureless and unified mass that stretches back to the triple arch structure at the opposite end of the amphitheatre. The geometric chunks of crowd in the stands mirror their counterparts on the raised dais emerging from the center of the field. The perspective of the scene takes the viewer back with the crowds, blurring further into dark patches that merge into a cloud or smoke from cannon salvos behind the arch. The obscured horizon hides any end to the crowd, suggesting that the masses do not stop at the limits of the Champ de Mars, but extend across France, even as its citizens and officials speak the oath of allegiance as one (image in Hunt 2002, 280).

Jean-Louis Prieur's *Fête de la Fédération* shows the same event, but from the opposite end of the Champ de Mars behind the triple arch. Prieur's depiction includes more individual features and outlines of the standard-bearers, cannoneers, and parasol holders (it rained heavily that day). The figures in the foreground are not brandishing swords but raising and extending their right arms toward the center of the field in a gesture of solidarity. Again in this print, the crowds disappear into a blurred horizon under the sky above all France (image in Roberts 137).

Monnet, painter to the King, completed the image that shows the Fes-

tival in the most detail, viewed again from the grandstands near the royal
seats on the École Militaire side of the Champ de Mars (Carlson 114). Framed
by the distant triple arch on the left and the pavilioned seating area on the
right, the citizen-spectators function as the most prominent subject of this
image. In the foreground, the spectators raise arms and hats. We see every
fold of the young girls' dresses, the wigs and bonnets of their parents, the
bayonets of the soldiers who cheer alongside the families. The raised dais is
found at the center of the painting, the lines of the marching national guard
symmetrically radiating from it. The smoke of cannon fire creates a striking
backdrop for the arch on the opposite side of the field, but does not obscure
the horizon as in Prieur and Girard's representations, thus leaving the clear
Paris outline in the far background. Interestingly, the King's painter gives us
the effect of a much more contained, and distinctly Parisian event, even
though the Festival is celebrating the federation of the nation (image in Carlson 114).

As is evident in the descriptions above, *The Fall of the Bastille* and the
Festival of Federation were not intended to be mirror representations of the
events they commemorated. They did not seek to accurately stage the events
as they had transpired. The setting in *The Fall of the Bastille* was not representational, but consisted of the space of the Notre Dame. The characters
in the evening ceremony were allegorical; the lines were not verbatim, but
consisted of the rhetoric of a civic ceremony grounded in scriptural passages,
conflating the present France and the biblical space of the book of Judith:
Persia and Jerusalem. Instead of portraying the storming of the prison as it
occurred in lived experience, *The Fall of the Bastille* and the Festival of Federation were careful articulations for specific purposes: (a) to affirm the moral
injunctions of Jean-Jacques Rousseau in his *Lettre à d'Alembert*, advocating
non-representational communal festival-spectacle-entertainment; (b) to construct a network of symbols designed to impose meaning to recent events of
the Revolution, which could be used by figures in power to sway and control public opinion memory; and (c) to rein in and stabilize the citizens' anxieties surrounding split loyalties to revolution and the King. Because the
King was still in power, the Bastille, as symbol of radical action and over-
throwing of the old regime, needed to be detached from public memory and
reorganized into a new narrative of continuity, reconciliation with the father-
figure, and re-inscription of Christian Biblical narrative. Mona Ozouf writes:
"[T]he Festival of Federation was the beginning, rather than a celebration,
of something. Images and reminiscences of the Bastille played a very small
part in it" (33).

It is clear that a simple restaging of the storming of the prison, without any sort of political spin or agenda, would be much too ambiguous to

include in a celebration of specific revolutionary ideals. But such representation was not rejected due merely to inefficacy in achieving the desired solidarity. The discourse promoting representation as inauthentic, distorted,
irrational, and therefore improper for the ideal citizen was put into highly
visible circulation by Jean-Jacques Rousseau forty years earlier.

The organizers of the mass spectacles such as the Festival of the Federation took many of their cues from the model of civic entertainment offered
in Rousseau's *Lettre à d'Alembert contre les spectacles* (1758).[6] Written in the
context of Geneva, which then had a ban on theatres, Rousseau upheld main-
taining the ban for the general good and morals of the citizens of the city.
Theatres were primarily irrational places. They were purveyors of inauthentic representation. Rousseau judged public theatres by the effect they had on
audiences, and was skeptical of any real benefit of catharsis in tragedy. He
feared more that the audience members, unable to discriminate between
good and evil in these venues devoid of real Reason, would see negative
examples of behavior in the characters and take them home. Furthermore,
in Rousseau's argument, theatres were dominated by the tastes and passions
of women, whom he believed were not fit to judge anything but the little
works which required "only quick wit, taste, grace, and sometimes even a
bit of philosophy and reasoning." Works of true genius were beyond them
(Rousseau 103). Finally, while the theatre buildings brought individuals
together physically, they served only to further alienate them from each other
by substituting fable for real social relationships of father, son, and citizen.
Once theatre has become a place of alienation, Rousseau argued, the republic becomes that way as well.

The alternative to these theatres, held Rousseau, could be found in the
example of civic entertainments or festivals throughout the rural countryside. Rousseau called for the further propagation of such open-air festivals
as a remedy for the sickness that had befallen the citizens with the vile effects
of the theatres:

> What! Ought there to be no entertainments in a republic? On the con-
> trary, there ought to be many. It is in republics that they were born, it is
> in their bosom that they are seen to flourish with a truly festive air [...].
> But let us not adopt these exclusive entertainments which close up a small
> number of people in melancholy fashion in a gloomy cavern, which keep
> them fearful and immobile in silence and inaction, which give them only
> prisons, lances, soldiers and afflicting images of servitude and inequality
> to see [...]. Let your pleasures not be effeminate or mercenary; let noth-
> ing that has an odor of constraint and selfishness poison them; let them
> be fee and generous like you are, let the sun illuminate your innocent
> entertainments; you will constitute one yourselves, the worthiest it can
> illuminate [125–126].

Rousseau advocates here for the open-air model of communal spectacle, freed from the physical constraints of dark theatres. Those buildings are not the realm of "happy people." Citizens of a republic instead belonged in the outdoors, where their innocent entertainments would constitute a "sun" capable of self-illumination.[7] He also alludes again to the effeminacy of the theatres, dominated by the tastes of women. Outdoor entertainments, he stresses, will not be subject to effeminate pleasures. Rather, they will re-inscribe proper gender roles for the citizens of the republic. In order to do this, however, the outdoor spectacles cannot rely upon the unreasonable and inauthentic representational practices associated with theatre. Instead, he calls for spectacles that do not practice representation:

> But what then will be the objects of these entertainments? What will be shown in them? Nothing, if you please. With liberty, wherever abundance reigns, well-being also reigns. Plant a stake crowned with flowers in the middle of a square; gather the people together there, and you will have a festival. Do better yet; let the spectators become an entertainment to themselves; make them actors themselves; do it so that each sees and loves himself in the others so that all will be better united [126].

For Rousseau, the citizens were not to remove their own reasons and passions and invest them in characters upon the stage. As Danton would suggest in Büchner's drama, one can no longer count on representation to communicate a pure truth. Rousseau rejects the distortion of representation in favor of the individual standing in solely for himself.

For Rousseau, the problem of representation spilled over into other realms of civic life. Therefore, it was representation itself, and not just the physical theatres, that plagued the happiness of the ideal citizen. Indeed, authenticity was at stake. In politics, Rousseau insisted on a rejection of the practice of representation. In *Emile*, he wrote "Neither a sovereign nor representatives." Baker notes Rousseau's insistence that representation is illogical in government, since a person, including the sovereign, can only represent himself:

> The logic that precluded the transfer of sovereignty to a monarch, Rousseau emphasized, also condemned the modern practice of representative government, which had its roots in feudal particularism. "Sovereignty cannot be represented for the same reason that it cannot be alienated. It consists essentially in the general will, and will cannot be represented: It is either itself or something other. There is no middle ground."... Hence Rousseau's celebrated assertion that the English, believing representative government had made them free, enjoyed their liberty only during parliamentary elections. Hence this argument that modern peoples, in substituting representative institutions for the direct demo-

cratic participation made possible by the ancient practice of slavery, had eliminated slavery at the cost of its own liberty [Baker 236].

The revolutionaries, following Rousseau, dissolved the corporate order of the ancient régime "into a multiplicity of individuals and then reconstitut[ed] national political existence on the basis of the participation of individual citizens in the common sovereignty inherent in the general will" (235). Nor, wrote Rousseau, should the citizens of Geneva take part in theatrical entertainments that would substitute their social roles as fathers, sons, and citizens with characters from the past or fabulation. In Rousseau's community events, the spectators would become the "actors" themselves in their own spectacle, not impersonating, but engaging in their own role in the history of the republic and as a unified, happy people.

The problem with representation in the theatres, as in politics, was that it did not allow transparency in citizens' lives, and transparency, held Rousseau, was what kept society in good working order. As Paul Thomas puts it, transparency allows for no "ulterior motives" (Thomas 669); moreover, "Rousseau wanted transparency in politics and language alike, and the Revolution made their symbiosis seem possible" (665). Ironically, argues Jean Starobinsky, while laboring to be true to Rousseau's template for public festival sans representation, the French Revolutionary festivals ultimately achieved the opposite effect. The festivals failed to give rise to any authentic presence of the people because in the end they "fell into the old trap of a performance. Reason turned out to be an actress from the Opera" (Vovelle 300).[8] The spontaneity of Rousseau's festivals gave way to artificiality when the production elements of ceremony were applied with growing complexity.

Hunt writes that festivals were a major site of symbol construction in the years following 1789. Every event of the Revolution — the fall of the Bastille, the massacre at the Champ de Mars, the fall of the monarchy, the fall of Robespierre, the rise of Napoleon, et cetera — were "vertiginous." Each required "proclamations, addresses, reports, and eventually festivals and revisions of festivals" in order to structure their meaning in the minds of the people (Hunt 1984, 52). The constructed symbols, argues Hunt, functioned as a medium for public discussion of political attitudes, and lent the revolutionary experience a "psycho-political continuity," reminding the public of the secular tradition of republicanism (55). As the spectacles and festivals became more elaborate, more and more symbols were required to communicate the complex construction of meaning.[9] Allegorical symbols, like the virginal Liberty and the tree of feudalism, replaced the saints and religious imagery, in accordance with a movement away from Catholicism toward civic religion. Since the new social order was no longer grounded in the Christian French and European past, but in reason and the rights of humanity, revolutionaries rejected references to Catholicism in favor of Roman and Greek models.[10] For instance, in David's *Festival to a Supreme Being*, dedicated to the people of France, the French people were represented allegorically as Hercules holding two tiny representations of Liberty and Equality in his hand. However, the circumvention of immediate French past in favor of classical history was not necessarily a glorification of the past: "The radicals [...] linked liberty, breaking with the past, and the model of the Ancients, which represented not so much the past as a model of a future society" (Hunt 1984, 29). This aspect, according to Hunt, distinguished the French revolutionary movement from both the American Revolution and the concurrent radicalism in England:

> [T]he French did not have behind them a long-standing tradition of popular literacy motivated by religious dissent, and there were no recognized birthrights of the "freeborn" Frenchman to sustain and animate revolutionary rhetoric. Instead, the French harkened to what I will call a "mythic present," the instant of creation of the new community, the sacred moment of the new consensus. The ritual oaths of loyalty taken around a liberty tree or sworn en masse during the many revolutionary festivals commemorated and re-created the moment of social contract; the ritual words made the mythic present come alive, again and again [27].

Thus, the labor to construct symbols harkening back to Ancient times did not directly correspond to a general spirit of nostalgia for a past age. Rather, the symbols were appropriated from the past and re-imagined in the present in order to represent the ideal of a future world.

The Festival of Federation, however, unlike the later festivals described in Hunt's analysis, did not happen after the fall of the monarchy.[11] Merely a year after the fall of the Bastille, the *fête* took place in a space of contested history and memory. With the King still in power, and the Revolution in progress, the practitioners and artists associated with both *The Fall of the Bastille* and the Festival of Federation did not have the augmented network of symbols to celebrate liberty that the July 14, 1793 Festival would be able to incorporate two years later. The anxiety of split loyalty to the Revolution or to the King needed to be dispelled in order to retain control. "It was necessary to bring the Revolution to closure," writes Warren Roberts, "ultimately this was the central purpose to the July 14 patriotic celebration" (Roberts 277). Therefore, the rhetoric of the drama, and the public spectacle the next morning, needed to be placed within the context of reconciliation, peace, and mourning for the lives lost in the past year's conflict. Rather than re-stage *The Fall of the Bastille* on the original site (which was now vacant), which would evoke or rekindle the chaotic revolutionary forces, the organizers selected the formal, non-representational space of the Notre Dame. Such a religious site could lend an atmosphere of solemnity and memorial, adding the element of ceremony to the commemoration. The attachment of scripture to the play distanced *The Fall of the Bastille* from the original event, and placed it into a ritual retelling rather than strict reenactment.[12] While later festivals broke completely with Christian references, *The Fall of the Bastille* was still inherently wrapped up in them.[13] The shift would come in the subsequent events of the Revolution: the fall of the monarchy and the removal of a patriarchal figure at the head of the state equated with a paternal God.[14] With the erasure of the father figure at the head, the female figures of Liberty and Equality could take his place.

Also important to remember is that *The Fall of the Bastille* corresponded to the patriarchal template of the monarchy lain over all public forms of representation in the late eighteenth century. The King had exerted control over all the theatres. By the year 1789, the number of legitimate theatres had been reduced to the Comédie Française and the Opéra. The representatives of their respective companies, the major players in *The Fall of the Bastille*, were employed only because the King allowed them to exist. In later festivals, this would not be the case. A January 1791 law would declare all theatres equal and free, and municipalities would replace the monopolies on theatre. But, for now, in 1790, by virtue of the fact that the king was still in power, the festivals needed to confirm that fact. Thus, a general appearance of tranquility was demonstrated in the following day's events of the Festival of Federation:

> "On the route, at windows, on the rooftops, everywhere men were beside themselves, elated with a judicious joy that resembled in no way the unrestrained joy of slaves" [...] and the king himself seemed to endorse the emergence of a new society [...]. The Festival brought the French family back together again, with the recognition that the father had given in to the pressing demands of his sons [Hunt 1984, 35].[15]

With the mood of reconciliation, the Festival of Federation temporarily soothed the anxieties of Revolution by constructing France in happy reunion between the newly empowered "citizens" (vs. subjects) and their king.

At least, this was the way it appeared on the surface in the staged celebration of reconciliation and federation. The combination of spectacle, symbolism, and oath taking seemingly united all citizens in France. But while the majority sang "Frenchmen, let us go to the Champ-de-Mars" on the way to the Festival, a counter refrain was sung from the margins and from below the surface:

Aristocrat you now are done for
The Champ-de-Mars has kicked you in the ass
We will sleep with your wives
And you will be hanged [Vovelle 293].

The verbal enunciation, however marginal, voiced a multiplicity of conflicting concerns. Ozouf describes the sense of foreboding and the spread of rumors in the days preceding the Festival. Many aristocrats fled Paris, fearing the prospect of the city occupied by thousands of "well-armed patriots." The patriots themselves were on guard, suspicious that the Festival "was a trap cleverly set for them by the aristocrats" (Ozouf 44–45). In the face of such tensions, then, it appears that the network of symbols in *The Fall of the Bastille* and the Festival of Federation was specifically constructed to shore up the political walls intended to keep back dissent and further chaos, and not at all as a device for simple recall. Restaging the destruction of the Bastille alone, without mediating and organizing how it was perceived and accessed would not have done the same job.

By looking at the practices during the years of the French Revolution not as a desire to represent the events as historically accurate portrayals, but as labors to reign in, organize, and disseminate public memory constructed in the present through the use of civic symbols, *The Fall of the Bastille* and the Festival of Federation can be understood not as a re-staging of a past event, but as an arrangement of archival records to stabilize power. The way to achieve this was to make it part of a festival in a Rousseaudian fashion. Participants would not lose themselves and their reason by identifying themselves and their history with characters from the past on the stage. Rather, they took part in a festival where they themselves became the subject of the spectacle. The previous year's fall of the Bastille was not an event to be restaged as it originally took place. New symbols were required, because verbatim lines from the fall of the Bastille a year earlier, calling for blood and for death to the oppressors, did not necessarily correspond to the "truth" that those in power desired to construct in July of 1790. Likewise, the symbols of *The Fall of the Bastille* and the Festival of Federation — the scriptural passages, the giant altar, the specially constructed bridge, the clasped hands, the tri-color banners — conveyed temporary meaning. These symbols would be replaced with the shifts and events to come in the next few years. With each subsequent festival, the archive would be created anew by an arrangement of historical records, to produce current meaning for the events of the Revolution. *The Fall of the Bastille* was not a restaging of a past event, but an invention of, to use Hunt's term, "a mythic present." In July 1790, the people saw themselves in a communal narrative of reconciliation in the moment.

To summarize, the play and the festival it initiated illustrate that the

meanings of the French Revolution needed constant reformulation and sta-
bilization by those in power in order to reign in the chaos of the social and
political events taking place. Each was a labor to soothe the revolutionary
passions of the citizens of France and to re-inscribe the power of the monarch.
The representational practices of the Festival were a practical application of
Rousseau's wish to remove the spectator from the theatres, where he or she
would be tainted by illogical events and alienation from their social roles.
Instead, through mass communal spectacles or entertainments, the citizens
would become the spectacle themselves, participating in a narrative of their
own history. During the Revolution, this history was constructed for the citizens by the authoritative bodies. Each history was an arrangement of signs
designated to control public memory to be used by those authoritative bodies to maintain control. *The Fall of the Bastille* was not a representation of a
past event, as much as it was an ideal representation of a future world, referencing the recent past as well as Biblical narratives, and, in subsequent festivals, classical mythology. Each subsequent festival was a totally new
arrangement of records, reproducing the archive of the Revolution every
time.

It is the verdict of both Thomas and Starobinsky that the Festival of
Federation failed to embody Rousseau's ideal of a celebration that would
make the citizen both the spectator and the spectacle, thereby defying the
imposed layers of inauthenticity employed by the theatres. The emergent
networks of symbols and allegory, unlike Rousseau's flower-crowned stake,
are representational by nature. The Festival did make the citizen into a spectacle, but in doing so, it aligned the citizen within a template — a tool for
the efficient overlay of meaning and a means for controlling public memory. To paraphrase Büchner's Danton, one may suggest that in order to really
get at the lived event that the Festival commemorated, one would need to
crack open the skull housing the people's memory and tear it from the fiber
of the public brain. But, just as a painted or sketched depiction of the Festival differed markedly among three witnesses to the event, it is clear that
neither could there be a singular public memory of the Bastille a year later.
That is why, despite their vastly different modes of presentation, *The Fall of
the Bastille* and the Festival of Federation alternatively produced and utilized
a specific arsenal of symbols available at the time. It so happened that the
particular state of affairs allowed for the inclusion of both Christian symbols and those from antiquity. The only element not allowed in this representational milieu was a depiction of the fall of the Bastille — the event it
commemorated.

Notes

1. See also Mona Ozouf, *Festivals and the French Revolution*, trans. Alan Sheridan (Cambridge: Harvard University Press, 1976); François Furet, *Interpreting the French Revolution*, trans. Elborg Forster (Cambridge: Cambridge University Press, 1981); and Hans-Jurgen Lüsebrunk and Rolf Reichardt, *The Bastille: A History of a Symbol of Despotism and Freedom*, trans. Norbert Schürer (Durham: Duke University Press, 1997).

2. Citing Michel Foucault, "Film and Popular Memory: an Interview with Michel Foucault," trans. Martin Jordin, *Radical Philosophy* 11 (Summer 1975).

3. Alan Sikes, in a presentation at the University of Minnesota, linked Danton's line to Foucault's argument that, during the late eighteenth and early nineteenth centuries, words lost their power to convey an essential truth of the objects they designated: "Withdrawn into their own essence [...] things, in their fundamental truth, have now escaped from the space of the table; instead of being no more than the constancy that distributes their representations always in accordance with the same forms, they turn in upon themselves, posit their own volumes, and define for themselves an internal space which, to our representation is on the exterior (Alan Sikes, [citing Michel Foucault, *The Order of Things: An Archaeology of the Human Sciences* (New York: Vintage, 1994)] unpublished presentation, University of Minnesota, 1998). Sikes continued that "Foucault argues that this notion of truth somehow anterior to representation gives birth to the Modern conception of 'Man,' a being who may employ representations in order to search for his own truth, but who can never completely understand the essence of his being [...]. Modern 'Man' is thus always somehow 'other' to himself, forever linked to another aspect of himself that he does not, cannot truly know. It is no coincidence, Foucault argues, that the 19th century culminates with the development of psychoanalysis and the insistence upon the existence of the unconscious mind" (Sikes, 1998 presentation).

4. Necker had tried to reform the fiscal system (1787–88) but these attempts failed with the aristocracy's refusal to surrender their privileges. Louis XVI dismissed Necker on July 11, 1789. Necker was recalled to office July 16.

5. Quoting from Louis Pericaud, Théâtre de Monsieur (Paris, 1908).

6. For an extended discussion of the history of the Revolutionary festival, see Ozouf 13–32.

7. According to Thomas, "the festival provide[d] a setting in which the participant-observer would experience no loss of self. The secret and the lie lose their medium of existence; jubilation negates words and judgement, verbal symbolism and discursive thought [...]. If indeed human society is filled with show, with artifice, with insincerity, with dissociations between the inner and outer, as Rousseau never tired of telling us it was, festivals can serve as a reminder that, and as a practical agency by which, these divisions can be overcome" (Thomas 666).

8. Quoting Jean Starobinsky, *Jean-Jacques Rousseau: Transparency and Obstruction*, trans. Arnold Goldhammer (Chicago, 1988).

9. Elsewhere, Hunt writes that the symbol construction snowballed between 1792 and 1799, and that, furthermore, the symbols went through various modifications. One engraving, for example, commissioned by the Directorial Government in 1788, had so many different symbols "that the government felt it necessary to publish a long description which explained the meaning of the allegory. How else were viewers to know that the crown and oak and laurel was

a 'symbol of the rewards given by the government to those citizens who distinguished themselves,' or that the shield was a symbol 'of the paternal solicitude of the magistrates,' or that the thunderbolt in the claws of a gallic cock was 'an emblem of the fate being prepared for the enemies of the Republic?'" (Hunt 2002, 283–84).

10. Ozouf writes, "Antiquity seemed to the men of the Revolution to be a quite new, innocent society in which words were a perfect match for deeds; when they did have to confront the decline of ancient society, they defused it by moralizing it, attributing the decadence of history to a taste for wealth and loss of virtue" (Ozouf, *Festivals and the French Revolution* 274–75, qtd. in Paul Thomas, "The Revolutionary Festival and Rousseau's Quest for Transparency," *History of Political Thought* 18 [1997]: 674).

11. The Convention would not abolish the Monarchy until September 21, 1792. The new revolutionary calendar began the next day (abandoned in 1804). The dethroned King then remained in prison for another three months before his execution.

12. Dissociation between the space of the commemoration and that of the original event was also employed, in order to "departition" the closed spaces of the Ancien Régime: "Organizers of the Revolutionary festivals, who saw themselves as inaugurators, as originators of the present, were also (understandably enough) more than a little preoccupied with symbols of a past it was their bounden duty to efface. Accordingly '[r]evolutionary festive space was always large and open; festival organizers preferred large, open fields or squares, where equality could be conveyed, and freedom by the lack of boundaries. Closed and vertical spaces were associated with hierarchy and lack of freedom, and [...] were avoided as much as possible'" (Thomas, quoting Ozouf 54, 672).

13. Warren Roberts points out that the symbols for the Festival of Federation were taken from both antiquity and Christianity in order to garner "the widest possible support" (i.e. clasped hands, triangles, obelisks, pyramids, angels, and compasses) (Roberts 277).

14. Ozouf posits a "transfer of sacrality" between Christian festival practices and those of Revolutionary France — a type of dechristianization and establishment of a new order — especially apparent around the time of the Festival of the Supreme Being in June of 1794 (qtd. in Vovelle 288–289).

15. Quotes taken from anonymous accounts, 1790.

Works Cited

Baker, Keith Michael. *Inventing the French Revolution: Essays on the French Political Culture in the Eighteenth Century.* Cambridge: Cambridge University Press, 1990.

Büchner, Georg. *Danton's Death. The Complete Plays and Prose of Georg Büchner.* New York: Farrar, Straus and Giroux, 1963.

Carlson, Marvin. *The Theatre of the French Revolution.* Ithaca: Cornell University Press, 1966.

Deleuze, Gilles and Félix Guattari. *What Is Philosophy?* Trans. Hugh Thomlinson and Graham Burchell. New York: Columbia University Press, 1994.

Foucault, Michel. *The Order of Things: An Archaeology of the Human Sciences.* New York: Vintage, 1994.

Hunt, Lynn. "Engravings." *The French Revolution: Conflicting Interpretations.* Eds. Frank A. Kaftner, James M. Laux, and Darline Gay Levy. Malabar, Florida: Krieger, 2002.

_____. *Politics, Culture and Class in the French Revolution.* Berkeley: University of California Press, 1984.

Ozouf, Mona. *Festivals and the French Revolution.* Trans. Alan Sheridan. Cambridge: Harvard University Press, 1988.

Roberts, Warren. *Jacques-Louis David and Jean-Louis Prieur: Revolutionary Artists.* Albany: State University of New York Press, 2000.

Rousseau, Jean-Jacques. "The Letter to M. D'Alembert on the Theatre." *Politics and the Arts.* Ed. Allan Bloom. Ithaca: Cornell University Press, 1960.

Sikes, Alan. Unpublished presentation. University of Minnesota, 1998.

Starobinsky, Jean. *Jean-Jacques Rousseau: Transparency and Obstruction.* Trans. Arnold Goldhammer. Chicago: University of Chicago Press, 1988.

Thomas, Paul. "The Revolutionary Festival and Rousseau's Quest for Transparency." *History of Political Thought* 18 (1997).

Vovelle, Michel. "Festivals" excerpted from *La Mentalité Révolutionnaire: Société et mentalités sous la Révolution Française. The French Revolution: Conflicting Interpretations.* Trans. and eds. Frank A. Kafker, James M. Laux, and Darline Gay Levy. Malabar, Florida: Krieger, 2002.

Athenian Prologue
to an American Theatre

Gary Jay Williams

When Freedom's flag was wide o'er Greece unfurled
And Delphi was the centre of the world,
The Drama first uprear'd the rustic stage...
(Deacon Kurtz, from the Prologue for
the new St. Louis Theatre, 1837)

After the Revolution, when Americans were building their new theatres in America's developing cities, they marked their openings with the performance of long dedicatory poems, commonly called prologues or addresses. In the traditional hierarchy of literary studies, such occasional poetry is usually relegated to the damp basement of ephemera. But when approached as a cultural practice, as a performative convention, the opening prologues are revealing, especially those written between the 1790s and the 1840s. At a time when the nation's identity was first under construction, in the midst of the national performative laboratory that was America, the prologues are representations of imagined communities.[1] They are American Enlightenment performances of a national imaginary. Their authors frame the new theatres in America's new cities as symbolic spaces for the representation of national and city identity. This essay offers an overview of the prologue practice and focuses on the way in which the American poets linked their vision of the new nation's theatre and drama with that of the classical past.[2]

Prologue Practices

There is, of course, a long history of prologues and epilogues attached to plays. This practice can be traced back to Greek and Roman drama. Pierre Danchin's recent annotated volumes collect over 2300 prologues and epilogues from just the English Restoration and the first third of the eighteenth century — the heyday of the genre.[3] Opening prologues belong to this genealogy and have a history of their own. The prologue with which Lewis Hallam opened his theatre in Williamsburg in 1752 came out of the same English tradition as Samuel Johnson's famous prologue for the opening of Drury Lane under David Garrick a few years before, in 1747 ("The drama's laws the drama's patrons give…"). After the War of Independence, American prologue poets employed the English conventions but developed them to perform visions of their own theatres as important sites for representing the new nation's identity.

The prologue practice became national in scope as the nation grew. I have found evidence of over 170 prologues that were written for the openings of American theatres between 1735 and 1909, the majority of which — and those of particular interest — were written between 1782 (after the victory at Yorktown) and the early 1840s. They were written for theatres in large, middle-size, and small cities including Boston, New York, Philadelphia, Baltimore, Annapolis, Washington, D.C., New Orleans, Pittsburgh, Albany, Hartford, Nashville, Charleston, Montgomery, St. Louis, and San Francisco. That constitutes a national American custom, flourishing over a period of sixty years. The practice begins to decline by the mid-nineteenth century for reasons I will suggest later. To be sure, there are wide gaps between the vision of the prologues and the material practices of the theatres they helped dedicate. Still, in the national imaginary of the prologue poets, their theatres were centerpieces of cultural identity.

Public competitions were often set up for the submission of the prologues. Theatre managers announced competitions in city newspapers, offering prizes of considerable value, such as the silver cups that Charles Sprague won for his winning prologues for the opening of the Chestnut and Arch Street theatres in Philadelphia in 1822 and 1828, respectively. The performances of winning prologues were advertised on playbills as part of the inaugural events for the openings of the theatres, leading actors delivered them, and city newspapers printed the prize-winning poems in their coverage of these occasions. Many amateur poets vied to be the civic muse on these occasions. In 1822, more than thirty authors besides Charles Sprague entered the Chestnut Street Theatre's competition.[4] Prologues were written by lawyers, judges, doctors, editors, doctors, actors, women writers on a few occasions, and, in at least one instance, a pub owner and farmer. They were sometimes published in books, their authors achieving some fame. The prologues of Charles Sprague, a banker from Boston who won five competitions, were regarded as the best since Alexander Pope's.[5] Sprague's collected works, which include his theatre prologues, went through five editions in the century.

In form, the American prologues are patterned on the Restoration and eighteenth-century neoclassical poetry; the works of Dryden, Addison, Steele, and Pope are among the models.[6] They are invariably written in heroic couplets, in lofty language, and frequently call on familiar classical names and myths — all attributes thought appropriate for the high civic occasion. They are as neoclassical in style as the architecture of the theatres they dedicated. Over the years, some prologues reflect a trend to that plainer, less "aristocratic" language that democratic America increasingly valued.[7] Washington Irving's prologue for the Park Theatre season in New York in 1807 opens with the line: "In drowsy days of yore — those stupid times/Ere fashion sanctioned follies..."[8] The prologue for the Tremont Theatre's opening under new management in 1839 declared, "Plain honest thoughts within our bosoms glow;/Unswathed by pedantry, unchilled by art,/Our verses speak the promptings of the heart."[9]

The American prologues, like their English models, are also heavily steeped in eighteenth-century ideas of natural law and moral sentimentalism. Humankind, created by God with reason, has inherent rights and duties, more fundamental than those governments give (or deny). The stable society is held together by respect for these. The exercise of virtue and benevolence was thought to flow from natural instincts, were each citizen but to attend to them. The ideal citizen was the man or woman of reason and a morally well-tuned sensibility. The rousing of spontaneous feelings of compassion, love, or benevolent acts was thought essential to personal social bonds and national stability. In this the theatre was a logical ally. Pope had said as much in his influential prologue to Joseph Addison's *Cato* (1713); speaking of the stoic, honest Roman he wrote: "Britons, attend; be worth like his approved,/And show you have the virtue to be moved."[10] In 1783, an American occasional prologue written for William Whitehead's *The Roman Father* made an explicit link between patriotism and the well of compassion in the human breast. In Annapolis, Mr. Heard, a member of the acting company, praised America's "champions of freedom" and asked audiences to:

> Attend this night our author's tragic tale,
> And let the maxim in our hearts prevail:
> He who can melt at sight of human woes
> Will fight the better 'gainst his country's woes.[11]

When American prologue poets write of the contributions their theatres will make to the nation, they often are restating the sentiments in the opening lines of Pope's prologue to *Cato*:

> To wake the soul by tender strokes of art,
> To raise the genius and to mend the heart,
> To make mankind in conscious virtue bold,
> Live o'er each scene, and be what they behold —
> For this the tragic muse first trod the stage,
> Commanding tears to stream through every age...[12]

We also must not overlook the obvious — the value to the age of the very act of the prologues' public delivery. Feelingly declaimed from the stage, they contributed to the public performance of virtue.

The Muses Are Moving to America

The linking of the classical past to the American theatre in the prologues occurs chiefly in the poets' frequent play upon a theme that was an eighteenth-century commonplace: the Westward progress of civilization. In the concept sometimes known as *translatio studii* or *translatio imperii*, civilization was thought to move Westward, like the sun, from declining ancient Athens to Rome, and from declining Rome to France and England. This became a literary topos in seventeenth- and eighteenth-century American poetry[13] and was used frequently in British prologues.[14] With the development of England's colonies in America, the topos was logically extended to the New World. In 1726, the Anglican minister, George Berkeley (who was with Addison on the opening night of *Cato*), envisioned colonized America as the source of the next great "golden age" of civilization in a poem that gave the progress topos its best known expression, "Westward the course of empire takes it sway," wrote Berkeley in his often-quoted final stanza: "The first four acts already past,/A fifth shall close the drama with the day;/Time's noblest offspring is the last."[15] With the new empire would come greatness in the arts and sciences. The idea was inured in Benjamin Franklin, who wrote to a friend, "'Tis said the Arts delight to travel Westward," and in John Adams, who wrote to his life-long friend, Dr. Benjamin Rush:

> There is nothing ... more ancient in my memory, than the observation that arts, sciences, and empire had traveled westward; and in conversation it was always added since I was a child, that their next leap would be over the Atlantic and into America.[16]

Adams did not expect to enjoy the arts in the America of his lifetime, but he believed his grandchildren would.[17] In all, America was the climax of a drama scripted by providence. Adams himself resorted to a theatrical metaphor when writing in a reflection about the response of his fellow colonists in 1765, the year of the Stamp Act: "They flatter themselves that America was designed by Providence for the Theatre, on which Man was to make his true figure..."[18]

In prologue after prologue, the muses are moving to America. Many opening prologues are structured as narratives of the ancient muses' migrations down through the ages and their ultimate arrival here. Robert Treat Paine Jr.'s 1794 prologue for the opening of Boston's Federal Street Theatre, which at 276 lines is the longest of the American prologues, traces the journey in the most detail. Paine's father was a Massachusetts lawyer, judge, and signer of the Declaration of Independence (not Thomas Paine, author of *Common Sense*). The younger Paine was educated in the Boston Latin School and at Harvard; he wrote Greek fluently, delivered a poem on liberty for his Harvard commencement, and later wrote dramatic criticism.[19] He was 21 when he won the gold medal for his Federal Street prologue. He invoked the classical past not only verbally, but specified (probably with classical and Renaissance traditions in mind) that his prologue was to be delivered by Apollo. The manager and leading actor of the Federal Street Theatre, Charles Stuart Powell, performed this service. He began:

> When first o'er Athens, Learning's dawning ray
> Gleamed the dim twilight of the Attick day;
> To charm, improve, the hours of state repose,
> The deathless father of the Drama rose.[20]

Paine went on to describe the Greek drama as evolving upward to the point where the ancient theatre became a "patriot stage," "a forum of the virtues," and a "Living school of Eloquence." This is, of course, a vastly simplified reading of Greek tragedy from Aeschylus to Euripides, in a very familiar tradition of moral and heroic uses of ancient Greece, from the Renaissance through the Enlightenment down to American conservatives in our time, such as William Bennett. After Athens, Paine tracks the muses' journey through Rome, the Middle Ages, Shakespeare's England, and the Restoration and eighteenth century. After Athens' decline, "Taste transplanted bloomed at Tiber's head," "Rome adopted Athens' orphan child," and "Roscius bodied all the forms of thought." After Rome's fall comes the "Cimmerian" gloom of the Middle Ages. The banished muses flee to Albion where Shakespeare sings, Garrick acts, and "Siddons looks a nation into tears." (Paine does not include France among the muses' stops; few American prologue poets do.[21]) Paine notes, "while Europe bleeds at every vein," the muse looks westward to America: "Behold! Apollo seeks this liberal plain,/And brings the Thespian Goddess in his train./O happy realm!" The Apollo on the Federal Street's stage then blessed the theatre:

> And now, Thou Dome, by Freedom's patrons reared,
> With Beauty blazoned and by Taste revered;
> Apollo consecrates thy walls profane —
> Hence be thou sacred to the Muses' reign!
> In Thee, three ages in one shall conspire;
> A Sophocles shall sweep his lofty lyre;
> A Terence rise, in chariest charms serene;
> A Sheridan display the polished scene...
> Thy classic lares shall exalt our times,
> With distant ages and remotest climes;
> And Athens, Rome, Augusta, Blush to see
> Their virtue, beauty, grace, all shine — combined in thee.

As with many prologue poets, Paine's linkage between a moral, heroic classical past and Boston's new theatre had immediate strategic reasons. Massachusetts had just repealed its laws prohibiting theatre, and Paine was assuring Bostonians that their theatre, which had been built by Federalist patrons, would also be a "patriot stage" and a "forum of virtues." The play that followed Paine's poem was *Gustava Vasa*, billed as "the truly Republican Tragedy."[22] Paine's defensive strategy is common in the prologues, in the colonial period as well as the post–Revolutionary War years. The linking of American theatres with a classical past constructed as moral model is only one of many ways in which the prologues assured local citizens of the moral efficacy of the stage. The assurances were sometimes quite literal, as in Charles Sprague's invocation for Philadelphia's Chestnut Street Theatre in 1823: "Within thy walls may youth and goodness draw/From every scene a lecture or a law."[23] Some were in a loftier vein, as in the prologue John Henry delivered for the Hallam Company in New York in 1785:

O be forever blest the Poet's art!
That tends to mend and humanize the heart;
That sets the passions on the side of truth,
And draws from paths of vice our wandering youth;
Protects religion and supports the laws,
And fires the soul in heav'nly freedom's cause.[24]

Many prologue poets construct a link between Athenian democracy and "heav'nly freedom's cause" in America, making the case that the arts will flourish where individual freedom flourishes. Where prologues once praised

enlightened royal patrons of the theatre, the American prologues now celebrate freedom as the nourisher of the art. Caroline Lee Hentz intertwined
freedom's progress with the topos of the progress of civilization in her prologue for the opening of the new theatre in Cincinnati in 1832. Actor-Man-
ager James H. Caldwell delivered it:

> What Grecian dome o'ertopp'd its gates of pride
> In more auspicious hour? The even tide
> Of freedom's most august and glorious day
> Pours on these classic walls its hallowed ray...
> But Freedom traveling in its strength unfurl'd
> Erewhile its banner o'er this western world —
> Religion, science, genius, wealth, and taste,
> Followed with gliding steps the path she trac'd...
> Here, too, the Muses, seraph pilgrims, came,
> Heralds and guardians of the drama's fame —
> Whose lyre, from land to land, from age to age,
> Has wak'd its noblest descant for the stage.
> Hail to this shrine!

In Albany in 1813, Solomon Southwick, editor of the *Albany Register*, associated Euripides specifically with a liberty like America's:

> In early Greece, the Tragic Muse first strung
> Her infant harp, and deeds of glory sung;
> Lur'd to her hallow'd fane Apollo's throng,
> Charm'd with her voice, enchanted with her song;
> Her fam'ed Aeschylus lit his classic page,
> And pour'd its beauties on the rising stage;
> Euripides arous'd the warm desires,
> Which holy freedom's kindling breath inspires;
> Made tyrants tremble, bid the slave be free,
> And blest the clime with love and liberty.[25]

In St. Louis in 1837, Deacon Kurtz established Athens as precedent for America in the opening lines of his prologue for the new St. Louis Theatre:

> When Freedom's flag was wide o'er Greece unfurl'ed
> And Delphi was the centre of the world,
> The Drama first uprear'd the rustic stage
> To smooth the manners and instruct the age...

Deacon Kurtz followed the ancient muse of drama to St. Louis:

> Throughout our land, where'er she chance to roam,
> She finds a *resting-place*, but here — *a home!*
> We dedicate to thee, oh! Goddess bless'd,
> This thy first temple in the far, far West![26]

The muse had had a home in Nashville, Tennessee, eleven years earlier, though, to judge from Anna Maria Wells' prologue for the new theatre there in 1826:

> In those proud days when polished Athens rose
> In arts and arms superior o'er her foes...
> And now ... the loved Athenian maid [the muse of drama]
> In all her native energy arrayed,
> Led by the Muses, to our shore has come,
> Here may she find a refuge and a home.[27]

These associations are akin to the comparisons Americans have commonly made between Athens and their cities or the nation as a whole. Thomas Paine wrote of America as the Athens of the future.[28] In the late eighteenth century, Philadelphia was commonly said to be the Athens of America, and Anna Maria Wells' Nashville, which built a replica Parthenon in the center of the city for its first centennial in 1897 (which still stands), has long been known as the Athens of the South. Interestingly, while such glowing equations of Athenian freedom with American liberty are familiar as efforts to provide classical precedents for a non-monarchical government, they do not at all reflect the complexity of the opinions of America's founders about ancient Athens. The ancient Greeks figured in both good and bad examples. "Altogether," writes Jennifer Tolbert Roberts in her book, *Athens on Trial*, "America's founders were deeply ambivalent about the utility of ancient history in general and Athenian history in particular."[29] John Adams had praise for Athens, but he and James Madison also believed, as Plato had, that popular sovereignty in Athens had resulted in a tyranny of the passions which had led to its fall. Like them, Alexander Hamilton in *The Federalist* argued strongly for a representative government to ensure a check on the giddy passions that prevailed in Athens' direct democracy.[30] As Roberts points out, the U.S. Constitution adopts the Roman term "senate" for the government's upper council, but contains no trace of Athenian institutions.[31]

Many early American writers and orators, like Mercy Warren, decried the luxury and licentiousness of ancient Athens, picking up a commonplace thread of criticism that ran through Enlightenment versions of classical history.[32] Royal Tyler gave these sentiments voice through the character of Colonel Manly, the Continental Army officer who is the central figure in his *The Contrast* of 1787. Colonel Manly criticizes his sister's luxurious lifestyle and protects a young woman from the advances of a pretentious, immoral seducer who is deceitful in the vein of English rakes. Manly warns Americans not to follow the path of ancient Greece, where, he believes, money and comfort brought moral degeneracy and "the common good was lost in the pursuit of private interest."[33] So does Colonel Manly define the manliness that makes him a model American, republican in his self-restraint and public spiritedness. Federalists generally preferred Sparta over Athens as a model and worried about an America that, in its affluence in some future era, would indulge in the morally corrosive arts. Some of that sentiment had its source in the American suspicion of European court decadence. The prologues seldom speak of the paradox that some Americans both expected and feared the flourishing of the arts, but they are products of it in their role as validators of the theatre.

In their vision of an American Athens, the prologue poets often prophesy that America will produce her own Sophocles and Shakespeare, as Robert Treat Paine had done: "A Sophocles shall sweep his lofty lyre;/A Terence rise, in chariest charms serene;/A Sheridan display the polished scene..." As great drama was a marker of great civilizations past, so should it be of the new nation and its cities. For the first opening of the Park Street Theatre in New York in 1798, Elihu Hubbard (an M.D.) developed the progress trope and predicted a time when "native bards" would flourish — American Shakespeares, Jonsons, Drydens, Cibbers, Otways, Farquhars, and Rowes.[34] Charles Sprague, in his 1822 prologue for the opening of Philadelphia's Chestnut Street Theatre, recounted the blessings of the muses in ancient times and in Shakespeare's Albion and prophesied a day when there would be American playwrights of genius:

> So from his mountain-perch, through seas light,
> Our untamed eagle takes his glorious flight.
> To heaven the monarch-bird exulting springs,
> And shakes the night-fog from his mighty wings.
> Bards all our own shall yet enchant their age,
> And pour redeeming splendour o'er the stage.[35]

Sprague's prologue was recited beneath a painting above the proscenium arch where Thalia and Melpomene made claims to the genius of Shakespeare. Shakespeare is so frequently evoked as a validator of the trope of the westward progress of drama that he was, in effect, a naturalized American, notwithstanding the fact that he had blossomed under a British monarch. Washington Irving's 1807 prologue for the re-opening of the Park Street Theatre in New York was devoted almost entirely to evoking memories of Shakespearean characters.[36]

The Dwindling Prologue and the Diminishing Link

But the grand ideals were overtaken as the nation and its theatres developed. In the new capitalist free market, many theatres were not even viable for long. Boston's Federal Street Theatre of 1794 went bankrupt one year after it opened. William Dunlap went bankrupt at the Park Street Theatre in 1805. Shortly after the Arch Street Theatre opened in 1828, it engaged in a in a cut-throat ticket price war with the Chestnut and Walnut Street theatres that resulted in the bankruptcy of all three within little more than a year.[37] In what has been characterized as the market revolution, the idealized identity of a city theatre as a civic or national institution, with Athenian precedents, quickly gave way to business realities.[38] One result of the rapid growth of roads and railways was that traveling star actors displaced local stock companies. Also, the prologues had laid claim to a national voice they had never had and to a vision of a homogeneous culture that was increasingly far removed from the realities of a society changing rapidly with every new wave of immigrants. From the first years after the War of Independence, the prologues had not really given voice to all Americans. Only ten of the 172 prologues of which I have found record were identifiably by women. African Americans as a subject are entirely absent from the prologues. Slavery is never mentioned. Native Americans are seldom mentioned, and in only three prologues (by Charles Sprague) are they represented as other than savages.

After the 1840s, prologues for theatres in the eastern cities begin to dwindle into moderately humorous patter pieces about the theatre itself— the actors, the local audience. The grand tradition lingered in Midwestern and Western cities as they built their first theatres. But these were echoes of an age that was passing and with it an ideal of an American theatre as a symbolic space for the representation of city or national identities. By the last quarter of the century, the prologue practice is a stale memory. In 1880, Fanny Morant of Augustin Daly's company came before the curtain to promise her New York audiences that her prologue would surely not be "like some fossil from the dust of time/ ... that grim bore, the prologue done in rhyme."[39] By then, the prologue — however inadequate to the task it was — no longer had its original function of trying to summon a community, a nation, into being. By then, the suggestion of linkages between the classical past and the American theatre were left largely to the figurings of Apollo, Thalia, or Melpomene in theatre murals or in plaster ancient masks of tragedy and comedy around proscenium arches; ancient Athenian theatre was little more than the source of architectural motifs, a decorative vocabulary long drained of meaning, a pale substitute for vital American theatrical encounters with the past.

Notes

1. The concept of imagined communities derives from Benedict Anderson's *Imagined Communities: Reflections on the Origin and Spread of Nationalism* (London: Verso, 1983). Also helpful is Anthony P. Cohen's *The Symbolic Construction of Community* (New York: Tavistock and Ellis Horwood, 1985). I borrow the phrase "national performative laboratory" from Marvin McAllister's *White People Do Not Know How to Behave at Entertainments Designed for Ladies and Gentlemen of Colour* (Chapel Hill: University of North Carolina Press, 2003) 1–9.

2. This essay derives from a work-in-progress, *Prologue to an American Theatre*. American theatre historians have made occasional deft use of passages from the opening prologues, but they have not been analyzed as a whole as a cultural practice. In 1887, Laurence Hutton assembled a collection for the Dunlap Society, entitled *Opening Addresses*, and Hutton and William Carey followed that with *Occasional Addresses* in 1890, also for the Dunlap Society. Their collections are diligent but without commentary. Thomas Seilhamer reproduced many colonial prologues as accompaniments to the chronological narrative of his three-volume *History of American Theatre before the Revolution* (Philadelphia: Globe Printing House, 1888–91).

3. Pierre Danchin, ed., *The Prologues and Epilogues of the Restoration, 1660–1700* (Nancy: Presses Universitaires [c. 1981–1988]), 6 vols., and *The Prologues and Epilogues of the Eighteenth Century, a Complete Edition* (Nancy: Presses Universitaires, [c. 1990]), 4 vols. to date, which cover the years 1701–1737. Other notable works on the subject are George Spencer Bower's *A Study of the Prologue and Epilogue in English Literature from Shakespeare to Dryden* (London: Kegan Paul, Trench, 1884), and Mary Etta Knapp, *Prologues and Epilogues of the Eighteenth Century* (New Haven: Yale University Press, 1961).

4. Thirty rejected poems, together with Sprague's, were published in *The Rejected Addresses*, presented for the Cup offered for the best address on the opening of The New Theatre, Philadelphia, to which is prefixed the Prize Address (Philadelphia: H. C. Carey and I. Lea, 1823). The preface to the collection explains that the thirty were only a selection. The model for this may have been the *Genuine Rejected Addresses* (London: MacMillan, 1812), published after the 1812 opening of the new Drury Lane, which included Lord Byron's winning prologue. For reasons too complex to explain here, a whole genre of satirical "rejected addresses" developed out of that occasion.

5. Edwin P. Whipple, Review of Rufus W. Griswold's *The Poets and Poetry of America* (1843), *Essays and Reviews*, 3rd ed. (Boston: Ticknor and Fields, 1856) 1: 40; *The National Cyclopaedia of American Biography* (New York: James T. White, 1896) 6: 230.

6. See, for example, the opening lines of Pope's prologue to Addison's *Cato*, cited in my ensuing discussion.

7. Kenneth Cmiel, *Democratic Eloquence, the Fight Over Popular Speech in Nineteenth Century America* (Berkeley: University of California Press, 1990) 55–93 (Chapter Two).

8. Hutton, *Opening Addresses* 22–26.

9. Hutton, *Opening Addresses* 89.

10. Joseph Addison, *Cato in Eighteenth Century Plays*, ed. Ernest Rhys, Everyman's Library (New York: E.P. Dutton, [n.d.]) 5.

11. Cited in Seilhamer, *History of American Theatre* 2: 91–92. This piece is not

precisely a prologue written to open a theatre or a season, but it was written specifically for the occasion of this performance of this play. Such occasional pieces are very closely related to opening prologues.

12. Addison, *Cato, Eighteenth Century Plays* 5.

13. Rexmond C. Cochrane, "Bishop Berkeley and the Progress of Arts and Learning: Notes on a Literary Convention," *Huntington Library Quarterly* 17 (May 1954): 229–49.

14. Examples abound in *The Genuine Rejected Addresses* (see note #4) from the prologue competition for the opening of Drury Lane in 1812. See, for example, the prologues on 8–11, 52–55, 76–79, 113–117.

15. George Berkeley, *Verses on the Prospect of Planting Arts and Learning in America*, in *The Works of George Berkeley, D.D.*, ed. Alexander Campbell Fraser (Oxford: The Clarendon Press, 1871) 232. The poem was first published in Berkeley's *Miscellany* in 1752. Cochrane (see note #13) points out that the last line reflects a skepticism that was unusual among versions of the theme. On Berkeley's London circle, see A.A. Luce, *The Life of George Berkeley, Bishop of Cloyne* (London: Thomas Nelson and Sons, Ltd., 1949) Chapter 4.

16. Franklin's letter to Mary Stevenson, 25 March 1763, in Leonard Labaree, ed., *The Papers of Benjamin Franklin* (New Haven: Yale University Press, 1966) 10: 232–33; Charles Francis Adams, ed., *The Works of John Adams* (Boston: Little Brown, 1856) 9: 600. The American adoption of the idea is also discussed in Joseph J. Ellis, *After the Revolution, Profiles of Early American Culture* (New York: Norton & Co., 1979) 5–6.

17. David McCullough, *John Adams* (New York: Simon and Schuster, 2001) 236–37, citing L.H. Butterfield, ed. *Adams Family Correspondence* (Cambridge, MA: Harvard University Press, 1963) III, 342.

18. L.H. Butterfield, ed., *Diary and Autobiography of John Adams* (Cambridge, Mass., 1962) 1: 282; see also 1: 257 for similar simile.

19. Dumas Malone, ed., *Dictionary of American Biography* (New York: Charles Scribner's Sons, 1934) 14: 157–158.

20. [Robert Treat Paine], *The Works in Prose and Verse of the late Robert Treat Paine, Jun. Esq. with Notes*, to which are prefixed Sketches of his Life, Character, and Writings (Boston: J. Belcher, 1812) 151.

21. See, for example, the mention of Racine and Corneille in Deacon Kurtz's prologue, in Sol Smith, *Theatrical Management in the West and South for Thirty Years* (New York: Harper and Brothers, 1868) 125, and in Edward Johnson's 1837 prologue for the opening of the St. Louis Theatre, in Hutton, *Occasional Addresses* 68.

22. Playbill for the opening night, 3 February 1794, reproduced in W.W. Clapp, Record of the Boston Stage (Boston: J. Munroe, 1853) 20.

23. *Rejected Addresses* (Philadelphia) 12.

24. Seilhamer 2: 183.

25. Hutton, *Opening Addresses* 27; *Dictionary of American Biography* 17: 413–24.

26. Smith, *Theatrical Management in the West and South for Thirty Years* 125.

27. Hutton, *Opening Addresses* 57.

28. Thomas Paine, *The Rights of Man*, Part II in *Common Sense and Other Writings*, ed. Gordon S. Wood (New York: The Modern Library, 2003) 154.

29. Jennifer Tolbert Roberts, *Athens on Trial, the Antidemocratic Tradition in Western Thought* (Princeton: Princeton University Press, 1994) 184.

30. *Federalist 9*, *The Federalist Papers*, ed. Clinton Rossiter (New York: New American Library, 1961) 71; Roberts 181.

31. Roberts 184.

32. Roberts 180–81.

33. Royal Tyler, *The Contrast*, in *Best Plays of the Early American Theatre*, ed. John Gassner (New York: Crown Publishers, Inc., 1967) 23 (3.2).

34. Hutton, *Opening Addresses* 18–21.

35. Charles Sprague, *The Poetical and Prose Writings of Charles Sprague*, new edition (Boston: A. Williams and Co., 1876) 93.

36. Hutton and Carey, *Occasional Addresses* 22–26.

37. Charles Durang, *The Philadelphia Stage from 1749–1855* (Philadelphia: *Philadelphia Sunday Dispatch*, 1854–55) Chapter 42; William B. Wood, *Personal Recollections of the Stage, Embracing Notions of Actors, Audiences, and Auditors, during a Period of Forty Years* (Philadelphia: H.C. Baird, 1855) 345–51; Bruce McConachie, *Melodramatic Formations, American Theatre and Society, 1820–1870* (Iowa City: University of Iowa Press, 1992) 22–28.

38. Sean Wilentz provides a good overview of the scholarship on the market revolution in "Society, Politics, and the Market Revolution, 1815–1848," ed. Eric Foner, *The New American History*, revised and expanded edition (Philadelphia: Temple University Press, 1997) 61–84.

39. Hutton, *Opening Addresses* 142.

Works Cited

Adams, Charles Francis, ed. *The Works of John Adams*. 10 vols. Boston: Little Brown, 1856. Vol. 9.

Addison, Joseph. *Cato: Eighteenth Century Plays*. Ed. John Hampden, *Everyman's Library*. New York: E.P. Dutton, [n.d.].

Anderson, Benedict. *Imagined Communities: Reflections on the Origin and Spread of Nationalism*. London: Verso, 1983.

Berkeley, George. *Verses on the Prospect of Planting Arts and Learning in America. The Works of George Berkeley, D.D.* Ed. Alexander Campbell Fraser. Oxford: The Clarendon Press, 1871.

Bower, George Spencer. *A Study of the Prologue and Epilogue in English Literature from Shakespeare to Dryden*. London: Kegan Paul, Trench, 1884.

Butterfield, L.H., ed. *Adams Family Correspondence*. 6 vols. Cambridge, MA: Harvard University Press, 1963.

_____. *Diary and Autobiography of John Adams*. 4 vols. Cambridge, MA: Harvard University Press, 1962.

Clapp, W. W. *Record of the Boston Stage*. Boston: J. Munroe, 1853.

Cmiel, Kenneth. *Democratic Eloquence: The Fight Over Popular Speech in Nineteenth Century America*. Berkeley: University of California Press, 1990.

Cochrane, Rexmond C. "Bishop Berkeley and the Progress of Arts and Learning: Notes on a Literary Convention." *Huntington Library Quarterly* 17 (May 1954): 229–49.

Cohen, Anthony P. *The Symbolic Construction of Community*. New York: Tavistock and Ellis Horwood, 1985.

Danchin, Pierre, ed. *The Prologues and Epilogues of the Restoration, 1660–1700*. 6 vols. Nancy: Presses Universitaires [c. 1981–1988].
_____. *The Prologues and Epilogues of the Eighteenth Century: A Complete Edition*. 4 vols. Nancy: Presses Universitaires [c. 1990].
Durang, Charles. *The Philadelphia Stage from 1749–1855*. Philadelphia: *Philadelphia Sunday Dispatch*, 1854–55.
Ellis, Joseph J. *After the Revolution, Profiles of Early American Culture*. New York: Norton, 1979.
_____. *Genuine Rejected Addresses*. London: MacMillan, 1812.
Knapp, Mary Etta. *Prologues and Epilogues of the Eighteenth Century*. New Haven: Yale University Press, 1961.
Hutton, Laurence. *Opening Addresses*. New York: Dunlap Society, 1887.
Hutton, Laurence, and William Carey. *Occasional Addresses*. New York: Dunlap Society, 1890.
Labaree, Leonard, ed. *The Papers of Benjamin Franklin*. 36 vols. New Haven: Yale University Press, 1966. Vol. 10, 959–99.
Luce, A.A. *The Life of George Berkeley, Bishop of Cloyne*. London: Thomas Nelson and Sons, 1949.
McAllister, Marvin. *White People Do Not Know How to Behave at Entertainments Designed for Ladies and Gentlemen of Colour*. Chapel Hill: University of North Carolina Press, 2003.
McConachie, Bruce. *Melodramatic Formations, American Theatre and Society, 1820–1870*. Iowa City: University of Iowa Press, 1992.
McCullough, David. *John Adams*. New York: Simon and Schuster, 2001.
Malone, Dumas, ed. *Dictionary of American Biography*. 22 vols. New York: Charles Scribner's Sons, 1928–58. Vols. 14 and 17, 1934.
National Cyclopaedia of American Biography. 53 vols. New York: J.T. White, 1893–1984. Vol. 6, 1896.
[Paine, Robert Treat, Jr.] *The Works in Prose and Verse of the Late Robert Treat Paine, Jun. Esq. with Notes*. To which are prefixed Sketches of his Life, Character, and Writings. Boston: J. Belcher, 1812.
Paine, Thomas. *The Rights of Man, Part II. Common Sense and Other Writings*, ed. Gordon S. Wood. New York: The Modern Library, 2003.
The Rejected Addresses. Presented for the Cup offered for the best Address on the opening of The New Theatre, Philadelphia, to which is prefixed the Prize Address. Philadelphia: H.C. Carey and I. Lea, 1823.
Roberts, Jennifer Tolbert. *Athens on Trial: The Antidemocratic Tradition in Western Thought*. Princeton: Princeton University Press, 1994.
Seilhamer, Thomas. *History of American Theatre before the Revolution*. 3 vols. Philadelphia: Globe Printing House, 1888–91.
Smith, Sol. *Theatrical Management in the West and South for Thirty Years*. New York: Harper and Brothers, 1868.
Sprague, Charles. *The Poetical and Prose Writings of Charles Sprague*, new edition. Boston: A. Williams and Co., 1876.
Tyler, Royal. *The Contrast. Best Plays of the Early American Theatre*, ed. John Gassner. New York: Crown Publishers, Inc., 1967.
Whipple, Edwin P. *Essays and Reviews*, third ed. 2 vols. Boston: Ticknor and Fields, 1856.
Wilentz, Sean. "Society, Politics, and the Market Revolution, 1815–1848." *The New*

American History, revised and expanded edition, Eric Foner, ed. Philadelphia: Temple University Press, 1997.

Wood, William B. *Personal Recollections of the Stage, Embracing Notions of Actors, Audiences, and Auditors, during a Period of Forty Years*. Philadelphia: H.C. Baird, 1855.

Herder and
European Theatre

S.E. Wilmer

In the eighteenth century, German intellectuals fostered a Romantic belief in the importance of the cultural traditions of the common people.[1] Influenced by the ideas of Rousseau, Friedrich Klopstock urged Germans to create their own works of art that would compete with, rather than imitate, the values of supposedly superior cultures from abroad (especially France, England, and Italy). Likewise, Johann Gottfried von Herder encouraged German-speaking people to take pride in their own cultural traditions and their native language. He urged them to acknowledge the importance of the German folk poets of the past: "These barbarians are our fathers, their language the source of our language and their unrefined songs the mirror of the ancient German soul."[2] But unlike Klopstock, Herder believed in national distinctiveness and a *Volksgeist* (spirit of the people) and encouraged all nations to express themselves in their own individual ways.

The ideas of Herder impelled intellectuals in countries throughout Europe to search for the unique aspects of cultural expression amongst their own peoples that would testify to separate and distinct identities. In seeking to formulate their own notion of what tied their people together and made them unique, cultural nationalists reinvented the past to some extent, often writing ancient national histories that came to justify the creation of separate nation-states.[3] In this essay, I will examine the development of nationalism and specifically its effect on the national theatres in Europe. Today, the links back to German Romanticism are barely visible in other countries because nationalist ideologies favor the notion that national identity emerges "organically" rather than being subject to rhetorical construction influenced by outside forces. However, one can demonstrate the influence of Herder's ideas by analyzing the similarities in emerging "national" cultural forms, especially in the practices of emerging national theatres. In order to do this, I will examine the emergent national theatres and compare certain common choices regarding language and repertory. It will thereby become evident how dramatists and theatre managers helped formulate a sense of national identity, partly through an emphasis on folk culture and national mythologies. The results were not always successful, nor the reception predictable, because these assertions of a shared mythic "national" identity had to be negotiated with the local audience and critics.

Unlike the solitary reader of a novel or a newspaper who reacts in isolation, the theatre-goer is part of a community of spectators who can express their approval or disapproval to the performers and to each other. As Stephen Greenblatt has shown, theatre "is a collective creation," both as "the product of collective intentions" and also because it "addresses its audience as a collectivity."[4] But theatre is also a place for interaction between performers and audience. In a manner consonant with Renan's notion of the nation as a "daily plebiscite,"[5] the theatre can act as a public forum in which the audience scrutinizes and evaluates political rhetoric and assesses the validity of representations of national identity. The theatre can serve as a microcosm of the national community, passing judgment on images of itself.

In the early days, national theatres, especially in emergent nations, maintained complex and contradictory relationships with the governments in power that were often in opposition to their aims. In Finland and Ireland, for example, operating under the control of the Russian and British empires respectively, both national theatres had to steer a careful path to avoid governmental interference. The Finnish Theatre had to submit all of its plays to the state censor. Likewise, W.B. Yeats and Lady Gregory guided the Abbey Theatre away from plays that were politically sensitive, partly because of an injunction by their English patron Annie Horniman who refused to support political drama. Such theatres, however, pursued what John Hutchinson has termed the politics of cultural nationalism. According to Hutchinson, "Cultural nationalism is a movement quite independent of political nationalism. It has its own distinctive aims — the moral regeneration of the national community rather than the achievement of an autonomous state — and a distinctive politics."[6] In this sense, the national theatres in such areas as Germany, Norway, Bohemia, Finland, and Ireland, in the period prior to becoming separate nation-states, were more cultural than political institutions. Although political nationalists sometimes used them for their own purposes, and although their very existence was predicated on the notion that they represented a distinct nation that could ultimately challenge the dominance of the hegemonic imperial power, the theatres were primarily myth-making, rather than "rationally" motivated organizations, and arguably fostered self-expression more explicitly than self-determination. As I explain below, the theatres used language, actors, and repertory to help construct a sense of national identity, especially through a reliance on local plays about historical, mythological, and rural characters.

Herder expressed his faith in cultural (rather than political) unity through the *Volk*. Lamenting the disrespect in Germany (by contrast with other countries such as England and Spain) for their own cultural past, and what he saw as the over dependence on foreign traditions that stultified the growth of German literature, he argued:

> From ancient times we have absolutely no living poetry on which our newer poetry might grow like a branch upon the stem. Other nationalities have progressed with the centuries and have built with national products upon the beliefs and tastes of the *Volk*. In that way their literature and language have become national. The voice of the *Volk* is used and cherished, and in these matters they have cultivated a much larger public than we have. We poor Germans were destined from the start never to be ourselves; ever to be the lawgivers and servants of foreign nationalities. [...] It will remain eternally true that if we have no *Volk*, we shall have no public, no nationality, no language, no literature of our own which will live and work in us. Unless our literature is founded on our *Volk* we shall write eternally for closet sages and disgusting critics out of whose mouths and stomachs we get back what we have given. [...] Our classical literature is like a bird of paradise, showy in plumage, pert in aspects, all flight, all elevation, but without any true footing on German soil.[7]

Herder was much impressed by the recovery in Britain of early folk tales and songs and in particular by the publication in the 1760s of the Scottish epic of Ossian, supposedly a third century Gaelic bard (who later turned out to be an eighteenth-century forger), as well as a collection of English ballads called *Reliques of Ancient English Poetry*, edited by Thomas Percy in 1765. Comparing German unfavorably with British literature, Herder proposed, "How much further we would be [...] if we had used these folk ideas and folk tales like the British and had built our entire poetry upon them as Chaucer, Spenser, and Shakespeare built upon them, took from them, and created on the basis of them."[8]

Herder called on Germans to look for the folksongs of the past, such as those from the Middle Ages. To set an example, he began collecting what he called the *Nationallieder* (national songs) of different nations in the 1760s, later encouraging Goethe to help him.[9] He published the first international collection of folk songs in Germany in 1778 and a second volume in 1779 as *Stimmen der Völker in Liedern*, coining the term *Volkslied* (folksong or folk poetry).[10] The collection was ready for publication in 1773, but, due to adverse reaction by various critics to his enthusiasm for folk poetry, Herder withdrew it from the publisher and later resubmitted it when his ideas began to gain more favor.[11] (He planned another collection, to be organized by nationality, period, and language, as well as a volume of folk tales, but did not manage to complete either of these projects.) He also emphasized the importance of folk literature, such as the Ossian tales in his *Über Ossian und die Lieder alter Völker* of 1771, referring to folk literature as *Nationalstücke*,[12] and encouraged Germans to make a "complete critical study of the chronicles and legends of the Middles Ages."[13] As a result of his endeavors and his admiration for folk songs and literature, Herder instilled a new respect for the German common people and German folk traditions, thereby helping to undermine the prevailing class distinctions of the day, and developed a persuasive notion of national cultural unity, which influenced other writers.

Influenced by the ideas of Herder, cultural nationalists in nineteenth-century Europe investigated and exploited folklore, myths, legends, and local history, and also romanticized the lives of the rural folk. Likewise, medieval epics such as the *Nibelungenlied* and the Nordic sagas were suddenly regarded as important and used as raw material for creating new works of art. In most European countries, the interest in folk culture did not start from scratch during this period, but had evolved over centuries. However, from the late eighteenth century, folklore and folk culture or ethnography (as well as philology) became important reservoirs for notions of national identity. In Greece in the early nineteenth century, nationalists looked back to ancient Greece and the Homeric epics as their cultural heritage, tracing their roots back more than 2000 years and overlooking the long intervening period of Turkish rule. In some countries nationalist feelings caused over-enthusiastic folklorists to manufacture their own heritage and create their own epics where none existed. In the late eighteenth century in Scotland, the notion of Scottish kilts as being distinctive for individual families was invented by British manufacturers eager to sell tartan clothing to Scots who took pride in what they supposed had been an ancient and suppressed tradition.[14] Similarly, James Macpherson created an international stir by supposedly discovering the epic *Poems of Ossian*, which he had written himself. In Germany, both Herder (as we have seen) and Goethe, not knowing it was fraudulent, used the Ossian epic for their own purposes. Goethe celebrated its sentiments by quoting it at length in his 1774 *Sturm und Drang* novel *The Sorrows of Young Werther*, and, Herder praised it as an especially fine version of Nordic folk poetry.[15] Likewise in Bohemia, where three writers, Josef Dobrovský, Jan Kollár and Pavel Josef Šafařík, were primarily responsible for spreading the ideas of Herder, the Czech nationalist Václav Hanka supposedly discovered manuscripts of Czech folk poetry from the Middle Ages (1290–1310) that were heralded as early examples of their folk heritage, but were later shown to be forgeries.[16] Similarly in Lapland, a Lutheran priest named Anders Fjellner composed epic songs that he attributed to the Saami cultural tradition.[17]

In the case of the Finnish *Kalevala*, Elias Lönnrot and others collected folksongs for many years and then Lönnrot revised the songs and structured them into narratives about individual heroes, publishing an early edition in 1835 and an expanded version in 1849. Using the Homeric epic tradition as a model, Lönnrot shaped his material so that it would flow chronologically, rhythmically, and poetically. In discussing the 1849 version, he explained that his work was not definitive but somewhat arbitrary, since he was unable to discover an original form for the work.[18] Nevertheless, enthusiastic nationalists testified to the authenticity of the *Kalevala* and proclaimed it as their national epic. Far from viewing the epic as the labor of a single individual, Finnish nationalists proclaimed the *Kalevala* to be the work of the Finnish nation and evidence of the importance of the Finnish language and culture. Furthermore, perhaps because it was more important to their construction of national identity to have ancient heroes than an ancient mythology, nationalists generally regarded the *Kalevala* characters as historical, and the stories as evidence of a long Finnish history that was now at last being written.[19] By 1900, the collection of Finnish folklore (or what Wilson has called "an imagined heroic past") had become a national movement.[20]

In Ireland in the late nineteenth century, a similar cultural movement gave expression to a separate identity for the island of Ireland, which at the time was wholly under the domination of Great Britain. In a pattern similar to the one in Finland, the Irish cultural movement reflected the need to reject the dominant ideology of the British colonial government and replace it with a new national ideology. As in Finland, Irish nationalists, influenced by the German example,[21] had collected folklore tales and published them to give a greater sense of an ancient history and culture in Ireland. Yeats, Lady Gregory, and others assembled folklore and legends in particular about the Red Branch Knights. The *Táin*, like the *Kalevala*, became recognized as an epic saga close in character to other national epics. Through his collection of folklore in *The Celtic Twilight*, Yeats attempted to create a sense of Irish identity as well as literary history. Similarly, Lady Gregory wrote that she wanted to "put together the Irish legends, into a sort of *Morte d'Arthur*, choosing only the most beautiful or striking."[22] Her *Cuchulain of Murithemne*, published in 1902, was an inspiration to Yeats for his plays about the same character.

Again, there was an element of myth making in the assertions about national identity. For example, Richard Warner, archaeologist at the Ulster Museum in Belfast, argued in 1999:

> In round terms, the image of the Irish as a genetically Celtic people, in fact the whole idea of a Celtic ethnicity and of Celtic peoples, Irish, Welsh and all the rest of it, is a load of complete cock and bull. [...] The average Irish person probably has more English genes than Celtic. The whole Celtic/Irish thing was invented in order to make the Irish different from the English.[23]

Even Lady Gregory wrote that she "never quite understood the meaning of the 'Celtic Movement' which we were said to belong to. When I was asked about it, I used to say it was a movement meant to persuade the Scotch to begin buying our books, while we continued not to buy theirs."[24]

Theatre was one of the principle and most visible forms of this cultural nationalist movement of "recovery" and mythification in emerging European states. In the late eighteenth century in Germany, while the ideas of the Enlightenment were still very much in vogue, Lessing in his *Hamburg Dramaturgy* advocated the need to avoid French neo-classical influences and to compose plays about humbler domestic characters: "The misfortune of those whose circumstances come closest to our own must naturally invade our souls the deepest."[25] His comedy *Minna von Barnhelm* (1767) indirectly called for German unity by representing the need for reconciliation between the opposing states of Prussia and Saxony during the Seven Years' War. Furthermore, it emphasized the importance of German culture, as was particularly evident in a scene where a German lady, in response to a Frenchman who asks her to speak in French, answers, "Sir, I would seek to speak it in France. But why here?"[26] At about the same time Johann Elias Schlegel's German folk play *Hermann*, about a Germanic hero who defeated the Romans, was first staged. In 1872, Herder's collection of essays *Von deutscher Art und Kunst* (Concerning German Style and Art), which included papers by Goethe on architecture and by himself on German folk songs, inspired the early Romantic *Sturm und Drang* literary movement of the 1770s. Under Herder's influence, Goethe dramatized German history in *Götz von Berlichingen* and began work on the German legend *Faust*. Schiller, whose *The Robbers*, *Don Carlos,* and *Wilhelm Tell* represented a call for freedom, advocated the use of the theatre for nationalist expression: "In the drama the national features must be marked in the most prominent manner." He added, "Let [our drama] be truly historical, drawn from a profound knowledge, and let us transport ourselves wholly back to the great ideas of old. In this glass let the poet enable us to see, though to our deep shame, what the Germans were in former times, and what they must be again."[27] Christophe Wieland, looking back a decade later, commented on the growing trend:

German history, German heroes, a German scene, German characters, customs and habits were something completely new on German stages. What could be more natural than that German spectators had to feel the most lively pleasure to see themselves transferred, like through a magic switch, into their own country, into well known cities and areas, amongst their own people and ancestors — amongst people they felt at home with and who showed them, more or less, the features that characterize our nation.[28]

Goethe and Schiller, who broke away from the *Sturm und Drang* approach to develop a more international and neo-classical style of drama at the Court Theatre in Weimar, nevertheless, wrote of the potential of theatre to galvanize the nation.[29] Goethe acknowledged the ability of such work as his *Götz von Berlichingen* to "awaken self-consciousness in a nation."[30] Likewise, Schiller proposed,

If in all our plays there was one main stream, if our poets reached an agreement and created a firm union for this final purpose — if a strict selection led their work and their brushes dedicated themselves only to national matters — in one word, if we had a national stage, we would also become a nation.[31]

Following the defeat of the Germans by Napoleon at Jena in 1806, Herder's promotion of individual nationalism gained widespread acceptance. Alain Finkielkraut argues that,

Broken up into a multitude of principalities, Germany regained its sense of unity through the *Volksgeist*. It was the Germans' response to a conquering France. [...] The nation found solace from the humiliation it was suffering through the marvelous discovery of its culture. To forget their powerlessness they embraced everything Teutonic with a passion. In the name of German specificity they rejected the universal values of the French used to justify the hegemony of France.[32]

The early nineteenth century saw the rise of new Romantic movements based in Heidelberg, Berlin, and Dresden, which emphasized German history, folk songs and folk poetry as well as philology. Achim von Arnim and Clemens Brentano published an important selection of folk songs, the Brothers Grimm began to collect and publish folk stories, and Johann Gottlieb Fichte published his nationalist philosophical tract, *Reden an die Deutsche Nation* (Address to the German Nation) in 1807. Kleist started the nationalist journal *Abendblätter* (Evening News) in Berlin as well as a society that included Fichte, Brentano, Arnim, and others which stimulated many German historical dramas. Kleist himself wrote *Die Hermannsschlacht* (Hermann's battle), which he dedicated to "my fatherland" to take advantage of the nationalist spirit of the times, and *Prinz Friedrich von Homburg.*[33]

The German Romantic movement of the late eighteenth and nineteenth centuries, as Marvin Carlson has pointed out, significantly influenced dramatic literature and theatre production in Europe, such as the work of Oehlenschläger in Denmark, Victor Hugo in France, Kisfaludy and Katona in Hungary, Pushkin in Russia, Alfieri, Manzoni, and Niccolini in Italy, Kivi in Finland, and Yeats in Ireland.[34] Oehlenschläger, whose *Hakan Jarl* was written under the inspiration of Fichte in Berlin, echoed Herder in commenting that every nation "ought to have its own peculiarly national dramas. The peculiarly national is the finest flower of poetry."[35]

Likewise, opera and symphonic poems proved to be a powerful medium for National Romanticism. In Germany, E.T.A. Hoffmann followed the eighteenth-century practice of using folk stories for themes in opera with his *Undine,* followed in 1821 by Carl Maria von Weber's *Der Freischütz.* Weber also flirted with the possibility of an opera based on the legendary character of Tannhäuser, anticipating the work of Richard Wagner. Franz Liszt developed the composition style of the symphonic or tone poem that used another work of art (such as a poem, play, story, or painting) as a source of inspiration and created a musical rendition of it, normally in one movement. Liszt used both German legends, such as Faust, and Greek myths for his source material, and inspired other Romantic nationalist composers such as Smetana and Sibelius to apply the genre to their domestic settings. Franz Schubert composed long song cycles to German Romantic poems, especially those of Wilhelm Müller.

Wagner developed the idea of a *gesamtkunstwerk* (total work of art) that would use folk legends as their subject. Unlike other opera composers, he wrote his own librettos, often exploiting German folklore. He celebrated the traditional poets and singing contests of Germany in *Tannhäuser* and *Die Meistersinger,* as well as employing old legends for *The Flying Dutchman, Parsifal, Lohengrin,* and *Tristan and Isolde.* Famously, he availed of the *Nibelungenlied* (though, perhaps surprisingly, the Nordic rather than the German version[36]) for his four-opera masterpiece *Der Ring des Nibelungen,* in which a strong sense of German geography is evoked with the images of the Rhein countryside in the final opera, *Götterdämmerung.* Wagner wrote in words echoing Herder, "To the operatic poet and composer falls the task of conjuring up the holy spirit of poetry as it comes to us in the sagas and legends of past ages." He also advised that artists focus on pre–Christian myths because Christianity had diluted the original popular spirituality: "Through the adoption of Christianity the folk has lost all true understanding of the original, vital relations of the *mythos.*"[37] Notorious for his anti–Semitism and notions of racial purity and the superiority of the Aryan race, Wagner took nationalistic feelings (and egotism) to the extreme: "I am the most German of beings. I am the German spirit. Consider the incomparable magic of my works."[38] As a vehicle for his own work, he created the festival theatre in Bayreuth with the help of his admirer and patron King Ludwig II of Bavaria, and he was crowned with a silver laurel wreath after its opening season in 1876.

In Italy, Verdi composed operas with libretti adapted from five of the plays of Schiller, one of which, *Giovanna d'Arco*, contained especially strong nationalistic sentiments to which the audience responded. Moreover, his *Nabucco* in 1842, created a powerful metaphor for Italians wanting to unite Italy and overthrow Austrian rule. The beautiful "*Va, Pensiero*" chorus, in which the Jews sing of freedom from Babylonian captivity, contained the poignant lines: "*o mia patria sì bella e perduta*" (o my country so beautiful and lost). Significantly the hero of this song was the oppressed masses rather than an individual. According to Charles Osborne, "With this one chorus in an opera on a biblical subject, Verdi immediately [...] became the composer of the Risorgimento."[39] After working on Shakespearean themes such as *Macbeth* and *King Lear*,[40] Verdi was encouraged to return to nationalistic subjects by the Italian poet Giuseppe Giusti, who wrote to him, urging him to express "the sorrow that now fills the minds of us Italians [...], the sorrow of a race that feels the need of a better destiny."[41] Against the background of the 1848 revolution and the Milanese uprising against Austrian rule, Verdi composed *La Battaglia di Legnano* to a libretto by Cammarano about the twelfth-century defeat of the German King Barbarossa by the Italian cities of the Lombard League. Verdi also used libretti adapted from two anti-monarchist plays by Victor Hugo: *Ernani* (based on *Hernani*) and *Rigoletto* (based on *Le Roi s'amuse*). *Le Roi s'amuse*, about a scandalously immoral king, had been banned in France after its first performance in 1832 and Verdi's opera was likewise censored by the Austrian authorities. After a few compromises, the production was allowed to go ahead and proved to be a great success in various Italian theatres, often with a change in title to avoid censorship.

Likewise, in Bohemia, Smetana invoked the folk legend of the origins of the nation in his opera *Libuše*, as well as Czech historical characters in *Dalibor*, and folk characters in *The Bartered Bride*. Although deliberately not quoting from folk songs, Smetana created music that seemed imbued with folk music. In *The Bartered Bride*, according to Harold Schonberg, Smetana exploited "Bohemian polkas and other dance music, though he did not quote directly. He invented all of the melodies. The opera is so spiced with the very spirit of the country that many find this hard to believe, but Smetana was proud of his ability to avoid direct quotation."[42] As well as in these operas, Smetana's nationalism was perhaps best expressed in his cycle of symphonic poems *Má vlast* (My country) which included his ode to the river that runs through Prague, *Vltava* (The Moldau). Following Smetana in a similar spirit, Dvořák used the Undine legend for his opera *Rusalka*. Of him, Schonberg has written, "Nearly all of his best melodies are nationalistic. He was at his best when Bohemia took over; when, un-selfconsciously, he wrote music that expressed his native land and his love for it. He, like Smetana, seldom used actual folk themes, but his nationalism runs just as deep as Smetana's, and perhaps deeper."[43]

In Finland, Sibelius was inspired by Wagner's example of basing operas on national folk legends and tried to write a full-scale opera using Karelian mythology to be called *The Building of the Boat*. However, after a trip to Munich and Bayreuth, where he hoped to gain inspiration from seeing *Parsifal*, *Lohengrin*, and other Wagnerian operas, Sibelius, it seems, despaired of competing with Wagner's success and abandoned the effort. However, he used much of his material for a series of tone poems based on the *Kalevala* hero Lemminkäinen known as the *Lemminkäinen Suite*. The overture for *The Building of the Boat*, for example, was renamed *The Swan of Tuonela* (echoing perhaps the swan imagery in *Parsifal* and *Lohengrin*.)[44]

In many cases, national theatres were established to further the aims of the cultural nationalist movements.[45] For example, the German National Theatres in Hamburg and in Mannheim (which hired Lessing and Schiller respectively as employees), the Norwegian Theatre in Bergen, the National Theatre in Prague, the Finnish National Theatre in Helsinki, and the Abbey Theatre in Dublin closely interacted with their respective cultural nationalist movements. In territories with emerging nationalist movements as well as in established nation-states, plays and theatre performances became important sites for expressing new approaches to national identity. Marvin Carlson suggests that,

> Few of the emerging national/cultural groups of the post-romantic period neglected to utilize the drama as a powerful tool for awakening a people to a common heritage and, not infrequently, encouraging them through an awareness of this heritage to seek both national identity and national liberty in opposition to the demands of dominant and external political and cultural influences.[46]

In *Imagined Communities*, Benedict Anderson emphasizes this notion of "awakening" as a common trope for nascent nationalism, the sense that the people of the nation are "awakened" to the call of their "natural" national allegiances.[47] In the nationalist drama and the work of many national theatres of the nineteenth and early twentieth centuries, one can see the attempt to "awaken the nation" to what was professed as its natural sense of nationhood and to promote and foster a notion of national identity.

The national theatres played an important role in trying to construct distinctive national identities as well as in asserting the cultural achievements of their nations. Yet they often experienced initial growing pains. The National Theatre in Prague, which was perhaps more politically motivated than others, was imagined as early as the eighteenth century. In 1793 the Czech nationalist Prokop Šedivý, basing his arguments on Schiller's, called for an independent Czech theatre to unify the nation. After the 1848 revolution, a committee headed by Františck Palacký, published an *Announcement* outlining their intentions to build a national theatre and simultaneously raising hopes for greater political autonomy: "Our national theatre will soon arise as a monument to our constitutional rights and equality."[48] Nevertheless, it took another thirty years to build the theatre, amidst considerable controversy. In Norway, the establishment of the national theatre in Bergen by Ole Bull led some critics to feel that the theatre was misplaced. The dramatist Bjørnstjerne Bjørnson, for example, while praising Bull's efforts, wrote that the national theatre should eventually be located in the nation's capital of Christiania (later Oslo).[49] Wagner, who became involved in the 1848 revolution and the uprising in Dresden against the Prussian King, proposed a national theatre for Dresden that would operate as a democratic institution with the director being elected, but his proposal was rejected.[50] Some countries such as Finland and Ireland had no history of indigenous drama before their nationalist movements began. The first major performance of a Finnish-language drama occurred in 1869, and Irish-language drama only began to be written at the beginning of the twentieth century. Nevertheless, well in advance of national independence, the national theatre companies in these two countries used the stage — even though theatre was an art form more associated with the cultural oppressor — to project notions of national identity in opposition to a dominant foreign culture.

The act of building a national theatre edifice was often a way of spreading the ideas of nationalism from the intellectual few to the masses and celebrating their communal endeavor. In Bohemia and Finland, for example, collections were made around the country for the construction of the theatre, and so the theatre became a commonly owned enterprise (at least in spirit if not in law). The foundation-laying ceremony for the Prague National Theatre took place at a time of patriotic protest as a result of the Czechs' disappointment in failing to gain autonomy on the occasion of the Austrian-Hungarian *ausgleich* (a compromise which gave Hungary special status). When the Prague national theatre was finally constructed twenty years later, the curtain tapestry facing the audience as they awaited the beginning of a performance reminded them of their spiritual ownership of the theatre in its depiction of images from the national collection of money for the new theatre.[51] According to the national theatre literature, the curtain also portrayed "artists and craftsmen" as well as "the coats of arms of the towns which the foundation stones for the National Theatre building came from."[52] The stones originated from "sacred places in the Czech national mythology and into whose mortar the leaders of the Czech people had poured water from the 'miraculous' Hostýn Spring."[53] Significantly, from the proscenium arch hung the slogan "Národ sobě!" (The Nation to Itself), and on the ceiling of the main foyer was painted a triptych of "The Golden Age of Art," "The Decline of Art," and the "Renaissance of Art," in which the national theatre building was shown being presented to the figure of Czechia. (Interestingly the design for another painting for the foyer depicting a Czech deity with a dog's head was rejected because such a pagan image was considered demeaning for the nation.) At the opening of the theatre in 1881 and at its reopening two years later, following a fire and massive renovation, Smetana's nationalistic opera *Libuše* was staged.

In Finland, in response to the Tsar's February 1899 Manifesto that threatened the country with a policy of Russification, nationalists seized the opportunity to assert their cultural independence by building a massive granite temple to their art near the center of Helsinki.[54] A national collection was made and the foundation-laying ceremony in 1900 occurred amidst a three-day singing event organized by the Fennomanic Society of Popular Education. The opening of the new cultural fortress in 1902, on the one-hundredth anniversary of Lönnrot's birth, heightened the sense of Finnish cultural achievement and brought together the new theatre and its ties to ancient Finnish culture and the *Kalevala* in a symbolic event. Because a statue of Lönnrot had failed to arrive in time from France because of poor weather conditions, it was particularly important that the theatre should be completed for Lönnrot's birthday. The workers worked feverishly to finish the building, and despite Russian governmental plans to delay its opening by demanding a sprinkler system, the building was finally declared safe by the inspectors on the evening before the event.

Naturally, the invitation list and the program for the occasion were major issues for the Board. Because of the political situation at the time, Finnish political figures argued that inviting Russian government officials (who in some cases had helped with providing money to complete the building) would be tantamount to treason, and they threatened to demonstrate and shame the Board at the celebration if the officials were invited. Such was the public interest in the event that the Board decided to hold two opening performances on the same evening, and the celebrations continued for five days. The program included Aleksis Kivi's *Lea* and a new *Kalevala*-based play critical of Russian oppression by J.H. Erkko called *Pohjolan häät* (The Northland Wedding) which the censor almost prevented. The occasion also featured patriotic songs and a piece by Sibelius based on the 47th rune of the *Kalevala* that predicts a new race of Finnish heroes. The Finnish Literary Society (of which Lönnrot had been the first president) declared that,

> In all civilized countries the national theatre is considered the most powerful representative of the national poetry and use of artistic language, and therefore the moving of the Finnish Theatre to its magnificent fortress is to be seen as a very important victory in the same direction as Lönnrot has influenced more effectively than any other.[55]

The linguistic identity of national theatres was often one of their most crucial aspects. In Prague, the theatre staged plays and operas in Czech to overcome the dependence on German culture. In Norway the National Stage in Bergen introduced the Norwegian language to demonstrate its ascendancy over Danish (and Swedish). In the Finnish theatre, although some of the nationalists (such as Topelius) favored two branches of a national theatre, one in Swedish and one in Finnish, this position was rejected by nationalists, who stressed the importance of creating a Finnish language theatre. In Ireland the situation was a bit more complicated. The Irish language, which had been discouraged under British rule and had nearly disappeared, was again a powerful tool in the hands of the Irish nationalists. Plays in Irish including Douglas Hyde's *Casadh an tSúgáin* (The Twisting of the Rope), which was staged by the Irish Literary Theatre in 1901, provided blatant expressions of a distinctive Irish identity and evoked strong nationalist feelings when they were performed. Moreover, in the future company, the Irish actors would be expected to perform both in Irish and in English. However, compared to other countries, fewer of the Irish nationalist leadership managed to master the Irish language, which was spoken by a small minority. In a sense a compromise was proposed in the use of a Hiberno-English language in drama, such as in the work of J.M. Synge, that inserted a mixture of Irish syntax and translated Irish expressions into English and thereby made the language a distinctive cultural hybrid. According to Declan Kiberd, "Synge saw that a deterritorialized Irish might yet deterritorialize English."[56] Moreover, this compromise enabled a wider market for Irish plays and for tours by the Abbey Theatre, not only in Ireland but also abroad and particularly to England and the U.S.A.

Often the building of a national theatre was accompanied by the demand and in some cases the development of an acting school, which would help educate the actors to speak correctly. In countries where the national language (such as Czech, Hungarian, and Finnish) had not yet been securely established as a medium for high culture, the correct use and pronunciation of the language on the national stage was a major issue in creating national theatres and ultimately became an important feature for the audience and a topic on which the critics frequently commented. In Hungary, the Parliament assigned the Academy of Sciences the role of establishing a national theatre as part of its function in "the institutional cultivation of the Hungarian language."[57] In Germany the term *Bühnensprache* (stage language) as a term for correct pronunciation indicates the role of the theatre in helping to standardize the German language.[58]

The repertory of each theatre was of course a major concern to the nationalists. The nationalist canon often included plays about historical or legendary figures engaged in the nation-building or national liberation process or in some way representing certain nationalistic ideals, such as *Wilhelm Tell* in Switzerland (and Germany), *Joan of Arc* in France, *Libuše* in Bohemia, *Boris Godunov* in Russia, and *Cathleen Ni Houlihan* in Ireland. In some cases national figures in one country were borrowed for similar purposes in another. Joan of Arc, for example was serviceable in several countries as a cross-cultural archetype. Schiller's play *Die Jungfrau von Orleans* (The Maid of Orleans) was used as the basis of a libretto for Verdi's opera *Giovanna d'Arco*, and was immediately appreciated in Italy for its nationalistic rhetoric. In a production of the opera in Palermo two years later, the police intervened, necessitating the performance of the music to a different libretto.[59]

As previously mentioned, the repertory also included characters from the local mythological and folkloric tales such as the Norse and Germanic epics in Scandinavia and Germany. More interestingly, the repertory also featured dramas about anti-heroes that sometimes caused controversy when they first appeared in print or on the stage (such as Ibsen's *Peer Gynt*, Synge's *Playboy of the Western World*, and Aleksis Kivi's novel *Seven Brothers*, which was later adapted for the stage). Often these plays about anti-heroes were sanitized in subsequent stage productions, and the characters were accepted as loveable national figures in spite of their roguish or amoral behavior (and, in some cases, the author's implicit attack on society). Sometimes, particular sections of such plays, for instance the fourth act of *Peer Gynt* (which featured an Ibsenian attack on Norwegian nationalists who wished to purify the Norwegian language of foreign influences), were omitted because of their problematic nature.[60]

While national theatre directors were often anxious to include both foreign classics as well as domestic drama in the repertory, they frequently ran the risk of offending nationalists who wished to promote the distinctiveness of the national culture. Echoing the sentiments of Herder as well as Hans Sachs' aria at the end of Wagner's *Die Meistersinger* that praises "holy German art," several eminent artists in Finland tried to create a sacred Finnish theatre style. Images from the *Kalevala* were deployed in drama, *tableau vivant* theatre performances (several with music composed by Sibelius for the occasion), and concerts, as well as in the celebrated paintings of Akseli Gallen-Kallela. The Finnish dramatist, Kasimir Leino, in an article entitled "Individual art and the Possibility of a Finnish Stage Style," accused the Finnish director Bergbom of imitating a foreign style and urged that theatre art be nationalistic and be created from domestic elements.[61] Likewise, Yeats was accused by nationalists in Ireland of being too influenced by Wagner and by Japanese Noh theatre.

At the turn of the century in the Irish Theatre, the issues of race, historical and mythical memory, religion, and language became critical in the debates over the repertory and the methods for illustrating the collective identity of the Irish people. In 1899, John Eglinton asked where the Irish dramatist should look for "the subject of a national drama. [...] Would he look for it in the Irish legends, or in the life of the peasantry and folk-lore, or in Irish history and patriotism, or in life at large as reflected in his own consciousness?" Eglinton recommended the path chosen by the Greeks and the Germans:

> The ancient legends of Ireland undoubtedly contain situations and characters as well suited for drama as most of those used in the Greek tragedies which have come down to us. It is clear that if Celtic traditions are to be an active influence in future Irish literature [...] we must go to them rather than expect them to come to us, studying them as closely as possible, and allowing them to influence us as they may. The significance of that interest in folklore and antiquities, which is so strong in this country, can hardly be different from that of the writings of [Johann Gottfried] Herder and others in German literature.[62]

Yeats and others recognized the power of the theatre to influence the nationalist movement, and they looked for appropriate symbols for a new national identity. In a letter to Gilbert Murray (suggesting a version of *Oedipus Rex* for the Abbey), Yeats wrote, "Here one never knows when one may affect the mind of a whole generation. The country is in its first plastic state, and takes the mark of every strong finger."[63] Yeats also indicated his debt to the ideas of German and Norwegian nationalists: "The national movement must learn to found itself, like the national movement of Norway, upon language and history."[64] In founding the Irish Literary Theatre, the organizers asserted that the theatre should project a new image of the Irish character, as opposed to the stereotype of the stage Irish buffoon which had been generated by the English theatre: "We will show that Ireland is not the home of buffoonery and of easy sentiment, as it has been represented, but the home of an ancient idealism. We are confident of the support of all Irish people, who are weary of misrepresentation."[65] At the same time, Yeats was never comfortable with simply presenting nationalist sentiments and often challenged his audience by using nationalist rhetoric for the theatre enterprise but presenting images on the stage that were discordant with that rhetoric.

As a result of German Romanticism, national theatres looked to mythical, historical, and rural characters in order to provide national protagonists who would help to define the character of the "awakened" nation. Cultural nationalists often blurred the border between folklore and history. As we have seen, some nationalists in Finland celebrated the characters in the *Kalevala* as historical. Likewise, Irish nationalists used folklore to create a national mythology about ancient Irish history that helped distinguish themselves from the English colonists. In Bohemia legendary stories about the origins of the Czech royal family became the subject matter of plays and operas. Plays dealing with folkloric heroes helped authenticate the folk culture and construct alternative histories to those that had been imposed by the dominant cultures. The legendary characters and stories that were created became an important source for inculcating notions of national identity. While Wagner exploited the *Nibelungenlied*, Finnish dramatists used the *Kalevala* and Irish playwrights the *Táin*. Yeats wrote a cycle of plays about Cuchulainn including the tragedy *On Baile Strand*. For inspiration, Yeats not only studied Wagner and Ibsen but also the *Kalevala*.[66] In Hutchinson's assessment, Yeats' vision of Irish theatre was attempting through an integration of the arts — poetry, music, stage décor, costume, and lighting — as in Wagner's music-drama, to suggest a higher symbolic reality. For Yeats the Irish theatre would be a national shrine, in which, presenting a unified cycle of plays based on Irish legend, focusing in particular on the warrior hero Cuchulain, he would project the Irish archetype into the national consciousness.[67]

In his play *Cathleen Ni Houlihan* in 1902, Yeats created a nationalist archetype, who was mythical but rooted in history. Yeats, who collaborated with Lady Gregory in writing it, set the play in the context of the 1798 rebellion led by Wolfe Tone, but avoided the obvious strategy of characterizing the male leader. Instead, he created a mythical figure of mother Ireland calling out her sons to fight for their country. As the spirit of a suppressed people longing for independence, she speaks in metaphors to an audience on stage as well as in the audience, urging them to fight for independence. She complains that there are "too many strangers in the house" and that her "four beautiful green fields" (the four provinces of Ireland) have been taken from her. She inevitably persuades a young man about to marry to go off with her to fight for the country as she warns, "They that have red cheeks will have pale cheeks for my sake, and for all that, they will think they are well paid. They shall be remembered forever. They shall be alive forever. They shall be speaking forever. The people shall hear them forever."[68] This national image conflated the historical with the mythical, historicizing myth and mythologizing history. Maud Gonne helped legitimate the character that she not only played but also simultaneously ghosted since she was not known as an actress but as one of the leading nationalists and one of the most radical opponents of British rule.[69]

As already discussed, European national theatres exploited their folk traditions and folk poetry as suggested by German philosophers such as Herder. In many countries, the early cultural nationalists who exploited these traditions belonged to the elite of society, but as cultural nationalism spread, they had to vie for authority with a second wave of nationalists who represented the middle or lower-middle class and the core community.[70] What often solidified the movements in the different countries was the notion fostered by cultural nationalists of a common identity amongst the various strata of society. As Wachtel has observed of the nationalist movements in the Austro-Hungarian Empire,

> The glue that held these movements together was cultural and linguistic rather than political, and it is the cultural basis for these movements that explains why, even today, those nineteenth century writers, composers, and artists who dipped into the wellsprings of the national folk culture for their inspiration are treated as national heroes throughout Eastern and Central Europe — Petöfi, Mickiewicz, Mácha, Prešeren, Smetana, and Dvořák are the George Washingtons and Thomas Jeffersons of the former subject peoples of the Austro-Hungarian Empire.[71]

To this list of national heroes could be added many others playwrights and theatre directors, including those whose work was initially rejected. Realism in a mythic-heroic world or positive images of rural life suited Romantic notions but too much reality or social criticism was problematic. As the Subaltern Studies Collective has argued, nationalism claims to represent and speak for all the people of the nation, but in reality it is very selective and excludes numerous voices such as the working class and women.[72]

Similarly, the ugly side of nationalism, particularly apparent in the fascist movements of the 1930s, used the symbols of national identity, fostered in the nineteenth century, to exclude dissident, alternative, multicultural, and multiracial elements of the population. It is not surprising that some of those people associated with the earlier national theatre movement became involved with fascist and right-wing organizations, and that Yeats, for example, wrote lyrics for the Irish Blue Shirts in the 1930s.

The notions of national identity remain a product of nineteenth-century myth-making by cultural nationalists who were influenced by the values and ideals of Johann von Herder and German nationalism and Romanticism. Although the social circumstances in the various countries were somewhat different in the late nineteenth century, the process was similar. The national theatres helped construct and promote notions of national identity by putting various types of national protagonist on the stage and trying them out in front of a live audience who could accept or reject them. In this sense, the theatres acted as a "daily plebiscite" in determining, inventing, and assessing national character and images of the nation.[73]

Notes

1. Some parts of this article appeared earlier in my essay "German Romanticism and its Influence on Finnish and Irish Theatre" 15–70.

2. Herder, *Sämmtliche Werke*, vol. 2, 246. Trans. Anna Lohse.

3. For example, Henri Pirenne in his *Histoire de la Belgique* tried to prove the existence of a Belgian people, hence nation, dating back to the Roman period. Benedict Anderson has observed, "If nation-states are widely conceded to be 'new' and 'historical,' the nations to which they give political expression always loom out of an immemorial past." Benedict Anderson, *Imagined Communities* 11. Also, Ernest Gellner argues, "The cultural shreds and patches used by nationalism are often arbitrary historical inventions. Any old shred would have served as well. [...] Nationalism is not what it seems. [...] The cultures it claims to defend and revive are often its own inventions, or are modified out of all recognition." Ernest Gellner, *Nations and Nationalism* 56. Although the dissemination of such political and cultural ideas throughout Europe was assisted by political events such as the American Revolution in 1775 and the French Revolution in 1789 (both of which promoted the importance of individual human rights), German nationalism stressed the sovereignty of the nation as opposed to the sovereignty of the individual. Rather than the Kantian idea that the common people should be voluntary participants in a state and could equally opt out of it and go somewhere else, Herder's ideas carried a notion of obligation on the part of the people to belong to a particular nation that was their natural place of belonging. This sense of obligation allowed intellectuals and political leaders later on to exert a certain coercive force in imploring the common people to sacrifice themselves for the greater glory of their nation, for their fatherland or motherland.

4. Greenblatt, *Shakespearean Negotiations* 4–5.

5. Renan, "What Is a Nation?" 154.

6. John Hutchinson, *Dynamics of Cultural Nationalism* 9.

7. Herder, *Sämmtliche Werke*, vol. 9, 528–9. Trans. Anna Lohse.

8. Herder, *Sämmtliche Werke*, vol. 9, 525. Trans. Anna Lohse.

9. Goethe collected twelve Alsatian songs on his travels in 1771 for the publication. See Ergang, *Herder and German Nationalism* 210.

10. According to Robert Ergang, Herder also coined the terms *Volkspoesie* and *Volksdichtung*. Ergang, *Herder and German Nationalism* 198, note 3.

11. See Robert Ergang, *Herder and German Nationalism* 203.

12. Ergang 197.

13. Herder, *Sämmtliche Werke*, vol. 16, 389. Trans. Anna Lohse.

14. See Hugh Trevor-Roper, "The Invention of Tradition" 15–41.

15. See Christa Kamenetsky, "The German Folklore Revival in the Eighteenth Century" 843.

16. David Sayer, *The Coasts of Bohemia* 144–147.

17. Interview with Professor László Keresztes, 8 April 2000.

18. See Wilson, *Folklore and Nationalism* 40.

19. See Wilson, *Folklore and Nationalism* 49–53.

20. Wilson, *Folklore and Nationalism* 206.

21. On reading Douglas Hyde's *Literary History*, Sir Fredrick Burton wrote to Lady Gregory, "Now true light has been let in and Irish history, archaeology, literature, and poetry are the gainers. Let us not grudge to the Germans their [n]eed of honour in having led the way." Augusta Gregory, *Our Irish Theatre* 42.

22. James Pethica, *Lady Gregory's Diaries* 290.

23. Qtd. in *Sunday Times*, Irish ed., 14 November 1999: 3. See also Simon James, *The Atlantic Celts*, which questions the existence of Irish Celts.

24. Gregory, *Our Irish Theatre* 21.

25. Lessing, *Hamburgische Dramaturgie* 14: 76. Trans. Anna Lohse.

26. Lessing, *Minna von Barnhelm* 90. Trans. Anna Lohse.

27. A.W. Schlegel, *A Course of Lectures* I, 30; II, 403.

28. C.M. Wieland, "Briefe an einen jungen Dichter" 3, 478. Trans. Anna Lohse.

29. Goethe, however, drew away from Herder's ideas later in life, arguing for an international rather than a national approach to literature. See Alain Finkielkraut, *The Defeat of the Mind* 37.

30. Goethe, however, considered some of "the martial feelings of defiance" as dangerous. Qtd. in Marvin Carlson, "Nationalism and the Romantic Drama in Europe" 141.

31. Schiller, *Werke in drei Bänden*, vol.1, 728. Trans. Anna Lohse.

32. Alain Finkielkraut, *The Defeat of the Mind*, New York: Columbia University Press, 1995.

33. It was not produced because it failed to please the authorities owing to weaknesses in the character of the Prince.

34. See Marvin Carlson, "Nationalism and the Romantic Drama in Europe" 139–152.

35. Qtd. in Marvin Carlson, "Nationalism and the Romantic Drama in Europe" 142.

36. *The Nibelungenlied* 215–216.

37. Qtd. in Harold C. Schonberg, *The Lives of the Great Composers* 257.

38. Harold C. Schonberg, *The Lives of the Great Composers* 264.

39. Charles Osborne, *The Complete Operas of Verdi* 52.

40. He worked on *King Lear* for many years but never completed it.

41. Qtd. in Charles Osborne, *The Complete Operas of Verdi* 189.

42. Harold C. Schonberg, *The Lives of the Great Composers* 366.

43. Harold C. Schonberg, *The Lives of the Great Composers* 368.

44. *The Swan of Tuonela* soon became recognized as Sibelius's "first incontestable masterpiece" and the series of pieces, known as the *Lemminkäinen Suite*, achieved a more marked success even than *Kullervo* had enjoyed." Rickards, *Jean Sibelius* 58.

45. Writing of the theatres in Northern and Eastern Europe, Laurence Senelick has argued, "Most national theatres arose in reaction to a dominant culture imposed from without; they were a means of protest as well as of preserving what were considered to be salient features of the oppressed group. Theatre was a catalytic factor in the formation of its identity. So, Norwegian theatre struggled to divorce itself from Danish influence, Finnish theatre renounced Swedish [and Russian] elements, Estonian and Latvian theatre tried to extirpate their German antecedents. The Austrian hegemony was opposed in Bohemia, Moravia, Slovenia and Hungary, while Slovakia and Upper Croatia tried to overthrow the yoke of Magyar culture; the Russian hegemony was violently rejected in Poland and Lithuania." Laurence Senelick, "Recovering Repressed Memories: Writing Russian Theatre History" (in *Writing and Rewriting National Theatre Histories*, ed. S.E. Wilmer, Iowa University Press, 2004) 50.

46. Marvin Carlson, "Nationalism and the Romantic Drama" 152.

47. Anderson, *Imagined Communities* 195.

48. Qtd. in Kimball, *Czech Nationalism* 39. See also František Černý, "Idea Národního divadla" 17–25.

49. Laurence Senelick, ed., *National Theatre in Northern and Eastern Europe, 1746–1900* 151.

50. See *New Grove Dictionary of Opera*, vol. IV, 1056.

51. This was in fact the second curtain because the first, with a different design, was destroyed in a fire shortly after the opening of the theatre in 1881.

52. The first curtain tapestry with a neoclassical image designed by Ženíšek was destroyed in the fire, and Hynais was commissioned to produce a new version for the reopening in 1883. The design proved quite controversial with the Committee responsible for the reconstruction. See *Národní Divadlo* 40.

53. *Národní Divadlo* 98.

54. Although the location was somewhat peripheral to Senate Square, it was located next to the central train station and across from the Atheneum art school. The organizers were disappointed that they could not obtain a more central location.

55. Aspelin-Haapkylä, *Suomalaisen teatterin historia* 4: 187.

56. Declan Kiberd, *Inventing Ireland* 174. See also Josephine Lee, "Linguistic Imperialism" 165–181.

57. Laurence Senelick, ed., *National Theatre in Northern and Eastern Europe* 287.

58. See Michael Patterson, *The First German Theatre* 9. For a discussion of the standardization of languages, see Ronald Wardhaugh, *Introduction to Sociolinguistics* 33–37.

59. Osborne, *The Complete Operas of Verdi* 108.

60. See Sarah Bryant-Bertail, *Space and Time in Epic Theatre* 122.

61. Reitala, "Kalevalainen esitysperinne Suomalaisessa teatterissa vuoteen 1912" 75.

62. Eglinton, "What Should be the Subjects of National Drama?" 386–8.

63. Yeats to Gilbert Murray, 24 January 1905, qtd. in D.R. Clark and J.B. McGuire, *W.B. Yeats: The Writing of Sophocles' King Oedipus* 8.

64. Chicago *Daily News*, 16 March 1903, qtd. in R.F. Foster, *W.B. Yeats: A Life*, vol. 1, 291.

65. Qtd. in Hugh Hunt, *The Abbey* 18.

66. Tawastjerna, *Sibelius*, vol. 1, 168.

67. Hutchinson, *Dynamics of Cultural Nationalism* 134.

68. Edward Said in his *Culture and Imperialism* discusses Yeats' poetry at length but fails to mention this play, which would undermine his argument that Yeats never approved of liberation. See, for example, 224.

69. Various actors longed to play the character after Maud Gonne, including Maire Quinn and even Lady Gregory. See Maud Gonne letter to W.B. Yeats, 3 January 1903, *The Gonne-Yeats Letters 1893–1938*, 161, and Mary Lou Kohfeldt, *Lady Gregory* 259.

70. For a discussion of the development of a mass nationalist movement in Finland from 1870 to 1900, see Liikanen, *Fennomania*.

71. Wachtel, *Making a Nation* 21.

72. See Ania Loomba, *Colonialism/Postcolonialism* 197–199.

73. Ernest Renan, "What Is a Nation?" 154.

Works Cited

Anderson, Benedict. *Imagined Communities*, rev. ed. London: Verso, 1995.

Aspelin-Haapkylä, Eliel. *Suomalaisen teatterin historia*. Helsinki: SKS, 1906–1910.

Bryant-Bertail, Sarah. *Space and Time in Epic Theatre: The Brechtian Legacy.* Rochester: Camden House, 2000.

Carlson, Marvin. "Nationalism and the Romantic Drama in Europe." *Romantic Drama*. Ed. Gerald Gillespie. Amsterdam: John Benjamins Publishing Co., 1994.

Černý, František. "Idea Národního divadla." *Divadlo v české kultuře 19.století*. Prague: Národní galerie v Praze, 1985.

Clark, D.R., and J.B. McGuire. *W.B. Yeats: The Writing of Sophocles' King Oedipus*. Philadelphia: American Philosophical Society, 1989.

Eglinton, John. "What Should Be the Subjects of National Drama?" *Modern Irish Drama*. Ed. John Harrington. New York: W.W. Norton, 1991.

Ergang, Robert. *Herder and German Nationalism*. New York: Columbia University Press, 1931.

Finkielkraut, Alain. *The Defeat of the Mind*. New York: Columbia University Press, 1995.

Foster, R.F. *W.B. Yeats: A Life*. Oxford: Oxford University Press, 1997.

Gellner, Ernest. *The Gonne-Yeats Letters 1893–1938*. Eds. White and Jeffares. London: Pimlico, 1993.

_____. *Nations and Nationalism*. Oxford: Basil Blackwell, 1983.

Greenblatt, Stephen. *Shakespearean Negotiations*. Berkeley: University of California Press, 1988.

Gregory, Augusta. *Our Irish Theatre*. New York: Capricorn Books, 1965.

Herder, Johann von. *Sämmtliche Werke*. Ed. Bernhard Suphan. Berlin: Weidmannsche Buchhandlung, 1877.

Hunt, Hugh. *The Abbey: Ireland's National Theatre, 1904–1979*. Dublin: Gill and Macmillan, 1979.

Hutchinson, John. *Dynamics of Cultural Nationalism*. London: Allen & Unwin, 1987.

James, Simon. *The Atlantic Celts: Ancient People or Modern Invention?* London: British Museum Press, 1999.

Kamenetsky, Christa. "The German Folklore Revival in the Eighteenth Century: Herder's Theory of *Naturpoesie*." *Journal of Popular Culture* VI.4 (Spring 1973).

Kiberd, Declan. *Inventing Ireland: The Literature of the Modern Nation*. London: Jonathan Cape, 1995.

Kimball, Stanley Buchholz. *Czech Nationalism: A Study of the National Theatre Movement, 1845–83*. Urbana: Illinois University Press, 1964.

Kohfeldt, Mary Lou. *Lady Gregory*. London: André Deutsch, 1985.

Lee, Josephine. "Linguistic Imperialism, the Early Abbey Theatre, and the *Translations* of Brian Friel." *Imperialism and Theatre: Essays on World Theatre, Drama and Performance*. Ed. J. Ellen Gaynor. London: Routledge, 1995.

Lessing, Gotthold Ephraim. *Hamburgische Dramaturgie. Lessings Werke*, Fünfter Teil. Mit Einleitung von Julius Petersen. Berlin: Deutsches Verlagshaus Bong & Co., 1910.

_____. *Minna von Barnhelm*. Eds. W.F. Leopold and C.R. Goedsche. Boston: D.C. Heath and Company, 1937.

Liikanen, Ilkka. *Fennomania ja kansa. Joukkojärjestäytymisen läpimurto ja Suomalaisen puolueen synty*. Jyväskylä: SHS, 1995.

Loomba, Ania. *Colonialism/Postcolonialism*. London: Routledge, 1998.

_____. *Národní Divadlo: History and Present Day of the Building*. Prague: Národní Divadlo, 1999.

_____. *New Grove Dictionary of Opera*. Ed. Stanley Sadie. New York: Macmillan, 1997.

_____. *The Nibelungenlied*. Trans. Helen M. Mustard. *Medieval Epics*. New York: Modern Library, 1963.

Osborne, Charles. *The Complete Operas of Verdi*. New York: Da Capo, 1977.

Patterson, Michael. *The First German Theatre*. London: Routledge, 1990.

Pethica, James. *Lady Gregory's Diaries, 1892–1902*. Gerrards Cross: Colin Smythe, 1996.

Reitala, Heta. "Kalevalainen esitysperinne Suomalaisessa teatterissa vuoteen 1912." Teatteritieteen pääainetutkielma, Helsinki University, 1990.

Renan, Ernest. "What Is a Nation?" *The Nationalism Reader*. Eds. Dahbour and Ishay. Amherst, NY: Humanity Books, 1995.

Rickards, Guy. *Jean Sibelius*. London: Phaidon Press, 1997.

Said, Edward. *Culture and Imperialism*. New York: Vintage, 1994.

Sayer, David. *The Coasts of Bohemia*. Cambridge: Cambridge University Press, 1998.

Schiller, Friedrich. *Werke in drei Bänden*. Munich: Hanser, 1976.

Schlegel, A.W. *A Course of Lectures on Dramatic Art and Literature*. Trans. John Black. London: J. Templeman, J.R. Smith, 1840.

Schonberg, Harold C. *The Lives of the Great Composers*. New York: W.W. Norton, 1970.

Senelick, Laurence, ed. *National Theatre in Northern and Eastern Europe, 1746–1900.* Cambridge: Cambridge University Press, 1991.

_____. "Recovering Repressed Memories: Writing Russian Theatre History." *Writing and Rewriting National Theatre Histories.* Ed. S.E. Wilmer. Iowa City: Iowa University Press, 2004.

Tawaststjerna, Erik. *Sibelius.* Trans. Robert Layton. London: Faber and Faber, 1976.

Trevor-Roper, Hugh. "The Invention of Tradition: The Highland Tradition of Scotland." *The Invention of Tradition.* Eds. Eric Hobsbawm and Terence Ranger. Cambridge: Cambridge University Press, 1983.

Wachtel, Andrew B. *Making a Nation, Breaking a Nation: Literature and Cultural Politics in Yugoslavia.* Stanford: Stanford University Press, 1998.

Wardhaugh, Ronald. *An Introduction to Sociolinguistics.* Fourth ed. Oxford: Blackwell, 2002.

Wieland, C.M. "Briefe an einen jungen Dichter." *Brief, Werke.* Munich: Carl Hanser, 1967.

Wilmer, S.E. "German Romanticism and Its Influence on Finnish and Irish Theatre." *Theatre, History, and National Identities.* Ed. Helka Makinen, S.E. Wilmer, and W.B. Worthen. Helsinki: Helsinki University Press, 2001.

Wilson, William A. *Folklore and Nationalism in Modern Finland.* Bloomington: Indiana University Press, 1976.

Historical Avant-Garde Performance and Japanese Nationalism

David Pellegrini

The historical avant-garde has assumed centrality in Western art history and criticism, as well as social histories of interwar Europe. One widely-accepted paradigm holds that the historical avant-garde transformed the aesthetic categories by which art had been (and continues to be) produced and received. Inasmuch as they incorporated their manifestos into performances and exhibitions, the avant-gardists have been credited with transforming the category of artistic intention. The emphasis on collective and mixed-media production, the aim of incorporating everyday life objects, and the problematization of the aesthetic category of meaning, are all considered the avant-gardists' most significant achievements. Also, because they sought active rather than passive responses to their works through shock and surprise, and for their categorical rejection of the institutions of art, they have been credited with transforming the category of reception.

To many scholars, the avant-garde's enduring legacy is due less to the notoriety of specific artists than to their concerted efforts to transform the social status of art. Bürger has emphasized the radical critique of aesthetic autonomy as the single most important criteria for avant-garde classification. The doctrine of aesthetic autonomy, which can be traced to the Enlightenment era writings of Kant and Schiller, placed high value on the separation of art from the social realm as an ideal in bourgeois society.[1] It is considered to have reached its apotheosis in the aestheticist movements of the late nineteenth century, most notably art-for-art's sake. To Bürger, the overarching goals uniting such disparate movements as Futurism, Dada, Surrealism, Russian Constructivism, and, to a lesser degree, Expressionism were the abolition of the institutions of art (such as museums, academies, the critical establishment, and cultural traditions) and the erosion of the separation between art and life.[2] Though unsuccessful in accomplishing either objective, the critique of aesthetic autonomy and the concomitant crystallization of art as a separate social sphere represent, for Bürger and other theorists, the true social and political significance of the historical avant-garde project.

While Bürger's model situates the avant-garde's significance primarily within the aesthetic realm, another recurrent issue in avant-garde theory and scholarship is the socio-political coordinates of these movements, most of which appear to have been spawned as much in reaction to social and political conditions, as for the fulfillment of the artistic goals of founding members. Each movement has been examined for what might be revealed about the national temperament of its country of origin at the time of its inception, and even more significantly, at the time of its decline. Most have been outfitted with "national" identities, and/or "nationalistic" proclivities, just as many avant-gardists have been interrogated for their politics. Despite near-parallel developments in Italian and Russian poetry and art, Futurism is routinely associated with Italian Fascism, and often considered exemplary of "fascist modernism." Russian Constructivism, on the other hand, is often characterized as reflecting a post–Revolutionary utopianism that became increasingly incompatible with Stalinism. Dada and Surrealism are alternately associated with anarcho-syndicalism and Communism, due as much to the political allegiances of leading artists as to the smear campaigns mounted by the Nazi cultural bureaucracy.

While consensus regarding the political quotient of the historical avant-garde is elusive, its incompatibility with totalitarianism is indisputable. A by-product of nearly a century of scholarly debate is that the historical avant-garde is one standard by which the relationship between art and politics is gauged. Though seemingly paradoxical, the avant-gardists' rejection of aesthetic autonomy is often construed as having paved the way for totalitarian cultural production. The avant-gardists' conflation of social and aesthetic discourse in the condemnation of art devoid of social consequences, and the categorical rejection of the bourgeois institutions of art would indeed become hallmarks of fascist culture. This pattern is evident, albeit with certain variations, in Russia, Italy, and Japan, although it is perhaps most clearly observable in Nazi Germany, where avant-garde techniques and discourses were re-deployed years after the highpoints of Expressionism and Dada. Similarly, the Futurists' glorification of technology and ultra-nationalism foreshadowed, then paralleled, Italy's military expansionism. In Russia, opposition to the iconoclastic avant-garde culminated in the adoption of socialist realism as the official style of Communist art and literature to be adopted by party-affiliated artists world-wide.

Although comparatively under-examined, Expressionism, Constructivism, Futurism, Dada, Surrealism, and indigenous movements such as Mavo, Action, and Sanka, all emerged in Japan during the Taishō era (1912–1926). Though they shared many of the aesthetic goals of their European counterparts, the Japanese avant-gardists reacted to a vastly different set of social and political conditions, as well as distinctive artistic traditions. The most obvious distinction is that the Japanese avant-garde was preceded by other developments that had equally decisive effects on the production and reception of art. Perhaps most significant, the doctrine of aesthetic autonomy developed in both traditional and modern Japanese aesthetics quite differently than it had in Europe, and carried with it diverse social and political valences. No less important was the relationship of the avant-garde to the processes of Westernization, particularly its reflection of the socio-political tensions that resulted from Japan's relatively rapid absorption of foreign arts practices. Of these, the co-existence of the social-utility model of art as promulgated by the Meiji oligarchy alongside modern conceptions of individualism and art-for-art's sake, is the most significant pre-condition for the emergence of the avant-garde. Still another distinction represents for many theorists the decisive break from traditional culture, often superseding the impact of the avant-garde, namely, the rise to predominance of Naturalism. This was especially true in theatre, which experienced the simultaneous absorption of mimetic and avant-garde performance practices, as well as the devaluation of traditional forms within a few decades.

The European avant-gardists sought to change bourgeois theatre by subverting representational modes, assailing the sensibilities of bourgeois audiences, and rejecting cultural establishments. Most often, this meant the rejection of mimetic codes, such as psychologically-based characterization and the dramaturgical conventions of melodrama and the well-made play. While Japanese avant-garde performance practitioners shared similar goals, it is important to remember that the high-point of Japanese avant-garde performance was concomitant to the institutionalization of *shingeki*, the staple of which was mimetic realism. That naturalism and avant-gardism were contiguous forces, as opposed to Europe where they emerged a generation apart, is one of the many qualifications that render the Japanese avant-garde unique.

This essay examines the sociopolitical coordinates of the Japanese avant-garde and its role in transforming cultural production in the prewar era. A central concern is the transformation of aesthetic values and its effect on the production and consumption of art in the context of modernization, Westernization, and pan–Asian expansionism. Within these contexts, the trajectory of Japanese avant-garde project performance illuminates how conceptions of national identity were formulated in the Taishō era, and how more virulent strands of ultra-nationalism came to be consolidated in the social and political realms during a time of militarism and war. In this respect, transformations in performance effected by the avant-garde and other cultural processes may be seen as mediating forces in constructions of national identity, Japanese cultural autonomy, and the social efficacy of art during an era of rapid change and conflict.

As in Western scholarship, Japanese theorists have assessed the emergence and decline of the avant-garde as a function of diverse social and political ideologies. Among the earliest theorists to take up the avant-garde was Nakano Shigeharu, who in the 1920s, sought to educate the Japanese public on the values of Marxist criticism, avant-garde and proletarian art, and Taishō mass culture. In contemporary theory, Karatani Kojin has implicated critical assessments of the avant-garde as evidentiary of an "inverted" relationship between traditionalism and avant-gardism, which, he believes, characterizes the history of Japanese cross-cultural exchange. Emanating from this hypothesis is a constellation of socially-charged discourses, including individualism and aesthetic autonomy, and their incompatibility with the Confucian subordination of the individual to the state codified in the Meiji era; the persistent efforts to legitimate Japan's cultural autonomy in contradistinction to the influences of China (on traditional culture) and the West (on the modern); and the continuities of traditional, even feudal cultural structures in the modern era. It is such categorizations that render the Japanese avant-garde project unique and also serve to frame this inquiry.

In effect, I seek to illuminate three areas of possible conjuncture between the historical avant-garde with constructions of Japanese nationalism, prior to and after the Pacific War. The first of these relates to the bureaucratization of Japanese culture and the avant-garde's role in these processes. This entails an analysis of the aesthetic and social goals of the avant-garde, as well as its reception in the aesthetic and extra-aesthetic realms. The second area concerns the degree to which avant-garde discourses and production were assimilated into Japanese fascism, and how it influenced the mechanisms of propaganda. The third area concerns trans-historical valuations of the avant-garde project, and what they reveal about the interrelationship of art and politics.

Before addressing any of these issues, however, it is necessary to be reminded of the prevailing social, cultural, and theatrical contexts within which the avant-garde emerged, as well as imported and indigenous movements, key personalities, and the avant-garde's relationship with the burgeoning institutions of modern Japanese theatre. Several propositions regarding the categorical parameters of the Japanese avant-garde project emerge from historical developments in the Taishō era. First, as the efforts of the Meiji bureaucrats to modernize Japanese culture indicate, art's existence as a social institution was obviously apparent prior to the rise of both aestheticism and the avant-garde. This is in direct contrast to Western categorizations that attribute this phenomenon to the avant-garde's critique of aesthetic autonomy. Second, while the autonomy doctrine had a precedent in traditional aesthetics, it assumed distinct contours in the modern period as the tensions wrought by Westernization and formulations of individualism competed with the state's compulsory subordination of the individual to the family-state ideology. Furthermore, modern aestheticism cannot be considered to have reached its height until the Taishō era, a period also marked by the emergence of the avant-garde. Third, the status of Naturalism as a movement, style, and social discourse that developed alongside of the avant-garde, is a unique phenomenon, and one which has caused it to be enfranchised by many scholars as part and parcel of the Japanese avant-garde project. Finally, because the processes of Westernization generated both positive and negative valences in aesthetic and sociopolitical discourses, including those advanced by the avant-garde, Westernization itself becomes a category by which the avant-garde must be evaluated in regard to its social and political coordinates.

Overview of Japanese Avant-Garde Performance

German Expressionist theory and art were introduced in a series of magazine articles in 1913 (Omuka 1996, 23). The Der Sturm Gallery of Berlin loaned a number of prints to the Hibiya Museum for a 1914 exhibition that had lasting impact on many Japanese artists. The Hibiya show featured works by twenty-six artists, including Kandinsky, Kokoschka, Pechstein, and Kirchner, all of whom were associated with Expressionism, as well as works by Cubo-Futurists, such as Leger and Boccioni (Linhartová 1986, 143). Murayama Tomoyoshi's first exhibition in Germany was held at the Twardy Gallery, which was associated with Kandinsky's circle. In Germany, Murayama also became acquainted with the Expressionist dramatist Georg Kaiser, the poetry and plays of Ernst Toller, and the theories and productions of proletarian director Erwin Piscator. In 1923, Murayama designed the stage settings for the Tsukiji Little Theatre's production of Kaiser's *From Morn to Midnight*, and translated a number of Toller's plays and a collection of his poetry.[3] Hijikata Yoshi, the chief financier and a principal director of the Tsukiji Little Theatre, was drawn to Meyerhold's Constructivist and environmental stagecraft, which he had witnessed in Moscow (Ortolani 249). Photographs of Murayama's set design for the Kaiser play reveal affinities to Constructivist design precept. In Germany, Murayama also met Marinetti, who gave him a copy of the Futurist "Manifesto of Tactilism," which highlighted the potential of Futurist art to evoke the physical senses — a subject Murayama took up in the essay "Structuralism and Tactilism" (Itabashi, N. pag.).

Though never an organized movement, Expressionism influenced dramatists and theatre practitioners for several decades. Eguchi Takaya, who studied under the German Expressionist dancer Mary Wigman, was an influential force in the modern dance movement (Munroe 192). Yamada Kosaku, who also traveled in Berlin, experimented with a fusion of dance, poetry, and drama inspired by Expressionism (Omuka 1996, 23). Kubo Sakae, one of the most important playwrights of the prewar era, translated Expressionist plays as a student of German Literature at Tokyo University (Keene 460). His most famous play, *Kazambai-chi* (Region of Volcanic Ash) (1937), and his many proletarian dramas, incorporated Piscator's Epic theatre techniques, such as the use of film, theme music, voice-over narration, and a clinical portrait of modern character.

Mori Ōgai translated Marinetti's First Manifesto of Futurism in 1910, only months after it was first published in Italy. Interestingly, the translation was published in *Subaru*, the journal of the *Pan no Kai*, which was devoted to art-for-art's sake (Omuka 1996, 20). In 1912, Marinetti sent Kimura Sohachi and Uryu Yojirō a wealth of information on Futurism, including photographs of artworks (Asano 52). In 1914, Sato Kyuji, a director at the Hibiya Museum, called himself a "fuchiwarist" and experimented with *miraigeki*, his version of Futurist performance (Omuka 1995, 25). In 1920, the Russian artist David Burliuk arrived with over five hundred artworks by Expressionist, Futurist, and Cubist painters — an event that gave an immediate boost to the recently formed Futurist Arts Association. Between 1920 and 1922, Burliuk engaged in a number of high-profile activities that attracted artists, theatre practitioners, and critics. Just two weeks after his arrival, Burliuk presented "The First Exhibition of Russian Paintings in Japan," which contained examples of avant-garde artworks that had appeared only in journals (Omuka 1985, 112). At Tokyo University, he demonstrated an act of provocation typical to Futurist performance when he threw ink on the walls of the lecture hall (Omuka 1996, 119). Another noteworthy Russian artist to visit at this time was Varvara Bubnova, who immediately published two magazine articles that reported on developments in post–Revolutionary art (Omuka 1986, 114).

Interest in Futurist performance peaked in 1921, with the publication of Kanbara Tai's translation of Marinetti's performance piece *Poupées Electriques*,[4] and two articles on Futurist performance events.[5] In 1923, Kanbara contributed two more articles on Futurist Theatre, and translations of Marinetti's "Futurist Synthetic Theatre" and "Theatre of Simultaneity" manifestos.[6] In one of these articles, Kanbara mentions that Tōgō Seiji had been involved in Futurist performances in Bologna in 1922 (Lanne 390).

Dada was introduced in an anonymous article about Kurt Schwitters in the *Manchōhō* newspaper in 1920. The first detailed information about Dada appeared in two articles in the 15 August 1920 edition of the *Yorozuchōhō* newspaper. The first article summarized Tristan Tzara's performance piece *M. Antipyrine*, while the second outlined the "First Manifesto of Dada."[7] Though informative, the articles left the impression that Dada was a kind of decadent "bolshevism" in art (Linhartová 1987, 34).

Dada, like Expressionism, was never an organized movement, although its influence in the field of poetry was so significant that the 1920s has been called the "era of Dada" (Ko 4). Dada followed one of two lines of development that mirrored those in the West: the formal experimentation of the Zurich phase of the movement or the political activism associated with the Berliners. Takahashi Shinkichi, the most popular of the Dada poets, typified the formalist strand with his wordplay and associative language (Linhartová 1987, 37). Other poets were associated with the anarchist literary magazine *Red and Black*. Onchi Terutake, a noted Marxist literary critic, considered himself a Dadaist and published a one-man poetry magazine, *DADAIS* (1925). Tellingly, Onchi disparaged Takahashi's work for what he perceived to be an "unsteady middle-class temperament," a charge that echoed the European Dadaists' criticism of the Expressionists (Ko 105–6).

Of all Western avant-garde movements, Surrealism was the longest-lived, especially when one considers its importance in the postwar era. Breton's "First Manifesto of Surrealism" (1924) appeared in the literary revue *Bungei tanbi* (Literary Aesthetics) in 1925. The early 1930s witnessed the full-blown emergence of Surrealism in the visual arts, especially after the self-styled Surrealist poet, Takiguchi Shûzō, published a translation of Breton's *Surrealism and the Painter*. Fukuzawa Ichirō, who would become the premier Surrealist painter, studied in Paris when it was the center of the movement (Takashina 1986, 23). The works of Ernst, Masson, Tanguy, and Arp were introduced in the Tokyo-Paris Exhibition of Rising Art in 1932, a time when artists such as Yoshihara Jirō, Koga Harue, and Migishi Kōtarō adopted Surrealism as their aesthetic credo. The "Surrealism Overseas" exhibition of 1937 (curated by Takiguchi), was the largest exhibition of its kind to that point. That the Surrealists were afforded a measure of freedom in the late 1930s has been explained by their tendency to avoid politics; the arrests of

Takiguchi and Fukuzawa in 1941, however, marked the end of the first phase of the movement in Japan (Munroe 24).

Omuka Toshiharu has attempted to disentangle the Japanese avant-garde from matters of European influence. He traces the origins of an indigenous avant-garde to the establishment of the *Nikakai*, which was comprised of young artists disenfranchised from the *buntens*. Yorozu Testugur, Kanbara Tai, and Fumon Gyō were among the artists to participate in the first *Nikakai* exhibit in 1914, which denied entries by artists exhibiting with the *bunten*. By 1920, however, the *Nikakai*, was the dominant group of progressive artists, and the "institution" against which the avant-gardists would most rebel. To Omuka, this resulted in the polarization of art production into categories of "system and anti-system" and "authority and anti-authority" throughout the 1920s (Omuka 1996, 21).

In 1920, a radical faction of the *Nikakai* led by Fumon Gyō established the *Mirai-ha bijutsu kyōkai* (Futurist Art Association). Affiliated artists included Yorozu Tetsugor, Kishida Ryusei, Onchi Koshir, and Tōgō Seiji and Kinoshita Shuichir (Omuka 1996, 24). Their first exhibition at a small framing store in Ginza displayed works that engaged a range of avant-garde impulses deriving from Futurism, Expressionism, and Cubism. From the start, the group was associated with political activism by the authorities, perhaps unjustifiably. In Kinoshita's reminiscences about the early days of the Futurist Art Association and its political dimensions, he wrote: "In those days Communism was not yet a major threat, Ōsugi Sakae and his group frequently had trouble with the police. Any "ism," therefore, was a red flag. The authorities assumed that all "isms" were involved in Communism and tried to suppress them. Even the Special Higher Police came to investigate us."[8] After the Futurist Art Association disbanded in 1922 due to internal conflicts, several members re-formed as *Akushon* (Action), including Kanbara Tai, Yabe Tomoe, Yokoyama Junnosuke, and Nakagawa Kigen. The members did not necessarily reject other groups, however, and even included *Nikakai* artists on its advisory board.

Mavo was formed in July 1923 by Murayama Tomoyoshi, along with Kadowaki Shinro, Oura Shuzo, Ogata Kamenosuke, and Yanase Masamu — all of whom had been associated with the Futurist Art Association. In contrast to *Akushon*, the Mavoists protested the exclusivity of the art establishment, and when none of their works were admitted to the *Nikakai*, they mounted a "mobile" exhibit in Ueno Park. Their first formal exhibit was held at a Buddhist temple in Asakusa (28 July through 3 August, 1923). In the catalogue, they included the *"Mavo no sengen"* (Mavo Manifesto),[9] which declared that while they were all practitioners of the "plastic arts," they rejected any association based on "style," and, furthermore, that they "would not seek to establish definitive artistic principles." They also professed their intention to transgress the formal bounds of institutionalized art by presenting lectures, plays, and concerts. As evidence of their populism, they offered "Friends of Mavo" status to anyone donating one yen a month in exchange for free admission to exhibitions and other events.

The *MAVO* journal was printed in seven installments between 1924 and 1925, and was published out of Murayama's home. Reproductions of the magazine reveal that, from the first issue, the group was interested in experimenting with graphic and typographical arts.[10] Each issue included critical essays, poetry, performance texts, and collages. The first edition was an eight-page octavo leaflet that featured Murayama's translations of Kandinsky's poetry, paintings and photography by Okada Tatsuo, and original poems by Yanase Masamu. The second edition, which was thirty-two pages, included polemical essays, ten linocut prints pasted on newspaper, illustrations of stage designs, and poems by Ernst Toller translated by Murayama.[11] The Mavoists mounted an exhibition of stage designs in 1924. In their live performances, they became renowned for presenting alternate visions of sexuality, such as Murayama's cross-dressing, and their "unabashed sexuality" caused them to be branded as *kyōrakushugisha* (hedonists) (Weisenfeld 69).

The demise of Mavo has been attributed a number of factors, the most significant of which appears to be the political radicalization of many of its members. After the anarchist–Dadaist poet Hagiwara Kyōjirō joined the group, Ogata, Kadowaki and Ōura all resigned (Weisenfeld 71). Yanase began to devote his energies solely to the proletarian arts movement, while Murayama became more active in proletarian theatre. Some of the Mavoists joined forces with former members of the Futurist Art Association and Action to form *Sanka Zōkei Bijutsu Kyōkai* (Third Section Plastic Arts Association) in opposition to the *Nikakai*. Although it only survived a year, Sanka represents the locus of avant-garde performance activities.

Sanka's first exhibition in 1925 was held at the Matsuzakaya Department Store in Tokyo, and attracted a large audience. Representative works included Kinoshita's "living" sculptures (*R.G.* and *Three Examples of Costume Construction*) which were among the first examples of live installation art in Japan. The group also organized an evening of performance, *Gekijō no Sanka* (Sanka in the Theatre Arts), considered to be the most significant event in Japanese avant-garde performance history. Premiering 31 May 1925 at the Tsukiji Little Theatre, the evening consisted of texts inspired by Expressionism and Dada, and played to a sold-out audience comprised of many well-known theatre personalities.

The first act was a performance piece by Yoshida Kenkichi entitled *Botan* (Button), subtitled, "The Opening Play of Opposition Between White and Red." In this piece, Yoshida, who would go on to write a book on stage design, *Butai sōchisha no techo* (A Stage Designer's Handbook) (1931), presented a seemingly random series of live and filmed images that incorporated the standard avant-garde performance technique of surprise.[12] Murayama appeared next, barefoot and wearing a dark tunic, and proceeded to "writhe across the stage like a snake" to Beethoven's "Minuet in G." A photograph shows Murayama donning what appears to be a feminine costume and a bob-styled wig. A number of Sanka artists followed, producing billowing smoke and deafening sounds, with one performer running up the aisles with a charred fish. In what was obviously an act of provocation, the performers pelted the audience with tangerines.[13]

Murayama's contribution was entitled "Prostitute Giving Birth to a Child," which has been re-constructed based on anecdotal evidence by Omuka:

> After an opening accompaniment similar to the well-known folk tune *Yagi-bushi*, the curtain rose and a child selling newspapers came out on stage. Then a prostitute with a distended belly appeared, wearing a pink, Western-style dress. This woman gave birth to children squatting directly on the ground, and the babies rose up into heaven.[14]

While it is difficult to wholly discern Murayama's intentions from the fragmentary documentation, the juxtaposition of disharmonious elements, such as traditional Japanese music and Western clothing, is interesting given Murayama's aversion at the time to some of his colleagues' tendency to appropriate Western avant-garde forms.

Yanase's satirical play *Mangeki+-+-x÷=Kyūbi* (+-+-x÷=Holiday), is the only recorded text from the Sanka performance that has survived, and was only recently discovered in a collection of documents donated to the Tokyo Metropolitan Museum of Art by Yanase's family.[15] In the margins of the original script are assorted jottings, illustrations of the stage design, and notes on the lighting and blocking. The cast list, which reads like a "who's who" of the Japanese avant-garde, also contains character names and brief character descriptions.

The text reveals many of Yanase's aesthetic and political aims at the time. The subtitle, "A play with smell, action, and light as focal point," points to his interest in tactility, while the first stage directions ("No conversations between actors are allowed; everything is to proceed in silence") indicate his emphasis on movement and gesture (Yanase 44). After a pantomimed introduction, the Scholar, Missionary, and Army Officer characters enter from the audience, all of whom should "appear to be" intoxicated. The performers' entrance through the audience, and the planting of others who eventually join the action, typify the avant-garde performance artists' aim of blurring the distinction between art and life. The final sequence of the play is comprised of images evoking the illusion of chaos onstage. A man from the audience joins the group of performers, who crawl on their hands and knees. The stage then gets flooded with smoke, a "magnesium light" begins to flicker, and parts of the set are hoisted by a crane-like device. As the smoke gets more intense, the Shadow-Man dances with joy, while the lights slowly dim; when the lights return, "the stage set has crumbled down over the dead bodies, props, etc." (Yanase 31–3). While it is not clear whether the apocalyptic imagery was an overt reference to the earthquake, or a prophecy of impending war, it is noteworthy that the piece requires the use of a number of special effects, including a crane and film projectors.

Interestingly, the original script contains a "seal of approval" from the Metropolitan Police on the back cover, dated 26 May 1925, four days before the Sanka opening. Throughout the text, the seal of a person named Terasawa appears, and on page thirteen another seal is stamped which reads: "Public Order Division of the Metropolitan Police." Given the implicit criticism of the military in this piece, it is a wonder that the text was allowed to be performed at all. It is perhaps because Yanase knew that the text would be scrutinized so closely that he relied heavily on gesture and improvisation. Ironically, the subsequent turn to proletarian art and agit-prop theatre by many of the Sanka performance artists may have been at least partially due to the fact that the performance was not halted by the authorities. Still among all of the avant-gardists, Yanase was singled out for harsh treatment by the police. In 1923, he was arrested, beaten and bayoneted by soldiers, and detained for five days, after which he left Tokyo for a time. Four years later, his political cartoons were banned from the "First Exhibition of the Japan Cartoon League." In December 1932 he was arrested once again for breaking the Public Order Maintenance Law, and was held at the Ichigaya Prison in Tokyo until September 1933, with a temporary release granted August so that he could be with his first wife for a few days before she died.

Critical reception to the Sanka performance was mixed. Many of the contributors had already established themselves as controversial figures, so their participation must surely have pre-conditioned audience and critical expectations. Even though he participated in Yanase's piece, Ogata criticized Sanka for its relative lack of social import, arguing that the works "did not appear to be strong enough to permeate into the kernel of the times, and [thus] cannot become the fuse for a social revolution, an individual revolution, nor a revolution in the life of the masses."[16] The second Sanka show was suspended due to internal disagreements among the artists along both stylistic and ideological lines. In a text published shortly afterwards, Murayama wrote of the class consciousness that many, but not all, of the members of the group upheld in their exploration of Constructivist art and performance: "The desire to arrive at the universal ... that one locates in Constructivism corresponds to the desire for collective and social power. As a result, Constructivism is the blood brother of Communism, which, like us, tends to the universal, and looks for a truthful objective."[17] By 1927, however, former Sanka members would be advocating for social realism and agit-prop over the more abstract tendencies associated with Constructivist performance. In Omuka's estimation, the disbanding of Sanka represents a signal event in Japanese avant-garde performance as it was increasingly absorbed into the proletarian theatre movement and *shingeki* (Omuka 1986, 125).

The most significant event in the early proletarian theatre was the establishment of the *Nihon Rōdō Gekidan* (Japan Labor Theatre) by Hirasawa Keishichi, a labor leader and writer. The company, which used amateur actors and played to factory audiences, lasted only two years due to the fact that Hirasawa was "arrested and evidently murdered by the Tokyo police" (Rimer 1974, 52). Meanwhile, a production of proletarian playwright Fujimori Seikichi's *Gisei* (The Sacrifice) (1926) was halted by the authorities one day before its scheduled opening at the Tsukiji Little Theatre (49). Akita Ujaku, who wrote Expressionist plays, formed the *Senzuka* (Pioneer Theatre), which was housed in a Shinjuku bakery. In 1926, Sasaki Takamaru, who had participated in the Sanka performance, founded the *Toranku Gekidan* (Trunk Theatre) to support the efforts of labor unions (52).

That same year, Murayama, Sasaki, and Senda Koreya established the *Zen'eiza* (Vanguard Theatre), which aimed to reinterpret classical plays. For the *Zen'eiza*, Murayama directed and co-designed (with Yanase) a production of *Don Quixote Liberated* by Lunacharsky — the Commissar of Enlightenment in post–Revolutionary Russia, who was an early patron of the avant-garde.[18] Murayama also directed Upton Sinclair's *Prince Hagen* (a favorite of Erwin Piscator), for the Tsukiji Little Theatre in 1927. When the Communist purge prompted the consolidation of efforts, the *Zen'eiza* split into smaller groups that were ultimately reorganized as the *Sayoku Gekiō* (Left-wing Theatre). In 1929, the Japan League of Proletarian Drama was formed, and dozens of other proletarian theatres emerged, many of them drawing inspiration, energy, and talents from artists associated with the avant-garde.

Increased police surveillance was routine in the early 1930s. A production of one of Murayama's plays, *Shimura Natsue*, caused a scandal when an actress was arrested onstage at the *Sayoku Gekijō* in 1932. Murayama himself was arrested during rehearsals for another production of this play.[19] With the suppression of Communism a top priority of the censors, the *Sayoku Gek-ijō* leaders re-named it the *Chūō Gekijō* (Central Theatre) in 1934. Upon his release from prison, Murayama organized the *Shinkyō Gekidan* (New Cooperation Group) in hopes of revitalizing the movement. Constantly under the threat of arrest, the theatre managers operated sporadically until 1940, producing some works by proletarian writers, and socially-significant (though less overtly political) realistic plays, such as those associated with the New York–based Group Theatre, including Clifford Odets' *Awake and Sing*, and Sidney Kingsley's *Dead End* (UNESCO 226).

Aside from the performance activities and events associated with discrete movements, avant-garde dramaturgical and performance techniques were incorporated into *shingeki* in much the same way that the European avant-garde was absorbed into theatrical modernism. It is also true, however, that given the transformation of the institutions of Japanese theatre effected by the turn towards realism, some scholars consider *shingeki*, like Naturalism, a constituent movement of the avant-garde. As Ozasa notes, "*Shingeki* was avant-garde precisely because it leaned towards realism. Avant-gardism and realism were the same — a fact long unrecognized by Japanese scholars" (221). Hōgetsu's production of Ibsen's *A Doll's House*, for example, "exploded the earlier and milder portrayals of estrangement in naturalist literature," so that, by all accounts, "audiences exited debating the characters as if they were real persons" (Nolte 99).

Osanai had limited the repertory of the *Jiyu Gekijō* to European drama, and tried to incorporate Stanislavsky's actor-training and directing techniques. He attempted to replicate this policy at the Tsukiji Little Theatre, which produced over fifty works by Western playwrights. His colleague Hijikata, however, gravitated to Expressionism and experimental performance inspired by his travels in Russia and Germany. The early phase of the Tsukiji Little Theatre, then, is justly hailed as a period of experimentation in a wide range of performance techniques. Hijikata's preferences were also informed by what he perceived to be the social and political power of theatre. For the opening production, he directed the Expressionst play, *Seeschlacht* (Sea Battle) by Reinhard Goering.[20] Hijikata's "rough and abstract methods of direction" were at odds with Osanai's naturalistic impulses, hence the conflict between the two legendary Russian directors played out on the stage of a single Japanese theatre company (Rimer 1974, 44). To these *shingeki* pioneers, Rimer adds Murayama, who, especially in attempting to integrate Piscator's Epic techniques, became an advocate for the supremacy of the director in the modern theatre (1984, 45).

On 19 August 1940, the two remaining leftist *shingeki* troupes, the *Shinkyo Gekidan* and the *Shin Tsukiji* were dissolved, and a number of their members arrested. The only modern troupe of significance to perform during the war years was the *Bungakuza* (Literary Theatre), which had no overt political affiliations and mainly continued a pursuit of the art-for-art's sake ideal (Ortolani 253).

What this brief overview reveals is that when the indigenous avant-garde movements coalesced, there were many cross-tendencies in all fields of culture, thus precluding any totalizing theories regarding the avant-garde's rejection of either aesthetic autonomy, or previous styles and movements like Naturalism. This is not to suggest, however, that the avant-garde did not exhibit characteristics that distinguish it from other cultural manifestations of the era. Of these, the attack on the institutions of art and the sublation of art and life emerge as the most important. Interestingly, however, these tendencies did not necessarily entail either resistance to bourgeois commodification or the rejection of mimesis. Whether or not one considers Japanese Naturalism to be a constituent movement of the avant-garde, it is important to remember that in the theatre, its proliferation in performance was coincidental to the emergence of the avant-garde, and was central to the transformation of the institutions and institutional codes of the theatre.

The Political Quotient of the Japanese Avant-Garde

While scholars highlight the avant-gardists' overt affiliation with leftist politics after the rise of the proletarian arts movements, Clark maintains that they primarily "focused the discourse on themselves and their own sympathies and identification, not on a social or international other given to them by the state or, more broadly and abstractly, by Japan's historical situation" (Clark 41). This is an important qualification, because while many avant-gardists rejected aestheticism, for the most part, they sought to uphold artistic subjectivity in the face of political demands for conformity and consensus. This distinction may also be perceived as a reaction to the state nationalism of the late Meiji era, with its constraints on art. Early Taishō theatrical censorship, therefore, is especially illuminating regarding the internal pressures associated with Westernization.

Generally, the political allegiances of the European avant-gardists were less ambiguous than their Japanese counterparts. By the time that Mussolini assumed power, the Futurists were already identified with military expansionism, hence, their allegiance to a leader they extolled as possessing a supreme Futurist temperament. Patterns in the historical reception of Expressionism suggest its commodification, as well as its susceptibility to being a pawn of diverse sociopolitical agendas. The Dadaists, for example, criticized

what they perceived to be the movements' assimilation into German bourgeois culture. It is also significant that the first generation of Expressionists
either fled Germany, or acquiesced to the mandate of creating heroic-folk-
ish art. By contrast, the Berlin Dadaists reacted to the failed November revolution by supporting the Spartacists and considered themselves
propagandists for social revolution. Two sub-groups subsequently emerged:
one for whom Dada represented a political weapon at the service of Marxism and the other which espoused sociopolitical anarchism (Sheppard 51).
In retrospect, Hans Richter explained the political vacillation of the Dadaists:
"At one moment, they were all for the *Spartakus* movement; then it was
Communism, Bolshevism, Anarchism ... [but] there was always a side door
left open for a quick getaway, if this should be necessary to preserve what
Dada valued most: personal freedom and independence" (Richter 109–112).

However credible Richter's observations may be given his considerable
contribution to Dada, they also appear to be in line with revisionist interpretations that fault the historical avant-garde, and other cultural, social, and
political movements of the time, for failing to brook the rising tides of fascism. Most often this has been accomplished by downplaying the expedi-
ency by which the fascist bureaucracy was able to eliminate any and all
opposition in the cultural sphere, especially the avant-garde. Such tendencies are no less prevalent in Japanese scholarship regarding the failure of
Taishō and early Showa intellectuals and artists to counteract the rise of mil-
itant nationalism and pan–Asian expansionism, or to effectively protest legislative curbs to their autonomy. This is nowhere more evident that in Arima's
assessment of the lack of political consequences of the Japanese avant-garde
and all other artistic and literary projects of the prewar period. For example, he notes that while Italian Futurism stimulated a baleful nationalism
that was to become a dominant ideology prior to and after World War I, the
Japanese Futurists, by contrast, "did their somersault in a political vacuum.
Their anarchistic nihilism had no serious social consequences except that of
isolating the artist from his surroundings" (Arima 68). While Arima's summary judgment may be partially correct, the notion that the avant-gardists
operated within a political vacuum is easily disputable, considering that the
decade prior to its emergence is often referred to as the "winter years of
Socialism," a label just as easily applied to anarcho-syndicalism, constitutional monarchy, and democracy. Arima himself notes that Ōsugi Sakae, the
anarchist who had committed himself to an "anti-art" credo, was strangled
to death by an army officer in 1923 (69).

In contrast to Meiji-era utilitarian humanism, which emphasized individual merit and ambition insofar as it benefited the state, Taishō formulations of individualism are noteworthy for their gradual absorption as an

aesthetic value. In effect, one can map constructions of individualism from the Meiji period, which essentially served to legitimate technological and industrial development; through the relatively benign reconstruction by artists demanding greater autonomy (including the avant-gardists) in the Taishō era; and finally its reconstruction in the *Kokutai no Hongi* (Foundational Principles of National Entity), promulgated by the military in 1937. Brooker notes that the section on aesthetic values in *Kokutai no Hongi* described the "Japanese way" as one in which the "individual or personal creativity" was "an inherited and well-learned artistic tradition," so long as the artist "mastered his tradition before expressing his personal attitudes in departing from the traditional norms" (257). Ironically, however, a return to tradition would entail the resuscitation of both art-for-art's sake and life-for-art's sake, as well as a positive valuation of China's influence, none of which would suit the military's propagandist goals. Brooker, therefore, interprets the *Kokutai* discourse on art as a "fraternalist" mechanism.

Based on Durkheim's model of mechanical solidarity, fraternalism is a supplemental theory of fascism that posits the existence of a collective consciousness extending from political personalities to each member of society in nation-building enterprises based on similarities in heredity, culture, morals, and ideology (Brooker 3). Fraternalism was higher in Japan than in Germany and Italy due to the centrifugal force of the *Kokutai* ideology. In respect to cultural forms, Brooker notes that the military bureaucratic regime's support of traditional Japanese aesthetic values is reminiscent of Germany's "reactionary anti-modernism." The return to tradition, therefore, served to justify the elimination of Western cultural forms and their influence, at the same time that it served to legitimate the *Kokutai* model of racial supremacy. As Martin notes, the *Kokutai* was the corollary to the National Socialist race doctrine, and its "manifest destiny to conquer the world" (194). It can also be perceived to be an outgrowth of the Anti-Comintern Pact of 1936, signed by the German and Japanese military as a protest against British predominance worldwide. This alliance would lead to the Tripartite Pact, ratified by Germany, Italy, and Japan in September 1940 in order to discourage the United States from entering a two-front war and to abandon Great Britain.

An equally valid reading of the *Kokutai*'s emphasis on tradition is that the plan's architects had not pre-modern aesthetic formulations in mind, but, rather, Meiji (and thus, pre-avant-garde) aesthetic values, which were predicated upon the demand that art existed at the discretion of the Emperor, at the service of the state, and for the moral edification of the people. As Ienaga notes, since the Meiji Constitution did not guarantee basic human rights, freedom of expression "could be virtually abolished by subsequent laws" (14). Scholars point to the Peace Preservation Law, initially passed to suppress socialism, as the most significant legislation upon which subsequent efforts to bureaucratize culture were predicated. As Rubin notes, because "no where in the Japanese tradition — and certainly not in the Meiji Constitution — do we find the sanctification of individual rights," it is not surprising that there was a dearth of criticism of censorship practices in the prewar era (1984, 27).

If it is true that the more radical strain of the Japanese avant-garde revealed the social inefficacy of aesthetic autonomy and individualism in the same way that the Dadaists had done in Germany, then any subsequent effort to curb individualism must have benefited from the Japanese avant-garde's auto-critique of art. And it was precisely these strains of aestheticist discourse, which despite the *Kokutai*'s avowal of "individual and personal creativity," in no way characterized art production from that point forward. On the other hand, individualism and artistic subjectivity were never wholly abandoned by the avant-garde (with the notable exceptions of the anti-art faction of Mavo and the proletarian avant-garde), thus redoubling its susceptibility to the statist, anti-individualist model of culture that was adopted in the late 1930s. As Munroe notes, the Japanese avant-garde reacted against the "conservative, hierarchical, and bureaucratic art establishment," which was above all associated with Meiji authoritarianism (22). Clark adds that while aesthetic innovativeness was as essential to the avant-garde project in Japan as it was in Europe, "its stylistic discourses came at the historical conjunction of a repositioning of the artist in relation to the work itself, which was no longer an extension of received or necessary national taste" (41). This displacement of the artist's role in society was marked by the adversarial stance of the avant-gardists towards the institutions of art, as well as a self-consciousness that necessarily delimited their sociopolitical objectives. And although a degree of individualism as an aesthetic value neither precluded the intentions of abolishing the institutions of art, nor sublated art and life, it did entail the retention of a key feature of the doctrine of aesthetic autonomy.

In his influential study of Japanese fascism, Maruyama Masao links the bureaucratization of culture in wartime directly to Meiji authoritarianism, noting that the Imperial Rescript on Education permitted no basis in principle for intellectual or creative freedom. Instead, the national polity absorbed "all the internal values of truth, morality, and beauty," such that "neither scholarship nor art could exist apart from these national values." Maruyama also points out that nationalistic slogans, such as "art for the nation" and "scholarship for the nation" were promulgated frequently throughout the prewar period (6). Such manifestations were significant not merely because art and scholarship had to be of practical use, but because the state became the arbiter of what constituted social utility and aesthetic value in these realms. To Harootunian, the Taishō substitution of an earlier belief in "the perfectibility of the moral faculties of the individual," with the "aesthetic perfectibility of the individual," ultimately led to "the deployment of culture as a surrogate for politics" (2000, 17). Undergirding this phenomenon was an implicit social contract whereby the state could expect a categorical abstention from politics and criticism by artists in exchange for a moderate level of artistic license. This is one explanation for the reluctance of intellectuals to take a public stand against government censorship. That the radical avant-garde and proletarian artists managed to produce their work, albeit sporadically, throughout the late 1920s, is remarkable. The relative swiftness by which they were eliminated is equally noteworthy, except if one considers that the Japanese military bureaucracy turned to Germany for models to regulate culture and propaganda.

In 1936, Japan's Natural Resource Bureau prepared the Summary Working Plan for Information and Propaganda, which centralized all censorship efforts. It was modeled after the Reich Chambers of Culture, established by Goebbels in 1933. The seven Japanese control mechanisms resembled the assorted Reich Chambers of film, radio, press, music, fine arts, and the theatre; but, unlike Nazi plan, the seventh was devoted to the wire service rather than a division for literature (Kasza 151–2). Despite the irrationality that characterized Hitler's polemical attacks on modern and avant-garde art, the aesthetic program articulated by the Nazi cultural bureaucracy regulated every facet of the institutions of art and theatre — the contours of which, according to Western avant-garde theorists, were most comprehensively revealed by the historical avant-garde's attack on aesthetic autonomy. It follows, therefore, that if the avant-gardist critique illuminated the social inefficacy of autonomous art, it also exposed the "dangers" of politically-engaged art. This would, of course, be capitalized upon in the construction of propaganda models by the agents of fascism in Japan.

In regard to what appears to be the reluctance of the public to accept the more radical faction of the avant-garde as a contributory factor in its failure to achieve its sociopolitical goals, Rimer raises the possibility of a "national sensibility" that explains why Futurism and Dada were less attractive than Impressionism and Post-Impressionism (1987, 78). Alternately, it may be that Impressionism was more appealing because it was perceived as being less contentious to the state. In his recollections of the public's response to a Futurist Art Association exhibition, for example, Kinoshita recalled that many of the visitors could not comprehend the more abstract representations of the human form, with many demanding their entrance fees back.

He also noted, however, that, "as expected," most of the "established" painters completely ignored the show (1970b, 8).

Another trend effecting the decline of the avant-garde was that most artists followed one of three paths by the late 1920s: an adherence to a politically-benign aestheticism, a rigid adherence to the dictates of proletarian art, or active participation in new efforts at establishing a "national" style of art. These directions represent, to one degree or another, a reaction by artists once associated with the avant-garde by the press, the public and the authorities. While many were forever tainted by their association with the avant-garde, those who opted for art-for-art's sake were granted greater artistic freedom for a longer period of time, especially the Surrealists. Moreover, avant-garde "converts" to nationalist propaganda efforts were as prized as political converts. Because the effort to eradicate the avant-garde was concomitant to the suppression of Communism, it is necessary to examine the linkages between the two, at least from the vantage-point of reception. This linkage was first made by Lenin, who in 1919 hailed the Communist Party as the "avant-garde of the proletariat," a formulation that became part of international discourse for more than a decade (Enzenberger 29). By the late 1920s, however, the doctrine that art should be subservient to party goals became doctrine, thus paving the way for the liquidation of avant-gardism in Russia, and by Communist arts federations around the world. Given that many Japanese artists were allied with the Party, it is necessary to position the avant-garde's demise in relation to their willingness to accept this mandate, particularly the Mavoists.

The emergence of the post–Revolutionary avant-garde in Russia was unique in that it had the near-unanimous support from the government in its goal to eradicate bourgeois culture through the innovation of forms that were more closely related to life praxis. Collectivization in the arts was bolstered by the establishment of an official commissariat of culture, and under governmental patronage, more than three thousand theatrical organizations sprang up within five years of the Revolution. The innovations of these theatre troupes, as well as those of key practitioners of Constructivist theatre, dance, and stage design had global impact, especially in Germany and Japan. Russian avant-garde performance practitioners innovated many strategies to eradicate the boundaries between the audience and performance, and to abolish authorial authority and the cult of genius by working collectively. This would change by the late 1920s, when the adoption of socialist realism as the prescribed style became doctrine. What the elimination of avant-gardism from the Communist cultural agenda demonstrates, among other things, is that the political reception of the avant-garde — even when it appeared to be in line with dominant political ideologies — was predicated less upon artistic content than on the social contexts within which it was received. In effect, far from having relevance only in the aesthetic realm or to the intelligentsia, two often-cited critiques of the avant-garde, perceptions of the avant-garde's radicalism by the Soviet cultural bureaucracy heightened its potential to subvert increasingly authoritarian goals. This represents one of the most compelling arguments for the sociopolitical valences of the avant-garde project, and one that can be extended not only to the effects of the Comintern on avant-gardist and proletarian arts practitioners worldwide, but also to the new cultural mandates established under authoritarianism in Germany, Italy, and Japan.

While the Japanese Socialist movement succumbed to the state socialism of the nationalists, Communism failed to become a mass political force in Japan, where "education, religion, the civil code, and social and business conduct all emphasized the virtues of loyalty, obedience and stasis at the expense of freedom, individual rights and equality" (Beckmann 149). The Communists also faced difficulties penetrating the "integrating and binding forces" of nationalism and Confucianism, tethered as they were to the cult of the Emperor. This is not to infer, however, that Marxist ideology and Comintern social and cultural policies did not influence a generation of intellectuals and artists, or that the government did not take the "Communist threat" seriously. The reception by which the first Sanka evening of performance was greeted, for example, reveals that the leftist political affinities of many of the avant-gardists were clear to the public and, more significantly, to the police.

Given these circumstances, it seems unjust to maintain that the avant-gardists did not resist the bureaucratization of culture. In 1928, the Censorship Reform League, which was comprised of left-wing dramatists, theatre workers, filmmakers, and writers, met at the Tsukiji Little Theatre to organize protest measures against the suppression of their work (Rubin 1984, 248). Three years later such a public display of resistance would be impossible, because, by that time, it was impermissible to even refer overtly to the political content of a play in a review (Powell 28). Following the Manchurian Incident of 1931, the government stepped up efforts to eradicate Communism and other leftist movements, including the proletarian arts federations. In 1931, the proletarian literary magazine *Shi, Genjitsu* (Poetry, Reality) was forced to cease publication due to governmental pressure (Keene 342). Proletarian and Marxist criticism were disallowed in the early 1930s, and writers were forced to publicly renounce their beliefs, or to refrain from publishing (580). The arrests of Nakano Shigeharu and over four hundred proletarian writers in 1932 testify to the determination of the Home Ministry to eradicate the Proletarian Cultural Federation (Rubin 1984, 249).

The proletarian arts movements faced stiff opposition, with most writers being "fatally censored and cut," and journals such as *Senki* prohibited from being sold (Arima 208). One reason for this was that a recurring theme in proletarian literature and theatre was an unflattering depiction of the military, as exemplified by Yanase's Sanka performance piece. Kobayashi Takiji's novel, *Kani kōsen* (Cannery Boat) (1929), highlighted the anti-labor policies of the military, which in the novel "brutally crushes a strike" (Ienaga 17). In 1933, Kobayahsi was tortured to death by the police. That same year, a radio performance by the Japanese Proletarian Cultural Federation League, prompted a warning to be issued to broadcasters by the Communications Ministry that read: "...regardless of whether the show is a lecture, news, fine art ... eliminate anything which introduces an extreme 'ism' theory, movement or actual deed related to the national polity, political system, the economy, morals, ... which aids or abets related groups and their members."[21]

Although the Peace Preservation Law (1925) was initially passed to suppress socialism, over the next two decades it would be the legislation upon which an elaborate system of thought control would be constructed, leading many scholars to consider it foundational to Japanese fascism (Ienaga 15). It was first levied against students and labor organizers involved in the planning of an economic revolution, known as the Gakuren Incident of 1925-26. It also enforced the national polity by indicting any form of critical inquiry into the political power structure as anti–Japanese. In 1928, it was further amended so that any speech, action, or writing that advocated for the abolition of private property or the monarchy was outlawed, with a specific provision for the illegality of the Communist Party (Kasza 41). It was also deployed to justify the arrests and torture of liberal journalists (Rubin 1985, 229). Five months after Kobyashi's murder, the joint statements of *tenkō* by Sano Manabu and Mabeyama Sadachika, two prominent Communist Party leaders, inspired a wave of conversions. With more than five hundred such conversions within one month, the Party was effectively terminated (Tsurumi 47). The promulgation of *tenkō*, or forced ideological conversion, emanated from the government's belief that political undesirables were remediable, and that high-profile cases could serve as vehicles of public-relations. Interestingly, *tenkō* was designed as a "father and mother type of policy," whereby a "thought offender" would be awakened to the "fact of being Japanese, put his ideas into daily practice, fully accept and understand the concept of the *kokutai*, and discard the unassimilable positions of Western culture" (Mitchell 137–8). Sano and Mabeyama were forced to publicly accept those features of Showa ideology that the Communist Party most vehemently rejected, namely the race doctrine and the Emperor system.

Tellingly, they had to stipulate that any social revolution, should it ever be enacted, would have to be carried out under the leadership of the Imperial Household, and, furthermore, that it would be based on "one-nation socialism," rather than "international socialism" (Tsurumi 47). These provisions indicate the military bureaucracy was keenly aware of the advantages of a selective absorption of socialist ideology within the parameters of the Emperor system, and thus a variation of the quasi-socialism espoused by the Nazis.

In *Jihitsu nenpu* (Chronology of My Own Hand), the Surrealist poet Takiguchi Shûzō recorded the details of his nine-month imprisonment:

> I was investigated about once a week. The center of the investigation lay on the single point of whether or not the Surrealist movement had any connection with Communism (of course, without basis). Among my handwritten texts a correspondence with Breton was found, and I was intensely pursued on this. In the summer [of 1941] I was put under prosecutorial detention and reinvestigated, but the argumentation got a bit more on track, and I could see a perplexed look on the young prosecutor as the give and take got confused when we mentioned the relation between real politics and the essential theory of Surrealism.[22]

Under the threat of police torture and death, an overwhelming majority of those prosecuted accepted the terms of *tenkō*: of about five-hundred members of the Proletarian Arts Federation and the Federation of Proletarian Cultural Organizations, more than ninety-five percent are believed to have undergone ideological conversion (Tsurumi 41). Murayama, who was subject to a series of arrests, was among those who chose *tenkō*, the terms of which caused him to renounce Communism and be imprisoned for two years. After his release, he wrote a series of "conversion novels," of which *The White Night* is considered to be an accurate portrait of *tenkō*. An excerpt from this novel describes the psychological effects of imprisonment, as well as a subtle indictment of the *kokutai* ideology:

> Sitting in the corner of his prison cell, visualizing the scene of torture by the police, he tried to torment his own body, and he ended up with the full recognition that he could not stand up to such conditions.... He stayed in this frame of mind for almost two years in the prison. After his second summer there, absolutely shut away from fresh air, his mind was eroded by something undefined and invincible. He felt as though his flesh and blood, or rather something mysteriously a part of his own father and mother, and of their forebears from time immemorial, whose faces, names, and lives had long since perished, was eating away his existence, which was after all an infinitesimally small particle of their posterity. However hard he tried to cry out to them,

to push them aside, and to drive them out, it was of no avail. In his
struggle with his invisible foes, day in and night out, he groaned,
struck his head with his fists, and scratched the wall with his nails.[23]

After being released from prison, Murayama turned to directing, but continued to get into trouble with the authorities. He continued to write plays
and novels through 1942 under a pseudonym. Further arrests finally forced
him to leave for Korea and Manchuria in the last months of the war. He
returned to Japan in December 1945, and re-formed the *Shinkyō Gekidan*
the following year. He continued to work in theatre world, became the leader
of the *Geijutsuza* (Tokyo Art Theatre), and in 1974 was presented an award
commemorating his four hundredth directorial effort.

The Assimilation of Avant-Garde Discourse and Praxis into Japanese Fascism

To some scholars, avant-garde discourse and praxis were foundational
to the fascist aestheticization of politics, even though most factions of the
avant-garde were opposed to authoritarianism, and the avant-garde itself
served as a foil for the legitimation of fascist arts policies. As Stollman has
observed, the transformation to National Socialism could not be effected
until aesthetic and political material was directed towards a specific function, namely when fascist politics made its social systems more transparent
and its politics more aesthetic (51). In this respect, identifying the congru-
encies between the aestheticization of politics and the politics of aestheticization is as applicable to prewar Japan as to Germany. Since art under the
Nazis could have no justification other than to reiterate Party goals,
autonomous art had to be categorically abolished. In that art was also supposed to express the "collective dreams" of the people, the Nazis, like the
avant-gardists before them, emphasized collectivity in art's reception, even
though they bestowed the mantel of genius upon artists willing to work
towards their goals. This does not mean, however, that the Nazis tolerated
subjectivism any more than aesthetic autonomy: Hitler could not accept any
argument that art was a realm unto itself and governed by its own laws.
Instead, the Party platform incorporated early on the stipulation that art was
to be a part of a national community, rooted in the German race, and at the
service of the state.

Although I have elaborated upon the factors that rendered the doctrine
of aesthetic autonomy and its relationship to the avant-garde unique in Japan,
such qualifications do not render Stollman's thesis any less viable when

applied to the military-bureaucracy's liquidation of aesthetic autonomy. One characteristic of international fascism was the promotion of an elitist form of populist nationalism. In Germany and Italy, the vision of a new state leadership entailed the proliferation of a revolutionary ideology allegedly emerging from the will of the people, rather than from a monopoly party (Griffin 16). By contrast, the Japanese military bureaucrats did not have to create institutions for the express purpose of establishing a "folkish" community as much as they needed to strengthen traditional social patterns with the active support of the population. Official Nazi art, more than merely embodying the dynamics of the *Volksgeist*, however, presented images of "contented burghers, military victories, and pseudo–Bruegel landscapes fixated in a secure, serene world, such as had been conspicuously formulated by the Naturalist painters of the late nineteenth century" (Pois 22).

In Japan, the elimination of "Western" ideas of individualism was essential to the military bureaucracy. The legislative ground upon which such policies were carried out was the Imperial Rule Assistance Association of 1940, which "rejected the Western model of political parties," while entrusting the nation to the "paternal care of the divine Emperor" (Martin 148). Headed by Prime Minister Konoe, the IRAA developed propaganda units such as the Culture and Research Department and the Industrial Patriotic Movement (Brooker 283). Significantly, the architects of the IRAA drew their inspiration and their institutional structures from the Nazis. The movement away from modern forms meant that more pressure was being exerted on Japanese artists to create imagery in support of the war efforts. The rejection of Westernization even included the purgation of the language, as all foreign-language instruction was banned, and Japanese neologisms were found to replace foreign words for "tools, activities and sensations that contact with Western culture had brought" (Field 114). In 1937, Konoe's Cabinet instituted the "Spiritual Mobilization Movement" to galvanize the public's acceptance of war by sponsoring rallies, lectures, radio programs, films and publications, and national days of mourning for the war dead (Mitchell 162). Between 1939 and 1945, the Greater Japan Arts Association was one of several organizations devoted to war art. In 1939, the army sponsored exhibits of artists devoted to war art, while artists who did not comply were routinely denied access to materials (Guth 20).

The Japanese folk-art movement, which had been popularized largely by the efforts of Yanagi Soetsu in the 1920s, had become a full-fledged sociocultural force in the next decade, and replicated patterns of modern cultural nationalism throughout the world. Harkening back to traditional handicrafts, which, as Kawakita notes, were "so closely connected with daily life that they have a built-in conservatism," the movement's proponents exalted the beauty of craft objects that were long common to the lower classes (132). Yanagi's efforts yielded a "kind of philosophy, if not a religion," that resulted in a greater recognition of the beauty to be found in everyday objects, based on the construct that "it was in the unsophisticated folk arts that the true tradition of the Japanese people had been preserved" (132–3). Both ideas can be traced to the avant-gardists' attack on the institutions of art, as well as the standard avant-garde practice of incorporating everyday life fragments into their art and performances. Such values transferred to the literary field as well, with former proletarian writers and critics finding a second career by extolling the virtues of folk literature at the behest of the military (Keene 580). If such pursuits bolstered claims of the superiority of the Japanese race by demonstrating that the common people had literary traditions that were even more important than those of the aristocrats and the intelligentsia, they were not wholly unrelated to the avant-garde's erosion of confidence in "high culture," even if the avant-gardists did not espouse racism. This is another example of how avant-garde practices could be re-deployed towards social and political ends that diverged widely from its original intents.

The Mavoists were noteworthy not only for their populism, and their efforts to erode the distinctions between art and life, but also because they were among the first artists to incorporate the burgeoning forms of mass media communication, such as newspapers, magazines, and photography into their works. In so doing, they managed to highlight the social tensions that "fueled reactionary appeals to reinstate traditional cultural forms," by alternately celebrating, exploiting, and critiquing the objects of the industrial age "by investing them with the power and social significance of art" (Guth 20). In purporting to be movements of the masses, fascist culture exploited the "supposedly eternal values of high culture" deployed throughout history to legitimate power and privilege. Without jettisoning the high status of traditional art, the Japanese military bureaucracy adopted strategies that merged the mass media and art by mass-producing traditional and new works created expressly for the regime in films, posters, postcards, ads, and magazines, thus conferring a shared ownership over select images.

It has become commonplace in contemporary scholarship to refer to historical fascism as an essentially "modern" project, and to apply such terms as "modernist fascism" and "fascist modernism" to interwar cultural manifestations in Italy and Germany. In fact, Hewitt extends this formula to the entire epoch: "If the period from 1910 to 1939 can be characterized as the period of the historical avant-garde, it must also be characterized as the period in which fascism emerged in its most fully developed forms" (27). He also maintains that "the avant-garde, no less than fascism, could think of itself as both the completion and the liquidation of historical sequentiality" (7). Such a formulation conforms with Bürger's analysis that the avant-garde project was the culmination of the bourgeois rationalization of the aesthetic sphere, although it allows for complex, even causal relationships between the avant-garde project and fascism. To Hewitt, the precondition for the historical recognition of the interrelationship between aestheticization and politicization occurred when the distinction between the two discourses became most apparent, specifically when the avant-garde attacked aesthetic autonomy, and fascism emerged as a viable political discourse (38). As Griffin notes, far from being a force of "anti-modernism," fascism was borne out of a collective desire for "a sense of transcendence [and] cultural optimism" that were highly compatible with the forces of modernization (14).

Although he stops short of equating avant-gardism and fascism, Hewitt argues that they must be viewed as "two contemporaneous developments in the self-consciousness of modernity" (2). Specifically, he concentrates on the convergences between the avant-garde's "poetics of performance" and the fascist "theatricalization of power" as a "virtual form" of fascist politics. The commonalities of both, namely the privileging of "performance over the finished art object," the merging of the spectator's consciousness with the performance, and the incorporation and celebration of technology, all serve to bridge avant-garde aesthetics and fascist spectacles of power. One compelling application of this formula is the dramaturgical and performative components of fascist rituals, such as political assemblies, party rallies, and military shows. The construction of a "civic liturgy" in Germany and Italy was accomplished through iconography and ceremonial rites that had their roots in Christian ritual (Griffin 25). The Nazi aestheticization of politics and the means by which it permeated social life were borne out in newly-created customs and celebrations, and a manufactured folklore that comprised the National Socialist "calendar." With their military exhibitions and war games, the party conventions were perhaps the supreme example of this phenomenon. By 1933, the *Thingspiel*, a pseudo-cultic, ritualistic performance, tailored for large arenas and amphitheatres, was touted as a veritable National Socialist art form. Over 60,000 people were in attendance at a 1933 performance in Berlin, which featured an estimated 176,000 SA members (Stollman 43–44).

Scholars have tailored the concept of fascist modernism to suit prewar Japanese cultural production, especially as they refer to the coexistence of a capitalist, technological modernity and a "totalizing drive to reunite its disunities within an archaic, continuous and harmonious culture" (Ivy 14–15). In this respect, prewar anti–avant-garde discourse and anti–Western discourse can both be seen as one version of reactionary modernism, just as the

Mavoists' celebration of technology can be seen as another. Similarly, the Japanese race doctrine inflected military-bureaucratic cultural policies, and anti–Chinese and anti–Western discourses. One early manifestation occurred when the military commissioned Mayama Seika to dramatize the life of a famous Japanese general, who, having been defeated and held captive by the Chinese army, returned to the site of his defeat and killed himself. Mayama's *Kuga Shōsa* (Major Kuga) premiered in November 1932 and is a "definitive exposition of martial values" at a time when the Japanese military needed publicity (Powell 1984, 128–30).

A canny awareness of the significance of aesthetic form characterized the military-bureaucracy's propaganda efforts, particularly when it concerned the divinity of the Emperor. For example, the campaign promoting the installation of the Shōwa Emperor included an extensively photographed world tour in 1921, and his presentation as "one of the glamorous males" in magazines that appealed to female readers (Silverberg 130). The Japanese censors were especially sensitive to the forms of mass communication. Radio broadcasters, for example, were told to modulate their voices and delivery by adopting a "coldly neutral" tone, and instructed never to use terms such as "extremely" or "absolutely" in regard to any topic. Popular songs intoned in an overly erotic style were banned, as were comedic films such as the *Keystone Cops*, because they were considered to be corrosive to the public's respect for the police (128–9). The privileging of form over content is, of course, a characteristic of most modernist art, but it is especially true of the avant-garde. Nevertheless, the fascist aestheticization of politics has been perceived to be a by-product of the avant-gardist manipulation of form, and is evidenced in Walter Benjamin's association of Futurism and fascism, and Georg Lukacs' critique of Expressionism.

A predominant theme in Japanese wartime iconography was its incorporation of medieval and feudal imagery, which served as idealized constructs of social and racial harmony. In Japan, where religion and politics were more fully fused than in either Germany or Italy, the state ethos was often expressed through medieval motifs. In 1924, the *Kokuhonsha* was founded to propagate Japanese racial supremacy, and resurrected the cult of the Samurai warrior code, which already permeated the military. Brooker notes that the fundamental lack of an ethical code in State Shinto was redressed as early as the Rescript on Education (1890), which fused traditional Confucian ethical beliefs with the family-state ideology, and paved the way for a future fraternalist religion in the Showa era that gave an advantage to the military bureaucracy. By contrast, National Socialism lacked an authentic ethical code and had to be constructed through performative rituals (Brooker 247).

Maruyama locates two major features in the "psychological structure" of fascist-nationalistic culture: the "tendency to symbolize the State as the direct extension of the primary group (family or village) in which the individual is submerged"; and the love of fatherland expressed as a "love of one's native place." He adds that this second feature was the Japanese version of "tribalism," which he considers foundational to fascist nationalism (144–5). Whereas the Nazi's "blood and soil" tribalism was meant to neutralize the inherent contradictions between a glorified primitivism and the Nazis' technologized bureaucracy, Japanese tribalism was deeply ingrained in modern society, and was prone to hypostatization in that modern organizations and institutions no longer performed their original functions (263–4). In both countries, a mythical past of national grandeur and racist homogeneity — the Germanic cult of the Aryan race and the godly descent of the Yamato race — became central doctrines. The German variant was founded upon "agrarian romanticism," which Martin defines as an irrational yearning for pre-modern times in societies, which had been totally altered by World War I. Though not entirely an effect of the war, this construct holds even greater currency in Japan given that approximately fifty percent of the population was agrarian, as opposed to only twenty percent in Germany. Another effective ideology was the glorification of technology, which in both nations was based on the view that war was "the father of creation and the mother of culture." Just as Prussian history provided the National Socialists with a template of traditional martial values, *bushido*, the feudal Japanese fighting code, was passed down from the samurai to the new Imperial army, apotheosized in the *kamikaze* fighting spirit (Martin 171–3).

The Japanese military-bureaucracy formed a number of organizations whose express purpose was to strengthen contemporary versions of a mythical Japanese past by, paradoxically, employing all the means of modern technology at its disposal. This was accompanied by a series of measures that strengthened and extended existing anti-subversion laws. The Peace Preservation Law, which was amended in 1941 to allow the indefinite detention of political prisoners, was followed by the National Defense Security Law (1941), the Provisional Law for Control of Speech, Publications, Assembly, and Association (1942), and the Special Law on Wartime Crimes (1943), all of which secured absolute control over all forms of mass communication (Ienaga 98–09). Still more groups were formed to support the war effort, including the Japanese Literary Patriotic Association and the Japanese Journalism Patriotic Association. Beginning in 1937, there were "War Art Exhibitions," "Holy War Art Exhibitions," and "Greater East Asian War" shows, all of which featured works by many well-known artists, who contributed paintings depicting heroism and military victories (123–4). In 1943, the Cabinet Information

Bureau banned more than a thousand musical compositions, and decreed that American and British works could not be performed or publicly aired. In 1944, steel guitars, banjos, and ukuleles were outlawed, and all art exhibitions were banned, with the exception of those organized by the Great Japan Patriotic Association (123).

In 1941, the IRAA published the "Basic Concepts of the Greater East Asia Co-Prosperity Sphere," which affirmed Japanese racial superiority in Asia: "Although we use the expression 'Asian cooperation,' this by no means ignores the fact that Japan was created by the Gods, or posits an automatic racial equality" (Ienaga 14). Six months after the outbreak of war, a group of intellectuals met under the auspices of the *Bungaku-kai* (Literary Society) to debate the issue of "overcoming the modern." These debates, which culminated in the Kyoto Conference of 1942, solidified anti–Western sentiments most virulently expressed by intellectuals advocating a return to the timeless essence of historical cultural artifacts as an antidote to modernization. The proceedings of these debates, published in the literary journal *Bungakkai*, concluded that since European and Japanese intellectual traditions were ultimately incompatible, it was necessary to return to tradition in order to achieve a rejuvenated "spiritual outlook" (Munroe 23–4). At base, however, was the conflation of rationalism, liberalism, and materialism into a higher communal and spiritual entity, and an analytical version of state discourse whereby the "oppositional relations situated within the fundamental axis of tradition — restoration and revolution, emperor worship and expulsion of foreigners, isolation and open country, nationalism and modernization, East and West — exploded at a single stroke."[24]

To Bürger, the Western avant-gardists failed to bring about a change in life praxis based on art, since it was itself institutionalized. An intervening development, however, was the totalitarian mandate that excluded art lacking any means end rationality. In Benjamin's view, the fascist aestheticization of politics entailed the liquidation of autonomy not in order for art be closer to life (however much the fascists may have argued that art was of and for the people), but because they recognized that art was a potent force in legitimating and sustaining the absolute power of the state. In this respect, fascism succeeded where the avant-garde project failed, but drew upon the innovativeness of the historical avant-garde project in fulfilling their aims.

Trans-Historical Valuations of the Historical Avant-Garde

It must be noted that assessments of the political aspects of the avant-garde have been conditioned by the ideological frameworks of various critical projects. While this may well apply to aesthetic discourse throughout history, it seems especially viable given the avant-garde's auto-critique of art, and the transformations it effected along the constellation of receptive modes. In general, it is possible to locate two strands of criticism of the Japanese avant-garde prior to the war, both of which can be characterized as being politically-motivated and, mostly, pejorative. The first line of discourse, which focused on the negative effects of assimilating Western forms, ultimately served to legitimate nationalism and, later, Pan-Asian military expansionism. The second strand featured the routine association of avant-garde art, literature, and theatre artists with subversive politics.

Many scholars have examined the similarities between avant-garde and totalitarian discourse and praxis. In the West, this line of inquiry harkens back to the Frankfurt School critical theorists, and Lukacs and Benjamin. In "The Work of Art in the Age of Mechanical Reproduction" (1936), Benjamin observed that through such techniques as montage, the Dadaists destroyed the "aura" of their creations, which they termed "reproductions with the very means of production" (Benjamin 237). Benjamin's approbation of the avant-garde, however, was qualified by his condemnation of Italian Futurism, which he associated with Italian fascism. Lukacs excoriated the avant-garde on formal grounds, and what he believed to be the counter-revolutionary propensities of all non-realistic art. He was especially critical of the Expressionists' concentration on surface appearances and their "fragmentary and chaotic subjectivity," which he believed rendered it incapable of capturing social reality with any accuracy. Lukacs considered Expressionism as a cipher for all anti-mimetic tendencies, a position he took up with even greater vehemence after the Nazis' rise to power and, ironically, after the movement had already been suppressed. In "Expressionism, its Significance and Decline" (1934) he explicitly indicted Expressionism as "only one of the many tendencies in bourgeois ideology that grow later into fascism" (87). His severe criticism of the avant-garde was adopted by both leftist and conservative critics, and was to become foundational to the adoption of socialist realism in Russia and by Communist arts federations around the world.

Interestingly, the doctrine of aesthetic autonomy was advocated by Taishō and early Showa theorists associated with the Proletarian Arts and Literary movement. Hirabayahsi Hatsunosuke, a noted Marxist literary critic, proposed that a degree of autonomy should be preserved for artists. Hira-bayashi maintained that because the anticipated dictatorship of the prole-tariat would only be a temporary phase toward a "classless paradise," art should guard against the "imprint of class prejudices" (Arima 182). Like Western aestheticists after Kant, he also felt that art could offer a kind of consolation that politics was incapable of providing, though he recognized that art alone could not effect the transformation of existing social condi-tions. Hirabayashi concluded, therefore, that until the time that art became genuinely autonomous in a classless society, it should "temporarily" become the handmaiden of politics (Arima 183).

Another important Marxist intellectual was Nakano Shigeharu — a poet, novelist, and critic active in the Communist wing of the Revolutionary Lit-erature Movement of the 1920s. Nakano theorized that Taishō culture was shaped by capitalists and Orientalists who appropriated Japanese traditions for new social and political ends, and characterized the era as one of a "cul-ture of production," conditioned by new forms of mass communication (Sil-verberg 9). Nakano was particularly critical of the propensity of these two processes to homogenize human experience and obliterate historical and cul-tural distinctions. Ever-conscious of his own social status as a writer, Nakano maintained that capitalism subsumed art and literature into a system of exchange that rendered the artist a producer of cultural commodities. Nakano offered two examples that related to the phenomena of Occidentalism and cultural commodification: the poetry of Paul Claudel and the Kabuki Reform Movement.

To Nakano, Claudel, who was at one time the French ambassador to Japan, represented the "model" Orientalist because he appropriated tradi-tional poetic forms; in so doing, he revealed how historical cultural mani-festations could be split into profit-producing units to be sold on the global market (Silverberg 1990, 19). Nakano took even greater exception to Claudel's re-popularization of forms that had their origins in feudal culture. That the residual elements of historical feudal ideology could thrive in the modern era becomes a central concern to another essay, "On Theatre" (1928), in which he maintained that the Kabuki Reform Movement was emblematic of how traditional cultural values could be recycled towards new political ends (111). Because he maintained that of all art forms theatre comes closest to approximating life, Nakano was less critical of the imprint of Western-ization implicit in *kabuki* reform than of what he perceived to be the reformists' anti-progressivism. While he called for the "aggressive establish-ment of a new revolutionary theatrical form," Nakano believed that *shingeki* was equally unacceptable, due to its origins in bourgeois Western culture (112). The only appropriate course to adopt in modernizing Japanese theatre, therefore, was for *kabuki* to be re-fitted with a "new proletarian language" that "accentuated form," but rejected "feudal content" (113). This is especially significant given the non-mimetic dimensions of *kabuki* when compared to the mimetic propensity of Western theatre. Nakano's proposed reforms, therefore, were consonant with the formal techniques of traditional theatre familiar to Japanese audiences and, ironically, closer to the techniques of the avant-gardists.

While it is tempting to compare Nakano's critique of Taishō culture to the critical theorists of the Frankfurt School, what is most significant is his situating feudalism as an analytical category in regard to modern Japanese culture. That feudal ideology was to emerge full-force in prewar art and propaganda renders it an especially potent critical category. In his critique of *kabuki* reform, Nakano also established a critical precedent in emphasizing form over content, that is not only appropriate to Japanese theatre forms, but one that he himself applied to the institutional frameworks of Taishō culture, and one which subsequent scholars have applied to war-era culture. Finally, it is worth noting that because of his political beliefs, Nakano's first collection of poetry was confiscated by the police in 1931, while his second collection was published only after twenty-three pages had been expurgated.

In the postwar era, theorists have located continuities of anti–avant-garde discourse in assorted contemporary critical, social, and political projects. Huyssen states that in the 1950s, the rediscovery of Dada was reinscribed into Western cultural politics as an antidote to an increasingly canonized modernism in poetry, narrative, and painting. Berman notes that in the 1970s, the historical avant-garde was denounced by both liberal and neoconservative critics alike: to the new right, the anti-bourgeois sentiments of the historical avant-garde informed the "excessive" influence of a new class of intellectuals that emerged in the 1960s, while leftist advocates of postmodern theory pronounced the obsolescence of the avant-garde's goal to radically transform social totality (43–4). Mann suggests that the legacy of a "half-century of revisions and counter-revisions in avant-garde scholarship is vital to the historical discourse of the avant-garde," thus resolving what he considers the paroxysm in avant-garde theory, specifically that for the avant-garde to have succeeded would mean the death of art (55). Huyssen adds that most academic criticism of the historical avant-garde has been "ossified into an elite enterprise beyond politics and everyday life," even though the transformation of both was central to the project (4).

It should be noted that if the Western avant-garde has been institutionalized due to nearly a century of scholarly and curatorial interest, it was only in the last couple of decades that serious scholarship has been devoted to the Japanese avant-garde. Rimer notes that although Western aesthetic and art historical projects were being undertaken with greater sophistication by Japanese scholars as early as the 1930s, few wrote for the general public on avant-garde art, with the result being that "there remains virtually nothing in the way of any synthetic analysis of modern Japanese art between the wars" (1987, 63). As recently as 1994, Munroe observed that "a comprehensive historical narrative and critical context for the advanced study of twentieth century art has yet to be established" (20). In fact, Omuka Toshiharu's pioneering studies and his detailed efforts to construct an historical narrative have contributed much to understanding the contexts, personalities, and activities associated with a host of Western-derived and indigenous avant-garde developments prior to the war. Still, there exists a noticeable dearth of Western scholarship, even in surveys of its international manifestations; this situation has been replicated in Western curatorial practices.

The institutionalization of the Japanese avant-garde on theoretical, if not altogether practical levels, can be attributed partially to the radical artists of the 1960s, who claimed the prewar avant-gardists as their aesthetic and ideological precursors. Amidst the student protests of the mid–1960s, one of the first exhibitions of 1920s art was presented at the Tokyo Kokuritsu Kindai Bijutsukan, entitled *Zen'ei kaiga no senkushatachi* (The Pioneers of Avant-Garde Painting) (1965). Some scholars have observed that Japanese modern art from the late Meiji period through the Pacific War has been ignored in the context of Japanese art history as a whole, due primarily to conflicting interpretations of Japanese modernism. Along these lines, Munroe notes that such misinterpretations as the Gutai being hailed as Japan's "first avant-garde movement" can be viewed as part of a "national revisionist effort to establish a history of Japanese modernism independent from the Euro-American narrative" (81).

In regard to summary judgments of Japan's prewar political history, Maruyama noted that while the conclusions of Western political science may be abstract, "behind them lie several centuries of historical developments in European politics"; thus, he is cautious about their applicability to "understanding and analyzing the hard facts of Japanese political development" (231). Many scholars of prewar Japanese culture have heeded this warning. For instance, although he denies the validity of the label "avant-garde" because of its origins in Western critical discourse, Inaga notes that the reception of the Japanese artists affiliated with such movements was marked by several paradoxes at home and abroad. He points out that in the West, these artists were recognized only when they played up their "Japaneity," and also that they were called upon to "represent the Japanese people" even though they had rejected traditional Japanese forms. Domestically, meanwhile, they were recognized as being internationalists inasmuch as they "affected to have freed themselves from Japan." For Inaga, this "tragic" situation reveals a brand of "two-faced opportunism" in which recognition could only be achieved internationally and domestically through acts of "cultural betrayal" (71). While Inaga does not single-out particular artists, his argument is compelling for a number of reasons. At the same time that he supports his position that formulations of the avant-garde are categorically paradoxical in Japan, he does argue for avant-gardist classification for cultural forms not tethered to Western influence, specifically, flower arranging, the Popular Crafts Movement, and creative engraving. The Popular Crafts Movement, for example, "sought to question the typically Western distinction between high and low art" without modeling itself on Western forms (72). Nevertheless, in its rejection of artistic authority, and also because of its inversion of the scale of aesthetic values in the focus on everyday life objects, the crafts movement was highly relatable to the avant-garde project. Inaga's hypotheses also do not account for the avant-gardists' own chariness about Westernization, nor their indictment of institutionalized Western forms. It also appears significant that Inaga references the Japanese folklore movement, which had been deployed most actively by the military bureaucracy to reify the "supremacy" of Japanese folk production. In both cases, Inaga re-deploys Japanese avant-garde discourse (and anti–avant-garde discourse) towards a critique of an over-reliance on Western forms and critical classifications. That this aim is not without ideological implications corroborates the fact that avant-garde discourse can be reinterpreted towards sociopolitical ends well beyond their originary impulses. It is for these reasons that Omuka prefers the more expansive term, *shinkō geijutsu undo* (New Art Movement) to designate the cluster of experimental art movements of the 1920s, including the Futurist Art Association, Action, Mavo, and Sanka.

What these theories sidestep, however, are the nuances of gradated sociocultural change, and the relative impotence of intellectuals and artists in the face of hostile legislation, police brutality, and a mostly indifferent public. Arima's assertion that the "anarchist-artists," associated with Japanese Futurism, were unable to transform either of their goals into social and political programs represents one such accusation. At the opposite end of the cultural spectrum, Arima points out that as influential as the *Shirakaba-ha* and other art-for-art's sake movements may have been in the Taishō era, with their internationalism and aversion to fanaticism, they too were ultimately unable to provide an effective voice of dissent to xenophobic nationalism (100). Even though noteworthy intellectuals were against the war, Arima attributes their failure to mount an "effective opposition" on the grounds that their reaction to the social situation was "more impressionistic rather than analytical" (126). He also notes that contemporary scholars indict the *Shi-*

rakaba-ha's inefficacy on four main charges: anti-mass elitism, the high cult of aesthetic experience, the consciousness of tradition, and the low appreciation of scientism in humanism and social behavior — all of which are markers of prewar intellectual conservatism (126).

Arima's judgment on the "stunning inability of Taishō intellectuals and artists to translate their ideals into social action" appears less stunning when one considers that their aestheticist leanings separated culture from the social and political realms axiomatically. This does, however, appear to once again corroborate Karatani's theory of the inverse relationship of critical categories derived from the West when applied to Japanese culture. Perhaps the most compelling postwar conflation of aesthetic, avant-garde, and political discourse can be found in Karatani's observation that "Japan has always been conceived of, by itself as well as by others, in aesthetic terms."[25] It is no wonder, then, that one of the most telling corollaries of Karatani's theory is his observation that "Nationalism comes into existence in the aesthetic consciousness; it is essentially grounded less upon intellectual/moral speculations than upon an emotional/corporeal community" (34).

As all of these instances illustrate, a predominant feature of historical and contemporary avant-garde theory is the overt deployment of aesthetic discourse towards extra-aesthetic goals. That such tendencies developed alongside, and in response to, the historical avant-garde, is indicative of the reflexivity inherent to the goals of transforming the production and reception of art. Furthermore, that such valences continue to be deployed by a wide range of critical and scholarly projects in the contemporary era suggests that the historical avant-garde project, far from being ideologically neutral, or ossified as an aesthetic-institutional category, has social and political ramifications well beyond the scope of the original project.

Notes

1. In *Theory of the Avant-Garde*, Bürger argues that in the *Critique of Judgment*, Kant reflected upon the "subjective aspect of the detachment [of art] from the practical concerns of life"; a position also taken up by Schiller in *On the Aesthetic Education of Man*, which argued that it is on the basis of autonomy that art can fulfill the furtherance of humanity as could be accomplished in no other way; see Bürger 1984, 44–46.

2. Bürger excludes movements such as Symbolism and Cubism not on the basis of such issues as form and content, but, rather, because these movements did not advance a social agenda.

3. Itabashi, Kuritsu Bijutsukan, *Guraffiku no jidai: Murayama Tomoyoshi to Yanase Masamu no sekai* (Tokyo: Itabashi Kuritsu Bijutsukan, 1990) N. pag.; translated for this study by Mikiko Hirayama.

4. Published in *Ningen*, March 1921.

5. These two articles appeared in *Yomiuri shinbun* (19 March 1921) and *Gendai no bijutsu* (October 1921).

6. These articles appeared in *Sintyoo* (March 1923) and *Asahi* (April 1923).

7. Murasaki, Ran, "Kyorokushugi no saishin geijutsu — sengo ni kangeisaretsutsuaru dadaizumu" (The Latest in Hedonism in art: the popularity of Dadaism after the war); and Hitsuji Akio, "Dadaizumu ichimenkan" (A View of Dadaism) (*Yorozuchoho*, August 15, 1920); qtd in Linhartová 1987, 34.

8. Kinoshita, Shuichirō, "Taishōki no shinko bijutsu undo o meguitte (4) Miraiha bijutsu kyokai no koro (sono ichi)" (Concerning the New Art Movement of the Taishō Period 4: The Days of the Futurist Art Association). *Gendai no me* 185 (April 1970): 7–8; translated for this study by Miki Hirayama.

9. "Mavo no sengen" (Mavo Manifesto) *MAVO* 1 (1923); translated for this study by Miki Hirayama.

10. A facsimile of the all seven issues was issued as *Mavo fukkokuban* (*Mavo* Facsimile). Ed. Odagiri Susumu (Tokyo: Nihon Kindai Bungakukan, 1991).

11. Ogadiri, Susumu, *Showa nungaku no seiritsu* (Tokyo: Keiso Shobo, 1965) 411–412; translated for this study with the assistance of Nao Kato.

12. Omuka, Toshiharu, "Taishō-ki no shinko bijutsu undo to 'Gekijō no Sanka'" (The Progressive Art Movement in the Taishō Period and the "Theater of the Third Section") *Art Vivant* 33 (July 1989): 84–8; see Clark 1994, 43.

13. Murayama, Tomoyoshi, *Engekiteki jidoden 1922–1927 II* (Theatrical Autobiography, II, 1922–1927) (Tokyo: Toho Shuppansha, 1971) 25; translated for this study by Miki Hirayama.

14. Clark, citing and translating Omuka 1989, 89; see Clark 1994, 43.

15. Hiroko, Katō, "Introduction," +-+-+-x+=Holiday," *The Bulletin of the Tokyo Metropolitan Museum of Art* (March 30, 1991): 47–50; translated by Miki Hirayama.

16. Clark, citing and translating citation of Okada's statement in *Mizue* (July 1925) in Nakamura Giichi, "Chogenjitsu-shugi no notsaraku' ronso" (Debate on the Fall of Surrealism), *Zoku Nihon kindau nijutsu ronso-shi* (History of Modern Japanese Art Debates, Continuation) (Tokyo: Kinryudo, 1982), 188; see Clark 1994, 43.

17. Murayama, Tomoyoshi, "Koseiha ni kansuru ikkosatsu—Keisei geijutsu no han.i ni okeru." (A View on Constructivism — the State of the Plastic Arts) *Atelier* (August 1925): 22, qtd. in Asano 1962, 62; translation mine.

18. Sofue Shuji, "Murayama Tomoyoshi," *Nihon Kindai Bungakukan*, N. pub., 14.

19. Sofue, Shoji, synopsizing "Shimura Natsue," *Murayama Tomoyoshi gikyokushu, I* (Collected Plays of Murayama Tomoyoshi, I) (Tokyo, 1971); Murayama restaged and designed this play in April 1970 for the Tokyo Geijutsu-za.

20. Goering was best-known as a proponent of Expressionism; *Seeschlacht* (1918), his best-known play, gained fame as the first play to deal directly with World War I, and to employ what would become trademark Expressionist dramatic devices, such as anonymous characters and telegraphic dialogue.

21. *Masu Medua Tosei*, v.1, document 48, 258, N. pub., qtd. in Kasza 1988, 92.

22. Nakamura, Giichi, "Chōgenjitsu-shugi no notsaraku' ronsō" (Debate on the Fall of Surrealism), *Zoku Nihon kindau nijutsu ronsō-shi* (History of Modern Japanese Art Debates, Continuation) (Tokyo: Kinryûdō, 1982) 223–4; see Clark 1994, 46.

23. Murayama, Tomoyoshi, *Byakuya* (The White Night), *Murayama Tomoyoshi Shu* (Gendai Nihon Bungaku Zenshu, Tokyo: Chikuma Shobo, 1957) 345–7; see Tsurumi 1970, 58–9.

24. Takeyuchi, Yoshimi, "Kindai no chokoku" (Overcoming Modernity), *Takeuchi Yoshimi zenshu*, v.8 (Tokyo: Chikuma Shobo, 1980) 64–5; see Karatani 1994, 3.

25. Interestingly, Karatani echoes the sentiment first expressed by Oscar Wilde in "Intentions: The Decay of Lying," in which he states that Japan was an aesthetic fiction: "I know that you are fond of Japanese things. Now, do you really imagine Japanese people, as they are presented to us in art, have any existence? If you do, you have never understood Japanese art at all. The Japanese people are the deliberate self-conscious creation of certain individual artists.... In fact the whole of Japan is a pure invention. There is no such country, there are no such people." Oscar Wilde, *The Artist as Critic: Critical Writings of Oscar Wilde* (New York: Random House, 1969) 315; see Karatani 1994, 38.

Works Cited

Arima, Tatsuo. *The Failure of Freedom: A Portrait of Modern Japanese Intellectuals.* Cambridge: Harvard University Press, 1969.

Asano, Tatsuo. "La Peinture a l'Epoque Taisho." Trans. Catherine Ancelot. *Japons des avant-gardes 1910–1970.* Paris: Éditions du Centre Pompidou, 1986.

Barshay, Andrew. *State and Intellectual in Imperial Japan: The Public Man in Crisis.* Berkeley: University of California Press, 1988.

Beckmann, George M. "The Radical Left and the Failure of Communism." *Dilemmas of Growth in Prewar Japan.* Ed. James Morley. Princeton: Princeton University Press, 1971.

Benjamin, Walter. *Illuminations.* Ed. Hannah Arendt. Trans. Harry Zohn. New York: Shocken Press, 1968.

Berman, Russell A. *Modern Culture and Critical Theory: Art, Politics, and the Legacy of the Frankfurt School.* Madison: University of Wisconsin Press, 1989.

Brooker, Paul. *The Faces of Fraternalism: Nazi Germany, Fascist Italy, and Imperial Japan.* Oxford: Clarendon Press, 1988.

Bürger, Peter. *The Institutions of Art.* Trans. Loren Kruger. Lincoln: University of Nebraska Press, 1992.

_____. *Theory of the Avant-Garde.* Trans. Michael Shaw. Second ed. Frankfurt: Suhrkampf Verlag, 1974. Reprint. Minneapolis: University of Minnesota Press, 1984.

Centre Georges Pompidou. *Japons des avant-gardes 1910–1970.* Paris: Éditions du Centre Pompidou, 1986.

Clark, John. "Artistic Subjectivity in the Taisho and Early Showa Avant-Garde." *Japanese Art After 1945: Scream Against the Sky.* Ed. Alexandra Munroe. New York: Harry N. Abrams, 1994.

Enzenberger, Hans Magnus. "The Aporias of the Avant-Garde." Trans. John Simon. *The Consciousness Industry.* Ed. Michael Roloff. New York: Seabury Press, 1974.

Field, Norma. *In the Realm of the Dying Emperor: Japan at Century's End.* New York: Vintage Books, 1993.

Griffin, Roger. "Staging the Nation's Rebirth: the Politics and Aesthetics of Performance in the Context of Fascist Studies." *Fascism and Theatre*. Ed. Gunther Berghaus. Providence: Berghahn Books, 1996.

Guth, Christina. "Japan 1868–1945: Art, Architecture, and National Identity." *Art Journal* 55.3 (1996): 16–20.

Harootunian, H.D. "Disciplining Native Knowledge and Producing Place." *Culture and Identity: Japanese Intellectuals During the Interwar Years*. Ed. Thomas J. Rimer. Princeton: Princeton University Press, 1990.

_____. *Overcome by Modernity: History, Culture and Community*. Princeton: Princeton University Press, 2000.

Horioka, Charles Yuji. "Consuming and Saving." *Postwar Japan as History*. Ed. Andrew Gordon. Berkeley: University of California Press. 1993.

Huyssen, Andreas. *After the Great Divide: Modernism, Mass Culture and Postmodernism*. Bloomington: Indiana University Press, 1986.

Ienaga, Saburo. *The Pacific War, 1931–1945*. Trans. Frank Baldwin. New York: Pantheon Books, 1978.

Inaga, Shigemi. "The Impossible Avant-Garde in Japan: Does the Avant-Garde Exist in the Third World?" Trans. Margaret J. Flynn. *Contemporary and General Literature* 41 (1993): 67–75.

Itabashi, Kuritsu Bijutsukan. *Guraffiku no jidai: Murayama Tomoyoshi to Yanase Masamu no sekai*. Tokyo: Itabashi Kuritsu Bijutsukan, 1990.

Ivy, Marilyn. *Discourses of the Vanishing: Modernity, Phantasm, Japan*. Chicago and London: The University of Chicago Press, 1995.

Iwamoto, Yoshio. "Aspects of the Proletarian Literary Movement in Japan." *Japan in Crisis: Essays on Taishō Democracy*. Eds. Bernard Silberman, et. al. Princeton: Princeton University Press, 1974.

Karatani, Kojin. *The Origins of Modern Japanese Literature*. Trans. Bret de Barry. Durham: Duke University Press, 1993.

Kawakita Michiaki. *Modern Currents in Japanese Art*. The Heibonsha Survey of Japanese Art 24. Trans. Charles Terry. New York: Weatherhill/Heibonsha, 1974.

Kasza, Gregory J. *The State and the Mass Media in Japan, 1918–1945*. Berkeley: University of California Press, 1988.

Keene, Donald. *Dawn to the West*. New York: Holt, Rinehart, and Winston, 1984.

Ko, Won. *Buddhist Elements in Dada: A Comparison of Tristan Tzara, Takahashi Shinkichi and Their Fellow Poets*. New York: New York University Press, 1977.

Lanne, Mitsuko, and Jean-Claude Lanne. "Le Futurisme Russe et L'Art d'Avant-Garde Japonais." *Cahiers du Monde Russe et Sovietique* 25.4 (1984): 375–402.

Lehmann, Jean-Pierre. *The Image of Japan: From Feudal Isolation to World Power, 1850–1905*. London: Allen and Unwin, 1978.

Linhartová, Vera. *Dada et Surrealisme au Japon*. Paris: Orientalistes de France, 1987.

_____. "Manifestes et Reflexions: 1910–1941; Textes Choisis, Traduits et Presentés par Vera Linhartová." *Japons des avant-gardes 1910–1970*. Paris: Éditions du Centre Pompidou, 1984.

Lukacs, Georg. *Essays on Realism*. Trans. David Fernbach. Cambridge: The MIT Press, 1980.

Mann, Paul de. *The Theory-Death of the Avant-Garde*. Bloomington: Indiana University Press, 1991.

Martin, Berndt. *Japan and Germany in the Modern World*. Providence: Berghahn Books, 1995.

Maruyama, Masao. *Thought and Behavior in Modern Japanese Politics*. Ed. Ivan Morris. London: Oxford University Press, 1965.

Mitchell, Richard. *Thought Control in Prewar Japan*. Ithaca: Cornell University Press, 1976.

Munroe, Alexandra. *Japanese Art after 1945: Scream Against the Sky*. New York: H. N. Abrams, 1994.

Munsterberg, Hugo. *The Art of Modern Japan: From the Meiji Restoration to the Meiji Centennial, 1868–1968*. New York: Hacker Art Books, 1978.

Nolte, Sharon. "Individualism in Japan." *The Journal of Asian Studies* 43.4 (1984): 667–684.

Omuka, Toshiharu. "Beruurin no miraiha kara 'Augusuto Guruppe'" (From the Japanese Futurists in Berlin to the "August Group"). *Geijutsu kenyuho* (Bulletin of the Institute of Art and Design, University of Tsukuba) 15 (1990): 51–73.

_____. "David Burliuk and the Japanese Avant-Garde." *Canadian-American Slavic Studies* 20.1-2 (1986): 111–125.

_____. *Taishoki shinko bijutsu undo no kenkyu*. Tokyo: Skydoor, 1995.

_____. "Twentieth-Century Art and Japan: A Focus on the Taishō Era." Hiroshima: Hiroshima Prefectural Museum, 1996.

Ogadiri, Susumu. *Showa nungaku no seiritsu*. Tokyo: Keiso Shobo, 1965.

Ortolani, Benito. *The Japanese Theatre from Shamanistic Ritual to Contemporary Pluralism*. Princeton: Princeton University Press, 1990.

Pois, Robert. "German Expressionism in the Plastic Arts and Nazism: A Confrontation of Idealists." *German Life and Letters* 21 (1968): 204–214.

Powell, Brian. *Kabuki in Modern Japan: Mayama Seiki and His Plays*. New York: St. Martin's Press, 1984.

Richter, Hans. *Dada: Art and Anti-Art*. New York: McGraw Hill, 1966.

Rimer, J. Thomas. "Tokyo in Paris/Paris in Tokyo." *Paris in Japan: The Japanese Encounter with European Painting*. Eds. Shuki Takashima, et. al. Washington University, St. Louis: The Japan Foundation, 1984.

_____. *Towards a Modern Japanese Theatre: Kishida Kunio*. Princeton: Princeton University Press, 1974.

Rosenfeld, John M. "Western-Style Painting in the Early Meiji Period and Its Critics." *Tradition and Modernization in Japanese Culture*. Ed. Donald H. Shiveley. Princeton: Princeton University Press, 1971.

Rubin, Jay. "From Wholesomeness to Decadence: The Censorship of Literature under the Allied Occupation." *Journal of Japanese Studies* 11.1 (1985): 71–103.

_____. *Injurious to Public Morals: Writers and the Meiji State*. Seattle: University of Washington Press, 1984.

Shaipro, Theda. *Painters and Politics: The European Avant-Garde and Society, 1900–1925*. New York: Elsevier Scientific Publishing Company, 1976.

Silverberg, Miriam. *Changing Song: The Marxist Manifestos of Nakano Shigeharu*. Princeton: Princeton University Press, 1990.

_____. "Constructing a New Cultural History of Prewar Japan." *Japan and the World*. Eds. Masao Miyoshi and H. D. Harootunian. Durham and London: Duke University Press, 1993.

Takashina, Shuji. "Introduction." *Japons des avant-gardes 1910–1970*. Paris: Éditions du Centre Pompidou, 1986.

_____. "Natsume Soseki and the Development of Modern Japanese Art." *Culture and Identity: Japanese Intellectuals During the Interwar Years.* Ed. Thomas J. Rimer. Princeton: Princeton University Press, 1990.

Tsurumi, Kazuko. *Social Change and the Individual: Japan Before and After Defeat in World War II.* Princeton: Princeton University Press, 1970.

Ueda, Makoto. *Literary and Art Theories in Japan.* Ann Arbor: University of Michigan Press, 1967.

UNESCO, Japanese National Committee. *Theatre in Japan.* Tokyo: Printing Bureau, Ministry of Finance, 1963.

Viatte, Germain. "Le Combat des Avant-Gardes." *Japon des avant-gardes 1910–1970.* Paris: Éditions du Centre Pompidou, 1986.

Weisenfeld, Gennifer. "Murayama, Mavo's Conscious Constructivism: Art, Individualism, and Daily Life in Interwar Japan." *Art Journal* 55.3 (1996): 64–73.

Yamada, Chisaburoh, ed. *Dialogue in Art: Japan and the West.* Tokyo, New York and San Francisco: Kodansha International Ltd., 1976.

Remembering and Forgetting: Greek Tragedy as National History in Postwar Japan

Carol Fisher Sorgenfrei

At precisely 2:05 P.M. on August 30, 1945, the door of the C-54 airplane *Bataan* opened and General Douglas MacArthur, Supreme Commander for the Allied Powers (SCAP),[1] stepped onto Japanese soil at Atsugi Airfield. The lanky American "…appeared on the ramp with a corncob pipe clutched between his teeth and dark green aviator glasses. So dramatic did he seem that some compared his posturing to that of a *kabuki* actor" (Okamoto 30). In that theatrical moment when MacArthur first set foot in Japan, the world changed. In all of recorded history, no foreign invader had ever before occupied or conquered Japan. Fifteen days previously, after relentless firebombing, followed by the atomic blasts that devastated Hiroshima on August 6 and Nagasaki on August 9, Japan had surrendered. World War II was over, and the Occupation was about to begin.

The goal of the Occupation was no less than to reverse two thousand years of Japanese thought by the imposition of American-style democracy. According to American propaganda, the Japanese people would be freed from slavery to religious fanaticism, the totalitarian past would be utterly destroyed, and the defeated nation would be blessed with all the gifts of democracy. However, as John Dower notes,

> …the contradictions of the democratic revolution from above were clear for all to see: while the victors preached democracy, they ruled by fiat; while they espoused equality, they themselves constituted an inviolate privileged caste. Their reformist agenda rested on the assumption that, virtually without exception, Western culture and its

126

values were superior to those of the "the Orient." At the same time, almost every interaction between victor and vanquished was infused with intimations of white supremacism... Like their colonialist predecessors, the victors were imbued with a sense of manifest destiny [211–212].

Under the Occupation, freedom of speech was supposedly embraced. However, censorship was the reality, and historical memory was revised and rewritten. Prewar Japanese militarism and colonialism, previously imagined as the benevolent actions of the self-styled savior of Asia, were now condemned. Japanese leaders — with the notable exception of the Emperor himself— were convicted of wartime atrocities, and seven were executed. Many ordinary Japanese citizens felt that "these seven had died as scapegoats" either "for the Emperor, ...for the great many responsible for the war, [or] ... for the Japanese people as a whole" (Tsurumi 1987, 15–16). Thus, although most Japanese felt "relief" that the Emperor was not prosecuted by the tribunal, "...it was considered a denial of the very logic of the trial for war crimes. This ambiguity is the most important aspect of the Japanese reaction" (Tsurumi 1987, 16). Were the Japanese to consider themselves victims or victimizers?

The sense of ambiguity regarding Japan's national identity reigned throughout the Occupation and continues to this day. Japan, once the land of samurai warriors, was forced to accept a new Constitution forever renouncing war and the use of military force. Nevertheless, when the Korean War broke out, America encouraged Japan to violate this imposed constitution by creating a defensive force called the National Police Reserve. Fifty years later, the contradictions remain. The anti–Communist sentiments of the 1950s have been replaced by fears of terrorism; and despite the postwar constitutional prohibition, in 2003 Japanese troops were sent abroad to participate in American-led military actions.

Against the backdrop of widespread protest demonstrations, on May 19, 1960, the Diet met at midnight to ratify AMPO, the security treaty between Japan and America. AMPO went into effect on June 19. It formalized Japan's status as a client nation and authorized the maintenance of a large American military presence in Japan, including nuclear submarines. AMPO is renewed every ten years, resulting in protests from both the left (who want the Americans out of Japan so that Japan cannot be used as a military base for international conflicts, as it was in Vietnam) and the right (who want Japan to renounce the Peace Constitution and military dependence on America by creating a true Japanese military).

In order to transform Japan into an American style democracy, the Occupation encouraged the publication and denunciation of wartime educational documents outlining the philosophical basis of Japanese militarism and of Emperor worship. At the same time, SCAP needed to reinforce Japanese national self-respect and encourage economic development. Therefore, a policy of selective memory — what might even be termed enforced intellectual hypocrisy — ensued.

For a number of years, the Japanese Ministry of Education approved including references to Japanese war crimes in junior high history textbooks. However, the increasing power of right wing nationalists in Japan — including educators at highly respected universities — led the Ministry of Education in April, 2001, to adopt a revisionist textbook that does not discuss the existence of "comfort women" (Koreans and others who were forced into sexual slavery) and that downplays Japan's crimes against its Asian neighbors. The educators responsible for this new textbook insist that there is no proof that these events actually occurred, and that the self-respect of Japanese children is undermined by suggesting that they did. The revisionist rhetoric is similar to that of Holocaust deniers in America and Europe; and the government's action is reminiscent of the Kansas decision in 1999 to ban science textbooks that include discussion of theories such as evolution and the Big Bang. The textbook issue continues to be politically sensitive, highly controversial, and unsettled; as in America, both sides of the political spectrum have passionate arguments. Although the Occupation officially ended in 1952, its influence endures. As Dower perceptively notes:

> Much that lies at the heart of contemporary Japanese society — the nature of its democracy, the intensity of popular feelings about pacifism and remilitarization, the manner in which the war is remembered (and forgotten) — derives from the complexity of the interplay between the victors and the vanquished [Dower 28].

Such contradictions have insured that the way the national past is represented is an issue of paramount importance.

Theatre, Memory, and National Identity

The question of facing up to the past, ignoring the past, or simply rewriting and revising the past is crucial for the Japanese sense of self. While especially contentious after the war, the issue is not unique to the contemporary period, nor even to Japan. In every age and every nation, victorious warriors and new governments have encouraged revisionism to bolster hegemony. Nevertheless, some cultural scholars maintain that the Japanese have always been able to shift ideologies rapidly, depending on the immediate circumstances, without feeling that they are behaving hypocritically. This behavior is related to *tenkō* (the recantation of former beliefs, or the coerced conversion under pressure). It can be perceived as a practical solution to life's insoluble conflicts (Tsurumi 1986, 1987).

How did theatre artists after the end of the Occupation respond to the contradictions created by the imposition of democracy, revelations of Japanese militarism and war crimes, and the nuclear attacks on Japan? How did the tendency to reverse position based on the needs of the moment — to commit *tenkō*— affect postwar theatre? One way to address this problem is to consider the Japanese theatrical engagement with the foreign "Other" in the guise of the West. To gain perspective on the past fifty years, let's look back for a moment to the time prior to the Second World War.

Since the late nineteenth century, Japanese playwrights and directors have increasingly felt compelled to reply to rapid and distressing social upheavals by finding dramatic analogues in Western performance. Soon after the overthrow of the feudalistic Tokugawa *shōgunate* in 1868, debates raged about how theatre might properly represent a nation that was frantically attempting to replace the old, closed Japan with a new "civilized" Japan that could compete with the industrialized, imperialistic West. It was commonly assumed that foreigners were offended by vulgarity and sexuality. One attempted reform was the "modernization" of *kabuki* by making it more realistic and more like Western drama. To do so required numerous strategies such as casting actresses instead of *onnagata* (male actors specializing in female roles), emphasizing inner or psychological truth (*haragei*) instead of stylized beauty, eliminating theatricalist staging, fantasy and explicit sexuality, introducing historically accurate costumes, and writing plays about contemporary events. The government, theatre owners, and even some major actors such as Ichikawa Danjûrô IX (1839–1903) joined forces in the attempt to transform *kabuki* from a vulgar entertainment for the masses to something that might be able to compete with Western opera in terms of elegance. However, like the cultural and social manipulation attempted later under the Occupation, such top-down reforms were not embraced by *kabuki*'s patrons.

In contrast, the call for more "realism" and for plays about contemporary life inspired the youthful, politically savvy creators of a new genre, *shimpa* (new school drama). Kawakami Otojirō (1864–1911) and his wife Kawakami Sadayakko (1871–1946) celebrated Japan's status as an imperialistic power with popular, patriotic productions such as *The Sino-Japanese War* (*Nisshin sensō*, 1894–95), billed as "reports from the battlefront." Their troupe also represented "the new Japan" on tours to America and Europe between 1899 and 1902. These tours featured exotic, semi–Orientalist, pseudo-*kabuki* plays, such as *The Geisha and the Knight* (*Geisha to samurai*). The Kawakami troupe depicted a paradoxical national identity that was simultaneously modern yet ancient, martial yet feminine (Kano 3–123, 219–230).

Back in Japan, theatrical attempts to emulate the West were evident in *shingeki* (new theatre). From its creation in 1906, *shingeki* focused on Western literary and philosophical theatre, specializing in translations and adaptations of European classics by authors such as Shakespeare and Ibsen. Matsui Sumako (1886–1919), who first portrayed Nora in Ibsen's *A Doll House* in 1911, is often considered the first modern Japanese actress as well as an exemplar of the "new woman" whose behavior, like Nora's, shocked traditional sensibilities (Kano 3–38, 123–230).

Fear that girls would emulate the decadent, westernized "new woman" and fail to become the "good wives and wise mothers" that Japanese nationalism required — coupled with the desire for economic gain — led to the development of the all-girls' review known as *Takarazuka*. It was originally conceived as a kind of advanced finishing school featuring training in traditional female arts (including singing, dancing, cleaning, and obedience to fathers and husbands). Public performances were envisioned as wholesome family entertainment; a student's success would be demonstrated by a good marriage. Although *Takarazuka* has become a wildly popular commercial success, it continues to support an essentially conservative national image (Robertson).

During the 1930s, as the Japanese government moved ideologically to the right, many *shingeki* artists moved to the left. In 1942, fourteen leading *shingeki* theatre artists who had advocated Marxist-socialist positions (and who had been in and out of jail over the previous decade) were convicted of crimes against the state. *Shingeki* was forbidden for the duration of the war. All fourteen eventually committed *tenkō* (that is, they renounced Marxism and swore unequivocal allegiance to Japan) and were released. Among these were the actor-director Senda Koreya (1904–1994), who had been in prison since 1940. Although reviled by some for his failure to uphold his principals, Senda prospered as a revered artist after the war. He spoke openly about his *tenkō* in a 1970 interview:

> I was not concerned with whether Japan won or lost the war. It was not important to me. When a person was faced with the problem of recantation, there were two basic things to be considered. One concerned your responsibility to your organization. The other had to do with your responsibility to yourself. ... The members of my troupe ... all recanted and went into the government's traveling companies, and some just went into commercial films. I didn't have anyone left

to fight for, so the problem boiled down to a very personal one. I thought it would be better to get out and start doing things again instead of sitting in a prison cell [Senda 63–64].

Despite its elitist, intellectual origins and its leftist tendencies, *shingeki* realism became the standard in twentieth-century commercial theatre, and continues to be so even today.

Consequently, *shingeki* was the main target when another new Japanese theatre movement appeared. *Angura* (from the English "underground") was born amid the social contradictions of the time, including widespread anger and massive protests over the passage of AMPO in 1960 and the anti-authoritarian, anti–Vietnam war demonstrations of 1968 (which began four months prior to the events in Paris, and which led to the closure of at least 116 Japanese colleges and universities by the end of the year). *Angura* advocated a youthful spirit and innovative modes of performance. *Shingeki*'s "old left" politics and psychological realism were seen as outmoded. Like their counterparts in the West, *angura*'s theatrical innovators were true artistic revolutionaries. Some attempted to destroy, re-invent, or re-define Japanese traditional performance genres such as *nō, bunraku, kyōgen, kabuki,* and various types of rural entertainments; some aligned themselves with, or set themselves against, the Western avant-garde; and some searched for totally new modes of expression and identity.

The Myth of Democracy

Among the most inventive and resourceful of these *angura* artists were those who sought inspiration from classical Greek tragedy as one way to grapple with the inexpressible ambiguities of Japan's past and present. Considering the conflicts surrounding open discussion of their nation' s recent history, they resorted to a time-honored practice of substituting an earlier and analogous era for the present. Like *kabuki* playwrights before them, they often turned to a romanticized (or intentionally anti-romanticized) version of the Japanese past. Unlike their predecessors, however, these *angura* dramatists also found analogies in the theatre of an exotic, alien Other — ancient Greece.

During the eighteenth century, *kabuki* had been prohibited from representing current events. The government had feared the potential impact of plays depicting outlawed behavior such as rebellions against unjust authority, personal vendettas, or lovers' suicides. To elude the censors, *kabuki* resorted to the use of alternative worlds (*sekai*) derived from Japanese history, myth, legend, or literature, as well as selective substitution (*mitate*) of well-known historical events into a contemporary context. For example, Japan's most famous revenge play, *Chûshingura* (The Loyal Forty Seven Ronin), depicts actual, well-known events of 1703, when a group of loyal retainers murdered the villainous nobleman who was responsible for the unjust death of their own lord. Early theatrical adaptations of the story were forbidden. Eventually, a team of playwrights was permitted to produce the play by making slight changes to the characters' names and by substituting incidents from a similar occurrence in the fourteenth century. The resulting double-consciousness is among *kabuki*'s distinctive characteristics. Some *angura* theatre artists, while rejecting the traditions of *kabuki*, nevertheless utilized the practice of alternative worlds and *mitate* in order to speak covertly about culturally sensitive (or even taboo) subjects.

Before analyzing specific works, I would like to consider some possible reasons for the exploitation of Greek tragedy. Certainly, the use of Greek tragedy by non–Euro-Americans to speak to their own cultures and histories is not confined to Japan. For example, Nigeria's Wole Soyinka, South Africa's Athol Fugard, and Indonesia's W.S. Rendra have adapted *The Bacchae*, *Antigone*, and *Oedipus the King* respectively. Unlike Japanese dramatists, these playwrights matured in former European colonies, cultures imbued with long traditions of classical European education. Using the classics of their former colonial masters as weapons against those masters helped satisfy the need for postcolonial peoples to "write back" to the Empire.

Why would the never-colonized Japan choose to adapt Greek tragedy rather than seek a more familiar style? And why did this preference occur only after the Occupation and during a period of rebellious, new theatrical ideas? Certainly *shingeki* had never expressed great interest in the theatre of ancient Greece.

Let's look for a moment at the historical uses of tragedy by ancient Greek society, and the perceived connections between the ideals of Greek and American democracy. Citizens of Athens had a civic responsibility to participate in theatrical festivals as actors, playwrights, producers, or audience members. The festivals — whatever remnants of religious activity remained or did not remain — were undeniably civic rituals that helped consolidate social unity. The festivals were, among other things, elaborate displays of Athenian power and expressions of Athenian pride. The audience, consisting of both citizens (that is, free adult males) and non-citizens such as women, slaves, and foreigners, were not passive recipients of the author's (or government's) vision. Rather, they were imagined to be participants in the creation of the event. They were active agents in determining how previously known myths (or the social contract, or "history") would be re-created and re-understood in contemporary society.

The ideal, or myth, of American democracy, too, was envisioned as public participation. According to this naïve view, American citizens elected — or served as — members of Congress or of local government. They were the voters — the ones who counted — and every vote could make a difference. Anyone, so the myth went, could become President. Like the audience members of Greek tragedies, they were romantically imagined to be individual citizen-participants in the experiment of democracy, direct agents of action rather than passive listeners. MacArthur offered Japan a variant of this ideal as an alternative to Japan's more feudal, totalitarian past.

It seems reasonable to assume that the early artists of Japanese *angura* may have turned to the imagined, idealized, and mythologized tradition of Greek democracy, supposedly embodied in the performance of Greek tragedy, as they struggled to embrace, understand, or come to terms with the imposition of American-style democracy and its contradictions. Although their opinions varied from Satoh Makoto's passionate "New Left" political activism to Terayama *Shûji's* visionary, apolitical "revolution of the imagination," all these artists advocated participation in theatre by non-professional actors as a means to enact personal and/or social change. For example, in Terayama's *Throw Away Your Books, Go Out Into the Streets* (*Sho-o suteyō, machi-e deyō*, 1967 and 1968; filmed 1971) run-away youths and disaffected students performed their own heartfelt poetry speaking as themselves, not as fictional characters. Kara Jûrō's Situation Theatre (*Jōkyō gekijō*) troupe referred to themselves as "beggars of the riverbed" (*kawara kojiki* or *kawaramono*), a pejorative originally applied to outcast *kabuki* actors in the early seventeenth century. In 1967, he set up his famous Red Tent in the precise location in Kyoto where legend says that the temple-dancer/prostitute Okuni performed the first *kabuki* play. His peripatetic tent theatre had more in common with itinerant carnivals than with staid professionalism. Similarly, Suzuki Tadashi's most important actress was for many years Shiraishi Kayoko, originally a non-professional whose powerful voice and presence mesmerized Suzuki, leading him to transform the very nature of his work. Shiraishi's voice has been described as "...deep and overwhelming but not musical. It is harsh and guttural, not from her throat or chest, but from caves that crawl with demons — a Delphic oracle who does not speak but is spoken through" (Faber, qtd. in McDonald 34).

These provocative alternative theatre troupes often set up shop in unfashionable little theatres, in converted warehouses, on street corners, in rural villages, in gay cabarets, in public baths, in tents — anywhere but the western-style proscenium theatres favored by respectable *shingeki*. Whereas Greek tragedy was performed in the context of civic festivals sanctioned by the state — and therefore might be seen as complicit with the conservative impulse to maintain or create stability — *angura* artists envisioned themselves as active opponents to the political and/or theatrical status quo. Thus they could identify with an imaginary, Platonic ideal of participatory democracy, regardless of historical reality or what must have seemed like the perversion of that ideal under the Occupation.

The emphasis on non-professional actors, the agency and empowerment of the audience, and participatory theatre in the service of civic unity and/or social change did not preclude an interest in the trappings of international success. Terayama, Suzuki, director Ninagawa Yukio and numerous *butō* troupes are among those whose works have been consistently invited to perform at major festivals and venues throughout the world. In 1981, Suzuki even established his own highly regarded international theatre festival in the village of Toga, a rural center that requires audiences to endure a complicated, three-hour journey from Tokyo.

Although originally community-based and devoutly anti-commercial, these artists and their companies eventually embraced a new type of professionalism by creating an elite class of performers, playwright/directors, and audience members in direct conflict with their original ideals. Consequently, the next generation of Japanese theatre artists, who came to prominence in the 1980s and 1990s, felt a need to rebel against *angura*. Perhaps such a development is inherently a part of success, and I certainly do not mean to suggest any sort of intentional hypocrisy in regard to *angura* or the passionate artists associated with such innovations.

Dionysus in Japan: Angura's *Adaptations of Greek Tragedy*

Terayama Shûji's *The Hunchback of Aomori* (*Aomori-ken no semushi otoko*, 1967) is a radical re-working of *Oedipus the King* (Sorgenfrei). This dark tale of incest and rape serves as an oblique metaphor for both Japan's relationship to the West prior to World War II, and for Japan's agonized sense of guilt, shame, and victimization resulting from the atomic bombing of Hiroshima and Nagasaki. Terayama's staging is eclectic, utilizing elements from such disparate sources as old-time Japanese carnival acts (*misemono*), parodies or reflections of *nō, kyōgen, shimpa,* and *kabuki,* Japanese children's songs, psychedelic music and lighting, and *naniwabushi,* a nearly vanished form of popular prewar radio storytelling/chanting, accompanied by the *biwa,* a stringed instrument.

The play ostensibly takes place during the Taishō era (1911–1926), a time of nostalgia for many older people during the postwar period. Taishō seemed to recall a moment when much of Japan remained in limbo between cultural isolation and rapid Westernization. The leading role of Matsu, a depraved middle-aged matriarch dressed in grotesque Western finery, was first performed by the outrageous male transvestite chanteuse Maruyama (later Miwa) Akihiro, whose cabaret act at the club *Ginpari* (Paris on the Ginza) had been scandalizing the Tokyo music world for a decade. This dowager was once an innocent maid raped by her master's son. When she became pregnant, they quickly married to avoid scandal. Their child was born a hunchback, and a servant was ordered to abandon it to die. However, he secretly adopted it. Now the boy, unaware of his heritage, has returned. The dowager, who may or may not know that she is the hunchback's mother, rapes and torments him. She fights with the virginal schoolgirl narrator/*naniwabushi* chanter over his love. The villagers, crippled old men and semi-blind old women, gossip about the rape and possible incest. No one knows the truth, because the town's family register was stolen to cover up the crimes of the past. Everyone's identity, everyone's paternity is in doubt. The ending — like the past — is ambiguous. Perhaps the hunchbacked boy was murdered by his mother, or perhaps she was not his mother after all.

The historical analogy is this: during the nineteenth century, Japan, like the poor maid, was offered great wealth but was ultimately raped and betrayed by the powerful master, representative of the West. As she began to emulate her despised rapist, she lost her soul and became a sadistic monster capable of inflicting rape, torture, and possible murder on her own children, the younger generation of Japanese. The hunchbacked orphan, whose deformity is analogous to Oedipus' deformed feet, is the innocent child whose birth is the result of rape by the West, depicted both as the rich, powerful, abusive, hateful male master, and as the desired, unknowable, terrifying, godlike female Other. The boy is contaminated, unclean, a social pariah — he is clearly related to the *hibakusha* (victims of nuclear disease resulting from the atomic blasts at Hiroshima and Nagasaki). He is tormented by powerful, desirable, horrible females — simultaneously mothers, whores, brides, virgins, delicate young things, and sadistic monsters — who seduce, torture, nurture, abandon, and murder him. These tormenting females are representative of the impossibility of spiritual and social integration with the West, with the Japanese past, and with the ever absent but ever desired mother. Those who should have protected the child abandoned him, and the government closed its eyes to the crimes of the powerful.

Although almost all of the plot elements of *Oedipus* appear, there is no suggestion of parricide. While Terayama's biography and his obsession with incestuous mother-son relationships may offer clues to this omission,[2] it is also interesting to speculate that the suggestion of parricide might imply the need to kill the image of the Emperor. The Occupation, in contrast, offered a sanitized picture of a gentle, fatherly Hirohito unpolluted by complicity in Japanese militarist atrocities. Although Terayama's politics are not made explicit, he is clearly nostalgic for a romanticized version of the Japanese past. In the play, multiple versions of the past are unraveled but no truth is revealed. The past is ultimately unknowable.

Satoh Makoto's *Ismene* (Goodman, trans. in Rolf and Gillespie) is part of a trilogy inspired by Sophocles' *Antigone*. Unlike Terayama's females, who seduce and destroy helpless young males, Satoh's heroines act out of pure instinct and may even offer a sense of hope to the world. They clearly suggest the agency of the citizens in an idealized democracy. Unfortunately, reality intervenes. Satoh does not refer to traditional Japanese theatre in this work. Rather, he deploys a style that might best be related to American or European Theatre of the Absurd combined with playful, somewhat improvisational acting. The play is set in a contemporary warehouse dominated by a Coca Cola vending machine, where Ismene, Elder Sister (Antigone), and their parents reside. Clearly, Satoh is not interested in duplicating Sophocles' version, in which both Oedipus and Jocasta are already dead. Nor does he wish to focus on Antigone's rash heroism, but rather on Ismene's cowardice and her belated attempt to join her sister by claiming responsibility for the forbidden burial of her brother.

In Satoh's play, the war with Argos has just ended. Elder Sister has been patiently waiting for Haemon to marry her, but after Creon's decree, she feels she must rebel. For her, it is not so much a conscious choice as it is an uncontrollable urge to do something, rather than remaining passive. Ismene is stunned. It seems that this exciting adventure, this action, will have horrifying consequences. Ismene is like a child, unable to act for herself, unable to do anything but dream of an ideal world and continue waiting for her savior to arrive. She is afraid to utilize her power as a citizen-participant. As in the original, she falsely confesses to being a partner in her sister's action, but the truth is revealed. Satoh focuses on her as a negative example. Elder Sister berates her parents for hypocrisy. Her father (Oedipus) should have killed himself when he realized that his past crimes were the cause of his people's misery. She maintains that his "penance" is meaningless. In the present, her father and mother (Jocasta) have gradually become addicted to Coca Cola, a clear symbol of American cultural hegemony in general, and, specifically, of the way war criminals became complicit with the Occupation.

When Creon, a former peasant soldier who is now the king, appears, his first action is to buy and drink a Coke from the ubiquitous vending

machine. It is soon revealed that the edict forbidding the burial of Polyne-
ices was not Creon's idea, but came from Oedipus. Thus the true criminal,
in the guise of retiring penance, is covertly running the show. Insisting that
he does not have the stomach for carrying out the death sentence, Creon
begs Oedipus to once again be king. Father (Oedipus) responds, "If I could,
I would, believe me. I'd give almost anything to regain power in Thebes.
But there's not much hope of that. No one would follow me. I've lost my
charisma. The people despise me" (357). In right wing rhetoric, the Emperor
is considered to be the Father of the Japanese people. Is Satoh suggesting
the corruption of SCAP's apparent cover-up of the Emperor's war responsibility? The play concludes on an ominous yet ironic note. Creon does not
condemn Elder Sister to death. Instead, she and Father — the dangerous rebel
and the hidden criminal — will be exiled. As they leave, two Coca Cola ven-
dors (Nobody A and Nobody B) come to move the Coke machine, which
will travel with the exiles to the next town.

Ismeme reflects the anguish of young Japanese leftists who failed to prevent passage of the despised 1960 Mutual Security Treaty between Japan and
America. The treaty represented the collusion of Japan's leaders with their
American conquerors — the domination of Japanese culture by brash American pragmatism, capitalism, and Coca-Cola. Ismene, like Satoh, grew up
in a world dominated by a war that she did not start, and cannot change.
Born in 1943, by 1960, Satoh was old enough to understand the need for
action and change but, like Ismene, he was too young to do anything but
watch in horror as the older college students he idolized rebelled and were
brutally crushed.

Director/playwright Suzuki Tadashi's trans-cultural adaptations of
Greek tragedy include numerous versions and revisions. His most well-
known Greek adaptations are *The Trojan Women* (*Toroia no onna*, 1974), *The
Bacchae* (*Bakkasu no shinjo*, 1978; bilingual version 1981), and *Clytemnestra*
(*'hi Kuritemunesutora*, 1983). He has also directed additional adaptations of
Greek tragedies, including numerous variations of *The Bacchae*, especially
after Shiraishi left his company.[3] While freely drawing from and mingling
the classic myths with contemporary references, Suzuki's storylines are generally closer to the original plays than the works of Terayama or Satoh. Nevertheless, he shares with them an interest in how Greek tragedy can directly
address the postwar Japanese condition.

Suzuki's actors draw from his unique training methods, including nine
different walking techniques and special vocal exercises. Elements reminiscent of *kabuki* and *nō* mingle with popular music. Each of these Greek adaptations specifically comments on the relationship between Japan and the
West. Suzuki's *The Trojan Women* takes place in a ruined Japanese cemetery.

A Japanese beggar woman (performed by Shiraishi) is confronted by ghosts; perhaps possessed by them, she portrays herself, Cassandra, and Hecuba. As Euripides' tale unfolds, we see the suffering of Japanese women at the hands of soldiers (who may be Japanese or who may be foreign), the atrocities inflicted on innocent civilians in the name of war, and the complicity of implacable, uncaring gods. Japan's immediate past mingles with the aftermath of the Trojan War.

The time is after a war, yet there is no peace. Monstrous soldiers are on a rampage of rape and murder. Suzuki uses the device of a possibly mad Japanese woman who transforms into archetypal characters from Greek legend to soften the attack on the Japanese military past as well as on the American atomic bombings. These soldiers are universal soldiers, for they are simultaneously ancient Greek victors, Japanese invaders of Asia, and conquering Americans. There is no doubt that they are filled with blood lust and are out of control.

While Suzuki portrays the universality of the horrors of war and of its aftermath, he very pointedly refers to the Japanese sensibility as victims of America firebombing and atomic bombing. At the same time, his critique of Japan and of America is not specific. Suzuki here utilizes ambiguity, nostalgia, and horror to condemn all war. Throughout the play, the impassive image of Jizō, a voiceless, golden-skinned Buddhist *bodhisattva* (saint), watches as samurai-like soldiers perform unspeakable acts, including rape and infanticide. He does not punish evil-doers, nor does he take sides. Suzuki seems to suggest, as he does in his subsequent *The Bacchae*, that if the gods exist at all, their behavior is both incomprehensible and totally lacking in compassion for the sufferings of humanity.

The Trojan Women is stunning partly for its sheer theatricality. Although not quite as startling, Suzuki's bi-lingual version of *The Bacchae* is more pointed in its political posture. Created with Milwaukee Repertory Theatre, this adaptation clearly suggests the painful ambiguities of Japanese responses to the immediate postwar period through casting, costuming, and language choices. The actress Shiraishi Kayoko, speaking Japanese and wearing Japanese garb, embodies both the androgynous, eastern god Dionysus and the female Agave, the mother who in divine frenzy beheads her own son. That son, the militaristic and inflexible Pentheus, is portrayed by an English speaking American actor wearing a costume suggestive of a Shakespearean king. The chorus members are Japanese. On one hand, there is the implication that traditional Japanese female divinity (and thus the Emperor, direct descendant of the sun goddess) has greater spiritual power than the destructive, male, American military force that led to the bombings of Hiroshima and Nagasaki. On the other hand, the play makes it clear that both the Japanese god and the American military commander are guilty of inhumanity in the name of war. Dionysus' crazed followers, the Japanese chorus of Bacchantes and Agave herself, like unthinking soldiers or kamikaze pilots, blindly obey orders that make them guilty of atrocities and war crimes.

Suzuki adds a coda to his deconstruction of Euripides. After the beheading, Agave/Dionysus (played by Shiraishi) and Cadmus/Tiresius (played by a male Japanese actor) transform, becoming anonymous Japanese prisoners of war. As they sit quietly eating rice balls, the American Pentheus enters, dagger in hand. As he repeats his opening lines and brutally stabs the prisoners to death, the cycle of blind violence seems about to begin again. The play, like Euripides' original, defies easy analysis or simplistic solutions.

Terayama, Satoh, and Suzuki all suggest that the gods, if they exist, are impassive, helpless, and complicit in cultural, personal, and national destruction. These gods, incarnations of the Japanese past, or of Greek and American ideals of democracy, are powerless to confront the reality of postwar Japan. For Terayama, the political agenda is muddled and unclear. Japan is the helpless victim of cultural rape. Terayama's ambivalence suggests a lean to the right, or at least nostalgia for the Japanese past, as well as queasiness about the Americanized present. Satoh, in contrast, is squarely in the camp of left-wing reform. Like Terayama, he is suspicious of the imposition of American culture, but unlike him, Satoh wants to find a way to use the ideals of democracy to create a new social structure. He feels angry and betrayed by a generation that failed to do so, yet hopes for some solution in the future. The adaptations of Suzuki suggest a third approach. His work criticizes both American and Japanese atrocities, but ultimately suggests a humanistic universality in which cultural differences dissolve. All war is bad, all soldiers commit war crimes. Perhaps theatre can offer us insights so that the past will not be endlessly repeated.

For these disparate artists of *angura*, the past inhabits the present; Japan, America, and Greece exist simultaneously. These plays transform the icons of European culture and humanism into specifically Japanese images of horror and degeneration. They function as devices to ensure public agency in order to examine the meaning of incomprehensible reality.

Notes

1. SCAP refers both to McArthur himself (Supreme Commander for the Allied Powers) and to his Occupation Government (Supreme Command for the Allied Powers).

2. Terayama's life strongly suggests the Ajase Complex, which has been suggested by Japanese psychoanalysts as more culturally appropriate than Freud's Oedi-

pus Complex. It is based on the Buddhist parable of Prince Ajase, whose mother conceived him only to keep the love of her husband. Because she feared the wrath of the sage she murdered so that she could become pregnant, she attempted to abort the child. When he was born, she tried to murder him. When Ajase became a teenager, he learned of her actions. His anger was so intense that he attempted to kill her in revenge. Guilt caused his body to be covered with oozing, foul smelling sores. But his mother devotedly cared for him. Eventually, mother and son became mutually dependant and forgave each other. (For the pathology, see Okonogi 1978, 1979, and Allison 3–5, 136–138; for Terayama's biography and plays, see Sorgenfrei.)

3. This includes *The Tragedy: The Fall of the House of Atreus* (1983) and the post–Shiraishi *Dionysus* (1990). In 1995, I attended a production of *Electra* performed at Teatro Olimpico in Vicenza, Italy. The program notes do not make clear if this work was derived from the earlier *The Tragedy: The Fall of the House of Atreus* or if it was a newer version.

Works Cited

Allison, Anne. *Permitted and Prohibited Desires: Mothers, Comics and Censorship in Japan.* Berkeley: University of California Press, 2000.

Dower, John W. *Embracing Defeat: Japan in the Wake of World War II.* New York: Norton, 1999.

Faber, Roderick Mason. "From the Tornado's Eye." *Village Voice* (June 1979).

Kano, Ayako. *Acting Like a Woman in Modern Japan: Theatre, Gender and Nationalism.* New York: Palgrave, 2001.

McDonald, Marianne. *Ancient Sun, Modern Light: Greek Drama on the Modern Stage.* New York: Columbia University Press, 1992.

Okamoto, Shiro. *The Man Who Saved Kabuki: Faubion Bowers and Theatre Censorship in Occupied Japan.* Trans. and adapt. Samuel L. Leiter. Honolulu: University of Hawaii Press, 2001.

Okonogi, Keigo. "The Ajase Complex of the Japanese (1)." *Japan Echo* V. 4(1979): 88–105.

_____. "The Ajase Complex of the Japanese (2)." *Japan Echo* VI.1(1979): 104–118.

Robertson, Jennifer. *Takarazuka: Sexual Politics and Popular Culture in Modern Japan.* Berkeley: University of California Press, 1998.

Rolf, Robert T., and John K. Gillespie, eds. *Alternative Japanese Drama: Ten Plays.* Honolulu: University of Hawaii Press, 1992.

Senda, Koreya. "Senda Koreya: An Interview." *Concerned Theatre Japan* 1.2(1970): 47–80.

_____. *SCOT (Suzuki Company of Toga).* Tokyo: SCOT, 1991.

Sorgenfrei, Carol Fisher. *Unspeakable Acts: Terayama Shûji and Postwar Japanese Theatre.* Honolulu: University of Hawaii Press, forthcoming 2004.

Tsurumi, Shunsuke. *A Cultural History of Postwar Japan: 1945–1980.* London and New York: KPI, 1987.

_____. *An Intellectual History of Wartime Japan: 1931–1945.* London and New York: KPI, 1986.

The Critical Absence of Indonesia in W.S. Rendra's Village

Evan Darwin Winet

Indonesia incorporates over thirteen thousand islands inhabited by nearly two hundred million people from over a hundred native ethnic groups who speak three hundred more or less distinct languages.[1] It is the world's fourth most populous nation and has the largest Muslim population of any nation on earth. Migrations and invasions of the western islands from mainland Southeast Asia, Hindu, Buddhist and Muslim India, the Arab world, and China, beginning in the first millennium, created various links between disparate societies. However, no common culture or history has ever united the archipelago as a whole, as Indonesia's tragic struggle over East Timor demonstrated. The ethnic groups of the Western islands (Javanese, Sundanese, Madurese, Balinese, Batak, Minangkabau, etc.) are closer in culture and traditions to the Malay populations of mainland Southeast Asia than to the native inhabitants of the eastern archipelago or to Chinese-Indonesians. The Netherlands India government, which took control of Dutch interests in the Malay archipelago in 1800, following the bankruptcy of the Dutch East Indies Company, created modern Indonesia through military expansion, extending their territory from coastal fortresses to the current Indonesian borders by the time of their rout from Java by the Japanese in 1940, and through social policy, by creating bureaucratic infrastructure and, most significantly, standardizing the Indonesian language. Following the war of independence (1945–1949), the Indonesian nation-state inherited the territorial boundaries, and, in many respects, the administrative bureaucracy of the Netherlands Indies.

Of course, the Indonesian nation-state's continuity with its European predecessors raises concerns about Indonesian nationalism itself. A pervasive suspicion of nationalism as the handmaiden of authoritarianism looms large in the imagination of the post-fascist West. In Indonesia, as in much of the post-colonial world, nationalism has frequently abetted neo-colonial despotism. However, despite the hypocrisies and abuses committed in Indonesia in the name of the nation, many new cultural and artistic traditions have emerged over the past half-century within national culture. National culture has facilitated participation in broader regional and global artistic communities, and many artists address their compatriots as well as global audiences from what they understand as distinctly Indonesian perspectives. Though they may draw from local practices, Indonesian artists frequently reject the parochialism of traditional, ethnic or religious affiliations, challenging assumptions that local practices are somehow more "authentic" than their own. It is also crucial to recognize that the nationalism of these Indonesian artists is not always the same as the "official" nationalism of the Indonesian nation-state, for many artists have worked to articulate alternative Indonesian nationalisms.

In modern theatre, no figure looms larger in this regard than W.S. Rendra. Son of a Roman Catholic missionary and a dancer at the court of Surakarta, Rendra was raised with a mix of Western modernist progressivism and Central Javanese traditional culture. He wrote his first play, *Kaki Palsu* (False Foot) in 1948 at the age of 13, and won awards for several dramas written in the 1950s.[2] Nevertheless, Rendra himself has admitted that he was not serious about theatre in the 1950s. He put a greater effort into poetry, publishing his first collection, *Ballada Orang-orang Tercinta* (Ballads of Beloved People) to national acclaim in 1957. In the early 1960s, Indonesia's increasingly powerful communist arts establishment (headed by LEKRA, the People's Cultural Organization) proclaimed Rendra's work counter-revolutionary. To escape police harassment and the banning of their literature, Rendra and Arifin C. Noer, who became another of Indonesia's leading playwrights, formed in 1961 a Drama Study Group in the Central Javanese city of Yogyakarta.

Here, Rendra first began experimenting with syncretic intercultural theatre techniques that would become commonplace in Indonesian theatre in the 1970s. In 1962, for example, Rendra adapted Eugene Ionesco's *Les Chaises* in a work he called *Kereta Kencana* (Golden Chariot). *Kereta Kencana* preserves the basic structure of Ionesco's parable: an ancient "general factotum" and his slightly less ancient wife host a post-apocalyptic dinner party for invisible guests, represented by assembled chairs. Much of Ionesco's play consists of the playing out of social games and codes between the couple.

However, Rendra fills the imaginative world of the play's elderly couple with imagery more congenial to his own romantic and mystical palate, and verbal etiquette more closely aligned to Javanese and Indonesian conversation patterns. The culminating suicidal defenestration of *Les Chaises* becomes for Rendra's couple a more mystically optimistic passage. They ascend via a "golden chariot," invoking the wondrous chariot of Krishna that carries Prince Arjuna in the *Bhagavadgita*. Existential oblivion is translated into mystical transcendence.

Although Rendra's theatrical work of this period was not overtly didactic, he did publicly criticize President Sukarno (who, following the disappointingly fractious 1955 elections, had increasingly abandoned the institutions of democracy) and communism, as Rendra had been unimpressed by a tour through the USSR, China, and North Korea in 1957. Furthermore, he was harassed and imprisoned twice more in 1962 and 1963, which apparently influenced him to flee the country. In 1964, he attended an international humanities seminar for anti-communist youth at Harvard University, and afterwards connived to remain in New York City. Fortuitously, Rendra stayed in the United States during the years of Indonesia's bloodiest reckoning: a failed communist coup in 1965, followed by witch hunts that destroyed the party in one of the most terrible genocides of the twentieth century and catapulted General Suharto to power. Rendra studied social sciences and humanities at New York University where he first began to think of art in relation to "structural analysis" and communal activism.[3] At the same time, he received his first — and only — formal theatre training at the American Academy of Dramatic Arts. Although American Method acting had been known in Indonesia since the 1950s,[4] it was here that Rendra first became acquainted with improvisational rehearsal techniques. When Rendra returned to Indonesia in 1967, he began to produce a kind of modern theatre Indonesia had not seen before: ensemble-based, improvisational, abstract, and theatrical, a theatre that privileged action over text, visual over linguistic composition, and the company over the individual actor.

Rendra's *Teater Bengkel* (Workshop Theatre) began in 1967 with rehearsals in the open *kampongan* (courtyards) of Yogyakarta, a style of working familiar to rural performance traditions, but radical for the urban modern theatre. The early pieces generated by *Bengkel*'s courtyard improvisations often lacked dialogue or distinct characterization, but thematized fundamental social struggles, especially that between individuation and socialization. For example, a figure might begin to perform an action or sound, and soon everyone would imitate, transforming individual expression into a social movement. Goenawan Mohamad called the work *mini-kata* (minimal word).

Dami N. Toda called it *teater puisi,* referring to the poetic quality of the theatrical movement itself. Trisno Sumardjo called it *teater abstrak,* Subagio
Sastrowardoyo called it *teater murni* (pure), and Arifin C. Noer called it
teater primitif,[5] all pointing to a significant shift from the literary, realistic
Indonesian theatre of the 1950s and early 1960s. There are certainly historical affinities between *Bengkel's* early experiments and the contemporaneous
work of Jerzy Grotowski, Peter Brook, and Eugenio Barba. Nevertheless, it
would seem that Rendra came to his own methods from the admixture of
his training in American social sciences and Method acting with the Javanese
kampongan culture of Yogyakarta. This was not so much an imitation of currents in the Western avant-garde as an original Indonesian inter-cultural and
intra-cultural experiment.

Indonesian artists and political activists met the first years of Suharto's
presidency in the late 1960s with a great sense of optimism following the
political turmoil of the preceding decade. By and large, they expected that
Suharto would put the nation back on course towards development and
democracy, and Suharto, for his part, seemed eager to inspire confidence in
his new regime. The *mini-kata* aesthetic suited such times. It was political,
but in an exploratory rather than an ideological mode. It gently represented
what many Indonesians regarded as the enduring political and social question for the nation, that is, how to balance leadership and freedom without
the use of polarizing language. Rendra came to be regarded as an artistic
prophet. In this extraordinary transitional moment, people in Yogyakarta
claimed him as "our Rendra," academics praised him as a cultural hero, and,
in 1969, the Indonesian government presented him with a National Arts
Award.

However, by the early 1970s, it became clear to progressive students that
Suharto had assumed a familiarly paternalistic and authoritarian stance, and
was settling into the role of a latter day Javanese king. They began to demonstrate against the same sorts of political and economic abuses and "prestige
projects" they had seen under Sukarno. In particular, the construction of the
Taman Mini amusement park on the Southern outskirts of Jakarta and the
open manipulation of the first post–Sukarno election in 1971 convinced many
student activists that the new regime was not committed to improving the
plight of the poor. Once again, so soon after being hailed at all levels of society as a cultural treasure of the nation, Rendra allied himself with the student movement and its critique of Suharto and found himself at odds with
official state nationalism. He was first detained briefly in 1970 for taking
part in a "night of prayer for the nation," beginning a new period of harassment.

In October 1971, he attracted nationwide media attention by conducting a "camp out" on Parangtritis beach south of Yogyakarta, attended mainly by young men. In an article written shortly after the event, Rendra distinguishes his program as a political and economic "alternative" to state programs: "We didn't ask for help from the government. Our organizational costs were extremely cheap. And we didn't have a complex committee." In this simple, self-sufficient non-governmental camp, Rendra and members of *Teater Bengkel* supervised a very loose program of improvisational and meditative exercises, always stressing "spontaneity," a value that Rendra described as crucial for people to be able to act independently and take responsibility for their own actions. The young participants were often very frustrated, not knowing what to do, and looking for a leadership that Rendra and the members of his troupe adamantly refused to provide. Rendra reflected that this was precisely the kind of struggle that these young Indonesians needed:

> I don't want to become their leader in the course of their maturation. I choose the role of sympathetic witness towards their rebellion, towards their self-definition. My sympathy and dialogue are available, but I cannot provide a prescription for a way out, because I am certain that the one who is involved is the only one who will discover the prescription, but only after fully experiencing the challenges of life.[6]

Whether productive or harmless, this was clearly intended as a challenge to Suharto's view of the people. The Parangtritis camp, at the time, served as an organized community on Indonesian soil, but uniquely unaffiliated with any governmental administration. In its self-sufficiency, it challenged the notion that Indonesian communities could not function without supervision from the central government. In its strict refusal to provide leadership to the participants, the camp challenged the most fundamental assumption of Suharto's government: that Indonesia needs a father figure to oversee all forms of development and to safeguard against social chaos. With Parangtritis, Rendra argued that communities could maintain themselves without leaders and without chaos so long as everyone took responsibility for themselves. To this end, the *Teater Bengkel* actors led by example.

The 1971 camp at Parangtritis questioned the very notion that the president, or any leader, is indispensable to the development of individual Indonesians. It represented deference to such a leader-figure, as an erroneous emphasis on the "authoritarian elements" that have characterized Indonesian political thought since the Javanese courts and the colonial governments. It modeled this progressive community within Indonesia, but outside the supervision of any state apparatus. And lastly, the camp presented young actors showing personal responsibility and creative spontaneity as a preferable model of maturation to that of the "Father of Development."

In 1973, *Teater Bengkel* produced Rendra's first original full-length scripted play since the 1950s and his most explicit expression of political philosophy yet. *Mastodon dan Burung Kondor* (The Mastodons and the Condors) takes place in an unspecified South American country in which a fascist military dictatorship is poised to fall to a Marxist student movement. The protagonist, Carlos, is a beloved national poet, whose moral authority each faction tries to appropriate to its own political ends. Carlos, however, refuses to take sides in this ideological conflict, prompting accusations from both camps that he is a mere decadent, self-indulgently composing love poetry rather than serving his country. Carlos retorts that poets indeed do have a vital role in the life of the nation, and it is precisely to remain aloof from ideology. The poet must instead serve the nation as a gadfly, a social conscience that challenges government to listen and respond to the needs of the people. As Rendra will argue in *Kisah Perjuangan Suku Naga* (Story of the Struggle of the Naga People), an enlightened nation respects the criticism of its artists rather than insisting that artists act as spokesmen for official policies. In *Mastodon dan Burung Kondor (MdBK)* the Marxists do overthrow the fascists, but turn out to be just as authoritarian as their predecessors. It appears that only the poet has kept the real interests of the people in mind. Although he has rejected official national ideologies, he is the only real nationalist.

Rendra employs several strategies in this play to evade the censors without blunting his critique. As he will do a few years later in *Kisah perjuangan Suku Naga (KPSN)*, Rendra allegorically displaces the scene of *MdBK* from Indonesia. He also shrewdly displaces the play's ideological progression. The transition from fascism to communism seems more closely aligned to Bertolt Brecht's Germany than to Rendra's Indonesia. Indeed, in 1968 Rendra directed his own versions of Brecht's *The Jewish Wife,* and *The Informant* and *Seeking Justice.* Further, by emphasizing the corruption of the Marxist students, Rendra plays into Suharto's legitimizing narrative as the deliverer from the chaos of communism. Nevertheless, audiences of radical young people in Yogyakarta were not confused by these modest subterfuges and responded to the performances of 1973 with raucous approbation. The Yogya police reacted by banning Rendra from performing in Yogyakarta, a devastating blow to Rendra personally and to *Bengkel*'s intimate connection with the local community. Rendra and his theatre moved their primary performance venue to the Ismail Marzuki Arts Complex in Jakarta. Ironically, censorship had driven him from the periphery to the very center of the nation.

Student demonstrations became more strident over the following years, encouraged by Soemitro, a high ranking general who openly criticized

Suharto. This escalation came to a climax in January 16, 1974, when students from the University of Indonesia in Jakarta demonstrated against corrupt dealings with global financiers and capitalists during a visit by Japanese Prime Minister Tanaka. The demonstrations moved from the campus into the streets, where they were joined by thousands of poor Jakartans. Peaceful marching turned into riots, leaving at least eight demonstrators dead. Following this confrontation, Suharto closed six independent newspapers and imposed draconian restrictions on student political life.[7]

The students marched out of their campuses and the *pemuda* (radical youths) criticized the president for failing to develop Indonesia towards greater democracy. The Father responded by suppressing and appropriating them, diminishing democratic freedoms on campuses and consolidating his power even further. The students felt that they had been manipulated to serve the competing interests of politicos and turned to emphasizing their popular moral authority as *pemuda,* refusing political alliances in order to represent the democratic aspirations of the Indonesian people with greater purity.[8]

In 1975, Rendra brought *KPSN,*[9] his second play of the decade, to premiere at the Open Theatre (an outdoor amphitheatre) of the Ismail Marzuki Arts Complex (TIM) in Jakarta. *KPSN* depicts President Suharto's domestic development policy as a predatory joint venture between the urban indigenous elite, global corporate investors, and global financiers. The victims and choral protagonists of the play, represent the community of Naga, a village threatened by a mining project that will evict them from their land and destroy their way of life. Whereas *MdBK* had explored the independence of the artist in relation to the universal corruption of government, *KPSN* challenged the domestic policies at the core of Suharto's claims to political legitimacy. Suharto's New Order government responded to Rendra as it did to the most dangerous political dissidents: frequent harassment, detainment, and bureaucratic impediments to his free speech, and, finally, in 1978, a comprehensive ban from performing in Indonesia altogether.[10]

At the opening of *KPSN*, a character identified as *dalang* (the puppet-master-storyteller of *wayang* performance) walks out onto the empty stage, and welcomes the audience, assuming the role of master of ceremonies:

> Good evening everybody!
> Allow me to begin my story.
> This story does not — I stress once again, does not —
> take place in Indonesia,
> So don't get uptight and censor the story.[11]

Instead, the *dalang* tells us, we are in Astinam, an imaginary land that turns out to stand in the same political and economic predicament as contemporary Indonesia. The *dalang* views with horror a succession of choral antagonists — machines and ambassadors from the global industrial capitalists, whose developmental ethos appears as an insatiable colonizing disease. He shows us the villagers of Naga, developing their own lands in harmony with nature, led justly and in accordance with tradition by Abisavam. Abisavam's son, Abivara, returns home from studying abroad, accompanied by his foreign friend (another Carlos). As educated progressives, they respect the traditions of the village, and advocate a metaphysically and socially harmonious form of development.

Meanwhile, in Astinampuram, the metropole that is "not Jakarta," the decadent Western affectations of the Queen and her cabinet have given them all Western afflictions. They conspire to develop the nation by building a lavish hospital suited only to treating these exotic diseases, while basic clinics remain unbuilt. As the *dalang* protests, he is branded a subversive. Then, we see that this elitist developmentalism has "possessed" the elected parliament, paralyzing their critical faculties. The *dalang* now realizes that the state views its governmental role as a military campaign against the people. Mr. Joe, an American ambassador, assists in constructing the hospital and unloading surplus American wheat in exchange for participating in the Joint Venture to mine copper from the hills outside the village. Of course, all these initiatives are undertaken in the peoples' interests and in the name of "development."

Back in Naga, Abivara refutes the ideology of elite developmentalism to his fiancée, who seeks to modernize their family by moving to town. In a parallel confrontation, Abisavam refuses to allow a widow, Aunt Supaka, to sell her land, which she does not know how to tend, to outside investors. The wise leader argues that the land actually belongs to the village and not to any individual. A foreign engineer for the Joint Venture arrives to survey the land, and the villagers attempt to explain to him that the land is culture to them, not mere geology. Carlos writes of the struggle in the world press, to enlist public opinion on the side of the Naga, but the Astinamese government censors the free press, and arranges a boxing match with Muhammad Ali to distract the public from politics. Abisavam and the villagers stand their ground, first against the Minister of Mines, then against military intimidation. They reject diplomatic advances from the President of Parliament, whom they see as a corrupted instrument of the neo-colonial state, no longer a true representative of the people.

Finally, the real authority arrives. The Big Boss of the international mining company checks up on his Joint Venture, urging his agent, Mr. Joe, to corrupt the Naga youth, starting with Abivara, through foreign education, an official position, or celebrity. When Joe explains that Abivara will stand firm against such tactics, they settle on their last resort: they brand him a subversive and deport Carlos. However, they acknowledge that in the face of international scrutiny they must suspend their Joint Venture, and leave the Naga alone. The Big Boss consoles himself that he will make greater profits through commodifying yoga.

As Carlos departs, he affirms his solidarity with the Naga and the *dalang* in a struggle for justice. Abisavam proclaims that this struggle must be waged without cease throughout the world and within the soul of every individual: "worlds without, worlds within, uniting in the soul."[12] In a startling final image, Indonesia makes its only unequivocal appearance in the play. The Naga villagers march around the stage in a triumphal parade of resistance against the arrayed forces of neo-colonial developmentalism, brandishing the red and white flag of Indonesia. The village becomes Indonesia only in that utopian unrealized gesture of resistance against the Indonesian state, in the moment of affirmation that the revolutionary ideal and potential of Indonesia is not yet present.

As in the work of other dissidents writing under censorious regimes, Rendra's referential evasiveness invites universalistic consideration of the oppression of the little people by global conglomerates and conspiracies. However, the play's unremitting specificity (both to *wayang* and to Indonesia) continuously returns the play to Suharto's Indonesia. For example, in one scene, foreign ambassadors parodying the USA, Germany, China, and Japan promise to build "Shopping Centres" for the people, in which to sell a list of foreign goods flooding Indonesia at the time, including some specific consumer products, such as a vitamin pill called "Tonikum." In a scripted "slip," an uncle asks of the Western journalist, "Can he speak Indon... I mean Astinamese?"[13] Rendra winks slyly at the censors while boldly portraying a story which may "not take place in Indonesia," but it takes place in a theatrical universe that unequivocally depicts current Indonesia. Against models of "strategic" obscurity often associated with radical art under totalitarian regimes, *KPSN* looks brazenly tactless. The play's bluntness evokes Aristophanic political comedy, and implies a climate for reception akin to Attic democracy even as it bluntly depicts a far more authoritarian regime.

The statement that the play does not take place in Indonesia is a provocation that is prodded repeatedly throughout the play. Through this prodding, Rendra never lets us forget for a moment that he is leveling criticism against the current regime. He does everything short of calling Indonesia by name, nearly speaking the word, and ultimately parading the flag around the stage. It is a bold strategic challenge to the censors. If these criticisms are suppressed, the state effectively admits that Astinam *is* Indonesia. And yet Rendra may be sincere in saying that this is not Indonesia, for it is certainly not the Indonesia for which the revolutionary generation fought the Dutch. Neo-colonialism appears so totalizing a force that "Indonesia" appears as little more than an instrument of foreign industrial capitalism. Moreover, the Naga tribe represents a vision of progress whose vitality does not exist at the level of the nation. Rather, it is a village with its own traditions that negotiates directly with the representatives of the rest of the world. Until there is a just Indonesia with true democratic representation, villages must look to themselves not as insurgents, but as adults. In yet another sense, the true Indonesia for Rendra can only be located in the mind and soul of each individual. In this spirit, *KPSN* repeatedly maps physical geography onto spiritual struggle.

Although the machismo that has earned him the nickname "peacock"[14] suggests a certain political recklessness, Rendra's antagonism towards the military regime seems considerably tamer than that of such contemporaries as Goenawan Mohamad, Pramoedya Ananta Toer, or Ratna Sarumpaet.[15] In fact, even when poking fun at the military, Rendra's jibes often imply a veiled respect.[16] In an interview with Wing Kardjo in 1968, he answers the question, "If you were neither poet nor thespian, what would you be?":

> R: I would want to be an architect or a general.
> K: What attracts you to being an architect?
> R: I imagine an architect as one who fantasizes as well as builds.
> K: And a general?
> R: Generals always amuse me. Caricatures, yet impressive. Furthermore, generals' costumes look jolly like theatrical costumes. Apart from that, their cars are always good and nearly always expensive.[17]

Rendra criticizes the conspicuous wealth and pretence of the military, while simultaneously claiming an ironic identity for soldiers and actors. Both these types of costumed performers enact jolly and impressive caricatures; thus Rendra implies that they are rival players on the same stages.

The third figure, the architect, suggests a macroscopic dimension to Rendra's view of the artist. As Rendra describes him, the architect weds imagination (*berfantasi*) to the act of building (*membangun*). The Indonesian word *bangun* (which denotes a wide range of meanings including to raise, to build, and to develop) resonates as one of the key mantra of Suharto's New Order. *Bapak Pembangunan* (Father of Development), reified from public speeches to the epithet under his portrait on the fifty thousand rupiah note, sloganized Suharto's economic legitimacy. As *Bapak Pembangunan* builds the "imagined community" of the nation,[18] so an architect builds imagined spaces, and the poet-dramatist builds spaces of the imagination.[19] And as the impressive caricatures of the military claimed the public spaces of the New Order nation, so Rendra as *Bapak Teater Modern* dispatched impressive caricatures to occupy the playhouses.[20]

It would seem that the New Order administration shared Rendra's fundamental intuition on the parallel roles of actor and soldier. However, the state could only interpret such duplication as competition, a threat to national unity (etymologically difficult to distinguish in Indonesian from "singularity").[21] Their progression from censoring specific productions to banning *Teater Bengkel* from performing in Yogyakarta, and ultimately from the nation, suggests both Platonic and military escalation. The Republican philosopher-guardians fear that they must expel the rival caricatures (whose performances are *too* impressive) from the walls of the city. Klaus Theweleit, in his study of Nazi soldier culture, suggests that, for soldiers, nations exist at eternally contested fronts, borderlands of integrity: "The nation is seen as an abandoned orphan — or one that would have been abandoned, had a handful of men not been there to hold the bastion." For the Nazis, such soldier culture pathologized the republican state apparatus as the decadent center far from the outer battlegrounds where the nation truly lived. However, in Suharto's Indonesia, the doctrine of *dwi-fungsi,* according to which soldiers also served as civic police and even held reserved seats in parliament, extended the battle for the nation throughout public space at the nation's center.[22] Every public space became a potential front in danger, and every deviant imagination shaping public space became a traitor to national integrity.

Rendra himself has never subscribed to this hybrid logic, but rather, as in the Kardjo interview, maintained an ironic attitude towards the relationship between soldiers and artists. If he criticized the government, he criticized what he considered a puzzling unwillingness to accept the positive role of satire in a harmonious nation. In August 1975, after the premiere of *KPSN* at TIM in July, the Jakarta Academy presented Rendra with an Award of Honor. In his acceptance speech, he defended *Teater Bengkel* through the logic of the traditional clown characters of Javanese *wayang kulit*[23] against the soldier culture logic which had banned him from Yogyakarta:

> My plays are no more than *goro-goro*. In the *goro-goro* Semar, Bagong, Gareng and Petruk indeed launch criticism from the standpoint of egalitarian justice; but they do not suggest any change of power. The *goro-goro,* which I have already staged in Jakarta, have never given rise to anarchy, because, in essence, I am against anarchy. Then why have those superiors that the letter from the police mentions banned my *goro-goro* that oppose anarchy? This has caused me much deep anguish.[24]

In the role of *wayang* clown, Rendra assumes an innocent candor towards the state. He reacts with puzzlement to the present regime's inability to respond to satire with the grace and wisdom expected of the mythic knights and kings. He reprimands the state in the name of what he presents as conservative Indonesian values. Nevertheless, in this speech as in the play itself, Rendra also posits identity between Suharto's New Order and the mythic order of the *wayang*, an identity often invoked by the state itself in its own legitimization games.[25] For the New Order military police, Rendra's introduction of actors onto the stage of national discourse turned the playhouse into a battle front. In May 1978, a bomb exploded at TIM during one of Rendra's poetry readings, justifying his arrest for "spreading hatred" against the government. It was the sort of precipitated crisis-containment scenario that has often been traced to military choreography in Indonesia (most recently in the May 1998 riots, and the East Timorese militia violence).[26]

Over the course of the 1970s, Suharto and Rendra confronted each other on an ideological terrain laid out by "development." The word itself took on such pivotal and definitive significance for them that it might be understood as a keyword in Raymond Williams' sense. That is, a word whose meanings are "inextricably bound up with the problems it was being used to discuss," a word whose examination shows "that some important social and historical processes occur *within* language, in ways which indicate how integral the problems of meanings and of relationships really are." Williams' own examination of "development" sheds some light on the disputed terrain of Suharto and Rendra. By Williams' account, the English word "development" began to take on its familiar modern meanings in the mid-nineteenth century when the sense of development appeared in an evolutionary and often teleological sense in application to societies and nations. By the late nineteenth century, the industrial and resource-oriented usages had appeared, and thus the sense of "undeveloped" cultures and resources. The notion of "underdeveloped" nations appeared after 1945 in the era of post–Bretton Woods global finance.[27] Given the concurrent appearance in the late nineteenth century of psychological development studies, the hierarchical chronology of our contemporary usage is unmistakable. Those nations/resources/people who have not "developed" remain immature, unsophisticated, and backward, a weak link in world progress. Through the lens of development, unmined hills, obsolete consumer goods, or adherence to traditional irrigation techniques are as embarrassing as a man who still behaves like a child.

Both Suharto and Rendra confronted a common post-colonial dilemma, trying to reconcile development as understood by post-war global financiers with the ideas of developing Indonesia into a modern nation contained in the sustaining principles of anti-colonial nationalism. Rendra's approach to development takes something from the nationalistic principles of modernization espoused since the 1920s, a notion of a modernization which, in S. Takdir Alisjahbana's words, receives "a fresh breeze from the West" which is understood to enrich local culture.[28] This theme of pre-war nationalism carried over into the post-colonial state agenda, and provides ideological legitimacy for New Order cultural policy. However, Rendra parts from New Order cultural policy on the notion that development is something that a centralized urban government carries out for the benefit of a rural population. Instead, Rendra espouses democratic decentralization of development and modernization. He differs from both Suharto and pro-developmentalists like Alisjahbana in affirming the continued vibrancy of village culture. In this, he allies himself with Sanusi Pane (who debated Alisjahbana in the 1920s and 1930s, claiming that indigenous culture already provides more locally appropriate alternatives to all the touted improvements of Western culture) and with critics who have decried slavish imitation of the West throughout the twentieth century. Rendra has taken a middle road in regard to this culture debate, advocating a democratically negotiated cultural hybridity that challenges the very meaning of "development," as it is implied in New Order social and cultural policy.

The infamous logic of the New Order suggests that the government must oversee development at every level of society because "*rakyat masih bodoh*" (the people are still ignorant). The Indonesian word *pembangunan* carries many of the same connotations as the English word it has been adopted to express. However, it carries these meanings through a specifically architectural metaphor. The root word *bangun* means to raise, build, erect, construct, or shape. It is something which can be done to shapeless things, to raw materials, to nations, to people. When Suharto fashioned himself *Bapak Pembangunan*, he consolidated the implications laid out by Williams. He cast himself as the father figure in relation to everything in Indonesia that had not been developed. Land and people became his children, which he needed to develop (in the sense of resources or psychology) or build up (in the sense of a house or a city). As Virginia Hooker points out in the introduction to *Culture and Society in New Order Indonesia*, Suharto has claimed that he is not merely concerned with developing Indonesia's various marketable resources, but *manusia seutuhnya* (the entire people), the character of the Indonesian people.[29] The territory that must be nationalized extends from social and physical geographies to corporeal and psychological ones.

Rendra certainly advocated the development of Indonesian society in all these ways as well, and one might easily imagine that his complaint with Suharto's regime is simply against the hegemonization of those processes. To be sure, the democratization of society and culture looms large in Rendra's agenda. However, he also prioritizes a development in analytic method according to Western notions of scientific objectivity, and believes that, if these methods are applied prudently to social and cultural problems, much of the material development championed by Suharto will be revealed as destructive and inefficient. Modern Indonesian theatre anticipates Rendra in these developments. The early revolutionary drama (the first modern theatre in the Indonesian language) frequently concerned a protagonist who represented a new modern individual forged in the selective adoption of Western cultural values, particularly those that help improve a life which is still essentially informed by indigenous values. For example, *Manusia Baru* ("New" or "Modern" Man, 1940), the last play written by Alisjahbana's interlocutor, Sanusi Pane, depicts the struggle of an Indian reporter to apply Western values of journalistic objectivity and transparency to depict the plight of striking textile workers.[30] Indigenous and foreign corruption conspire against him, and his response requires an unswerving commitment both to reason and the vision of a prosperous Indian nation rooted in indigenous values. Rendra places similar protagonists at the center of *KPSN,* in the pair of Abivara: the local son. who has returned from study abroad with analytic methods to serve local development, and Carlos, Abivara's foreign journalist friend, who seeks to build a joint-venture with the village, rather than with the Astinamese government. These twin characters enact an alternate model of global cooperation, locally managed and free of the totalizing evolutionary hierarchy of post–Bretton Woods development. *KPSN* also parallels *Manusia Baru* in its displacement of national setting. *KPSN*'s Astinam — a thin reference to Astina, homeland of the Mahabharata heroes — is a mythic analogue to India, the most popular of many sources of Indonesian traditional culture. Both Pane and Rendra denied that their plays took place in Indonesia, but relocated them specifically to settings historically linked to Indonesia as its ancestor. This transplantation affects the territorial meaning of *KPSN.*

Other sources evident in Rendra's dramaturgy appeared in later periods of Indonesian theatre. During and immediately after the war, Indonesian drama frequently depicted the struggles of patriots. Although these plays lost some of the complexity of pre-revolutionary drama in grappling with the paradoxes of Western influence, they established a recurring trope of Indonesian national character, as manifest in the action of struggle against colonialism. This trope was invoked in the legitimizing narratives first of Sukarno, in his tireless campaign against *nekolim* (neo-colonial imperialism), and later of the New Order military, in its struggle to maintain the order and stability of the nation against communists and other supposedly subversive elements. Until the social upheavals of 1998, despite continuous terror and abuses, soldiers commanded a popular respect, inherited from the heroes who secured independence from the Dutch. Rendra casts *KPSN* in the familiar mold of the revolutionary struggle plays, but displaces the army corps as the subject of *perjuangan* in favor of the village community. Of course, the nobility of the resolute farmer defending his rights against the colonialists was nothing new, but to depict *perjuangan,* as carried out by the people against the supposed soldier-heroes, was certainly a representational coup and a territorial counter-invasion.

Rendra's territorial confrontation with the soldiers paralleled a general spatial struggle in the arts, which began almost as soon as Suharto took power. In his 1981 article on the popular *Lenong* drama, Umar Kayam divides New Order Indonesian theatre into two categories defined spatially: *kampungan* (village) and *gedongan* (building). *Kampungan* theatre, or the theatre of the *kampung* (villages, family compounds), comprises all theatre performed in traditional rural spaces. These are typically open pavilions or courtyards that are accessible to all people regardless of class and usually free of admission. It is theatre conceived both as inclusive of all sectors of society and community-based. In its inception in Yogyakarta, *Teater Bengkel* followed this model. Rendra's *kampung* became a well-known public space in Yogya, and people would often look in from the street while Bengkel rehearsed.[31] Rendra's Naga were loosely inspired by a small *kampung* of that name about ninety kilometers southeast of Bandung, about halfway between Yogya and Jakarta. Kampung Naga clearly appealed to Rendra, as a small village that had kept resolutely to its ancestral traditions, accepted the fruits of development in a limited fashion on their own terms, and remained staunchly independent of the government (commercially as well as physically Naga can only be reached by descending a steep six-hundred meter stairway). As touted in an economy and tourism magazine,

> They will accept no material assistance from outside the community, not even funding extended by the regional government for renovation of the village; not even electricity. Battery-operated radios and small television sets are sufficient to keep in touch with the outside world.[32]

Ironically, by 1997, the very cultural independence and resilience that insulated Kampung Naga from government ventures had made them an attractive venue for that quintessential form of Indonesian development: that is cultural tourism.

While *Teater Bengkel* thrived in the Yogya *kampung,* a new theatre culture emerged in Jakarta that Umar Kayam would term *gedongan,* the theatre of buildings.[33] Jakarta's energetic new governor, Ali Sadikin, included the arts in his program to reconstruct a city ravaged by Sukarno's neglect and the 1965 massacres. He established the Ismail Marzuki complex by converting the city's old zoo into TIM, an extensive arts complex with four theatres, gallery spaces, a planetarium, and a cinema. The Jakarta Arts Academy, with faculties teaching performing, plastic, and media arts, was built in adjacent facilities. What's more, Sadikin responded to artists' pleas to provide them a haven safe from the paralyzing surveillance and censorship suffered under LEKRA by establishing the Jakarta Arts Council (DKJ), an independent body of artists fully entrusted with administering the center. Thus, in 1968, Taman Ismail Marzuki became South-East Asia's first national arts complex, a distinction rendered extraordinary by its unprecedented liberal bureaucracy.

The program of the Arts Center as well as the preoccupations of arts and literary journals of the period suggest a twofold search for alternatives to socialist realism:[34] a re-investment in Western sources stressing existentialism and absurdism (Camus and Sartre in the literary journals, Beckett and Ionesco on the stage) and Indonesianized productions of Shakespeare and the Greeks;[35] and the development of new artistic work, derivative of Western theatre as it had always been, but Indonesianized through regional performance conventions and local references. To stage these experimental modern performances, as well as traditional performance from throughout Indonesia, TIM incorporated stages to accommodate every anticipated spatial configuration: Graha Bhakti Budaya (a proscenium auditorium seating approximately 800 spectators), Teater Arena (an indoor arena stage), Teater Tertutup (a flexible black-box theatre), and Teater Terbuka (an open amphitheater seating 1500 spectators). However, as the design strove to accommodate traditional and experimental Western and Indonesian spatial paradigms, the configuration of open space evoked a large-scale implementation of the *kampung* layout. At Sadikin's prompting, the architect, Tjong Pragantha, visited a modern arts complex in Hawaii and also conducted a survey of architectural styles in Indonesia to arrive at his hybrid design:

> Designing the architecture of PKJ-TIM seemed a difficult challenge for me ... because it had to reflect the uniqueness of Indonesian architecture. ... We built the architectural model of PKJ-TIM in the manner of *continuous space architecture*. Its key is located in the plan of the plaza. We borrowed the basic idea from the architecture of Java and Bali.[36]

Although TIM comprised Jakarta's most prominent *gedongan* theatre complex, it did so on grounds modeled after a *kampongan* spatial model. When the police evicted Rendra from his Yogyakarta *kampong*, Teater Bengkel performed *KPSN* at *Teater Terbuka*, the most open and *kampong*-like space there. All the same, like all TIM's stages, walls separated it from the surrounding environment in unequivocally *gedongan* fashion. In a modern theatre complex, on a stage referencing though not replicating traditional space, with a set combining Western experimental *mise-en-scène* with rural Javanese material culture and symbols of that culture, in one of the showcase development projects in the urban capital of Indonesia, a traditional Javanese narrator assured censors in classical Greek tones, "This story does not take place in Indonesia."

As opposition to the New Order steadily increased from the late 1980s into the 1990s, Rendra became one of the regime's most celebrated victims. On these credentials, the Jakarta Arts Council (DKJ) invited *Teater Bengkel* to revive *KPSN* for the first Indonesia Art Summit (an annual festival in Jakarta) after Suharto stepped down in May 1998. With modest compromises to circumstance (many new cast members, a simplified choreography due to the absence of the original choreographer, Julie Taymor, and adjustments for a proscenium stage due to the fact that the Open Theatre had been demolished in 1997), *Teater Bengkel* replicated its 1975 production for the 1998 festival. The script underwent some minor and non-substantive tinkering, preserving the original *mise-en-scène* almost fully. The production played for two evenings (29–30 September) to crowds exceeding the auditorium. Monitors set up outside allowed an uncounted excess crowd to watch. Much of this audience was, undoubtedly, composed of middle-aged and now middle-class Indonesians who had participated in the student movement in the 1970s. In any case, they responded with great enthusiasm, as did the press.[37]

However, the social context of this revival hardly replicated that of the original production. Whereas *KPSN* premiered in 1975 before a regime demonstrably willing to suppress criticism, by late 1998, Indonesia enjoyed a level of artistic freedom that most young artists had never before experienced. In fact, newspaper critics were already complaining that the denunciation of Suharto's New Order had become passé (only half a year after it had ended).[38] I asked Jose Rizal Manua, a veteran member of *Bengkel,* if he thought that in such a climate, with Suharto deposed and *reformasi* in the air, *KPSN* was not simply another piece of triumphal nostalgia preaching to the choir. "Are its criticisms still relevant?" I asked. "Masih," he assured me, "Still."

Between 1975 and *Suku Naga*'s revival in 1998, both *Teater Bengkel* and TIM had "developed." After Rendra began performing again in 1985, a prominent investor, Djody Setiawin, sponsored *Bengkel*'s relocation to

Depok, a relatively upscale community on the outskirts of Jakarta. Many critics and old admirers judged Rendra hypocritical for accepting the aid of an investor and moving into an exclusive development. However, in 1991, Rendra moved a little further out from Depok to the village of Cipayung where he established something of a *pesantren*, a mystical boarding school, for *Teater Bengkel*. Since then, new *Bengkel* recruits have trained and worked on the extensive grounds, while numerous old *Bengkel* actors have settled nearby, partially transforming *kampung* Cipayung into *kampung* Rendra. The rehearsals for the 1998 revival of *Suku Naga* took place here, in fields cultivated by the performers themselves, or in the Aula, an open Javanese pavilion fitted with curtains, lights, and handmade bleachers in which new *Bengkel* members spend an initiatory 90-day monastic seclusion. As in Yogyakarta before, *Kampung Rendra Cipayung* offered a kind of hyper-realistic setting for the rehearsals of a play about defending *kampung* life, in a *kampung* an hour from the center of Jakarta by commuter rail, ideologically somewhere in between the city and rural West Java.

However, the performance space and context had changed and the gap between *kampungan* and *gedongan* was much greater in 1998 than in 1975. In 1987, the restored Dutch colonial Schouwburg opened as *Gedung Kesenian Jakarta* (the Jakarta Arthouse), a more technologically sophisticated, Western, and expensive venue catering to Jakarta's burgeoning middle class. In 1996, anticipating the construction of a new modern theatre building that would incorporate a two- to three-thousand seat proscenium theatre and several smaller stages, TIM's Arena, Tertutup, and Terbuka were all demolished leaving Graha Bhakti Budaya TIM's only remaining performance venue. However, the Asian monetary crisis (*krismon*) struck in 1997, indefinitely postponing all such grand construction projects. As of my last visit in October 1999, the site of these three lost theatres and the interconnecting plaza space so central to TIM's spatial hybridity are a vast pool, filled by the rains and fished in by local people. As Suharto resigned in 1998, and theatre artists began contemplating how to create new work appropriate to Era Reformasi, two stages remained in Jakarta, both Western in their configuration: the neo-classical Schouwburg and TIM's proscenium theatre.[39]

Despite the sound rejection of all things Suharto in the popular imagination, *KPSN* was clearly still iconoclast in September, 1998. Early euphoria in 1998 about Era Reformasi soon settled into a more sober assessment that President Habibie continued Suhartoism without Suharto.[40] The global developmental and financial conspiracies, the abuses of power, and the infantalization and victimization of poor rural communities did not simply disappear without Suharto at the helm. He left a thick legacy of *korupsi, kolusi,* and *nepotisme* permeating every level of Indonesian society. To the student movement, as to Rendra's Naga, democracy consists in the ongoing struggle against the monopolization of the nation at the center. Arguably, the play had become more relevant in 1998, in a climate in which claims to democracy from the *rakyat* (the people) stood an unprecedented chance of being heard.

The two 1998 performances of *KPSN* played to capacity houses.[41] Ironically, the "virtual spectators" forced to watch the production on monitors outside the auditorium experienced the open space of the *kampungan,* whereas "the lucky ones" watched the *kampungan* in the same Javanese and Western setting used in 1975, as if transposed onto an incongruous Western reservation. Investors had relocated the *kampung* onto a proscenium stage in order to make room for a new and improved *gedong.* The issues raised by *KPSN* concerning the dangers posed by corporate development to the people of the *kampung* are evident in the production site itself. Economic recovery for Indonesia will surely involve the resumption of many "joint-ventures" such as the one that eliminated TIM's *kampungan* stages.

About a month after the 1998 production, Rendra worked to implement the ideology of *KPSN* in his own *kampung.* He hosted a gathering in his home in which Cipayung garment workers, suffering severe shortages of rice and cooking oil due to the monetary crisis, could meet with representatives from the government in Jakarta. Members of Bengkel helped to distribute these basic materials (*sembako*) to the most needy. Most significantly, however, the politicians and the villagers discussed how to reform representative government, so that management would become open and all discussions about financial interactions transparent. As Rendra enthused, "Now is the time for everyone to work together to bring about cooperative practices. For us, the most appropriate form for economic democratization is one which is cooperative." Throughout the discussions, Minister Adi Sosono deferred to Rendra as "*Kepala* (Headman) *Suku Naga.*"[42] Kampung Naga, Rendra's utopian image of Indonesia, was harvesting real Indonesian development from its own fields.

It seems that in "Era Reformasi" the thespian has prevailed over the generals while suffering at the hands of the architects. At the end of the twentieth century, the Indonesian military retreated from fronts that they had fortified for thirty years at the nation's center. After several violent suppressions of demonstrations in May 1998, the Indonesian military's popular prestige sank lower than it had since Independence as the leadership was purged at the highest levels. Prabowo Subianto, Suharto's son-in-law and commander of the elite KOSTRAD forces, notorious for civic abuses, was among the first of the old regime to lose his job. General Wiranto, despite shrewd maneuvering in the cabinets of B.J. Habbibie and Abdulrahman Wahid, was finally ousted early in 2000. Though still far from being the representative democracy for which the student movement struggled, the Indonesian government has become more representative than ever before.[43] More fundamentally, however, Indonesia's army lost popular respect after they violently suppressed demonstrations in 1998. At the height of the unrest, the military police feared to wear their uniforms in public, and army morale plummeted. Student demonstrators wore t-shirts with such challenging slogans as, "We will return to the classroom once the soldiers return to the barracks," and various groups, from PDI (Megawati's party), to PRD (the political party of the student movement), to non-partisan crowds, maintained a foothold on the streets of Jakarta and Yogyakarta.

In the crowded commuter trains that connect Cipayung to Jakarta, there are signs, which read "Jangan meluarkan anggota *badan*." It means, "Don't stick out body parts," but might be more creatively translated as "Don't expel members of the body/corps," an admonition to protect the integrity of the people shuttling in this quintessential mechanized conduit between *gedongan* and *kampungan*. Against this boxcar *kampung*, *KPSN* might be seen in 1998 as challenging the self-censoring audience to imagine that such "development" does not take place in Indonesia. Indonesia does not exist in tribal reservations built by investors, or in "cultural preserves" as the article on Kampung Naga advertised. In his 1975 speech to the Academy, Rendra expressed doubts that artists could successfully live in such *gedongan* as TIM, becoming "half-institutionalized." He thanked them for honoring him there, and excused himself to return to the wind, to his mystical *kampung* that has yet to be realized. Rendra's actor emerges into the world from meditation at the edges of power, as an impressive caricature to imagine and build Indonesia and struggle for it at the contested fronts: stages, which one day suffer political satire, another day bombs, and, on yet another day, the haunting absence of a rain-filled crater. I met Rendra in June 1999, returning from a conference of artists discussing the shape of Indonesian art after Suharto. He laughed remembering them asking for his own position. "*This*," he spread his arms to indicate the grounds of his *kampung*, its cultivated nature modeling the greater nature, its individual microcosms extending into the cosmos, "*This* is my *position*."

Notes

1. This article was researched through the generous support of the Henry Luce Foundation in association with the Research School of Pacific and Asian Studies at Australian National University. I would like to acknowledge the following members of Teater Bengkel who shared their *kampung* with me, and endeavored to answer

my questions: Willy Rendra, Zen Kuraida, Dewi and Otig Pakis, Fredy Suryadi, Amien Kamil, Amin Setiamin, Suzan Piper, Arief Margareth, and my deepest gratitude to Jose Rizal Manua, who first invited me in. I would also like to thank the members of W.B. Worthen's "Space and Performance" seminar at the 1999 ASTR conference for their comments on an earlier draft.

2. Information on Rendra's life prior to the late 1960s is drawn largely from his 1999 interview with Walter Isaac Cohen (Rendra and Cohen, 1999).

3. See Rendra 1983 (b).

4. See Winet 2003.

5. Toda 1984, 39.

6. Rendra 1983(a), 24, 26.

7. Saunders 1998, 18–19.

8. For more on the student movement revival in the early seventies, and the 1974 Malari riots, see Aspinall 1993, Budiman 1973, Crouch 1974, and van Dijk 1975.

9. I distinguish Rendra's original scripted plays, *Mastodon dan Burung Kondor* (1973), *Kisah Perjuangan Suku Naga* (1975), and *Sekda* (*Sekretaris Daerah*, or "regional secretary," 1977), from his numerous translations and adaptations of Western plays, as well as the improvisatory *mini-kata*. Rendra wrote several original plays in the 1950s and several more in the 1980s. However, this period from 1967 to 1978 is generally looked upon as the height of his career as a dramatist.

10. This ban silenced Teater Bengkel at its peak. However, Rendra continued to train, rehearse, and work with actors from his home compound in Yogya, and later in Depok and Cipayung, and continued to write and publish poetry and criticism. The ban was lifted in 1985.

11. Throughout this article, I cite Max Lane's generally excellent and widely available translation of *Kisah Perjuangan Suku Naga*. Due to the ban on publication of Rendra's works in Indonesia, the original Indonesian script has yet to be published. All references to the Indonesian version are based on a photocopy used by actor and designer, Jose Rizal Manua, for the 1998 production.

12. Rendra 1975, 72.

13. Rendra 1979, 19.

14. For example, in January 1991, after negotiations with the Minister of Security and Politics, Rendra arranged to read his poetry at TIM. When he arrived on the night of the performance, local police confronted him: "We are not going to say no, but we have no time to write a permit. Go ahead if you dare." Rendra proceeded to perform that evening without police interference, but it was never clear what was safe and what crossed the line. Jansen 1992.

15. Goenawan Mohamad (1941–), editor of *Tempo* magazine and a freelance essayist, is an outspoken critic of New Order human rights abuses. Pramoedya Ananta Toer (1925–) is often cited as one of Asia's likeliest candidates for the Nobel Prize for Literature; his unswerving devotion to exploring Indonesia's troubled history has gotten him imprisoned by the Dutch, Sukarno, and Suharto. Ratna Sarumpaet (1949–) once studied with Rendra before forming her own theatre troupe, Satu Merah Panggung, best known for her 1993 play, *Marsinah: Nyanyian dari bawah tanah* (Marsinah: Songs from the Underworld), in which a raped and murdered labor activist returns to accuse the New Order.

16. In the context of popular Indonesian sentiment with which Rendra consistently allies himself, this ambivalence is not at all unusual. Unlike in the Soviet Bloc nations that nurtured absurdism, the Indonesian people by and large have con-

tinued to respect the military as the *pahlawan* (heroes) who won the war of independence against the Dutch and continue to defend the integrity of the nation. The recent discrediting of the armed forces in the course of the events leading to Suharto's resignation in May 1998, has destroyed a popular coupling of nationalism with respect for soldiers which had weathered three decades of military abuses. It seems a resilient attitude though, as evidenced by the tentativeness of popular support for the student movement as well as the widespread lack of empathy for the East Timorese struggle against Indonesian military power.

17. Rendra and Kardjo 1968, 288.

18. I refer to Benedict Anderson's description of the nation as an identity that does not simply exist in a historical, ontological sense, but that must be "imagined" in a continuous and active fashion. Anderson 1983.

19. *Bengkel* means "workshop" in a sense most commonly applied to auto mechanics. The name refers to the idea of the experimental actors' "laboratory," which Rendra brought back from his years in New York, but the term deviates from the common avant-garde notion of scientific experimentation in imagining performance through a metaphor of "building." Although Rendra has echoed Stanislavsky and Grotowsky in calling for "scientific" rigor in the actor's process, his choice of metaphors casts the actor more as engineer than scientist. In a forum at TIM in 1982, Rendra reflected on his development from his poetry in the early 1960s, at which time he says "My spirituality and intellectuality were still quite stoned." In New York, he became acquainted with "social and political science and economics." He describes the influence of these disciplines on his theatrical work in terms both architectural and developmental: "Only after 1971 was I able to begin seeing the problems of social, political and economic injustice in terms of structures. With the *Bengkel Teater* (Theatre Workshop) I began to develop myself, holding discussions and small, restricted seminars, keeping newspaper clippings as documentation and making study tours to the villages." Rendra 1983(d), 46. In 1980, he published the poetry he wrote in this most politically active period from 1971 to 1978 under the title *Potret Pembangunan Dalam Puisi* (A Portrait of Development in Poetry).

20. Far from being a whimsical fabrication of post-modern theorizing, this stage metaphor in application to Indonesian public and political life has become an ubiquitous cliché. Beginning with Clifford Geertz's famous formulation of Bali as a "theatre-state" in which performance does not represent the state but actually constitutes it (Geertz 1980), theatrical terms have been employed to dizzying lengths in descriptions of Indonesian power politics. Indeed, I would argue that Indonesian public performativity often warrants theatrical metaphors. However, these commentaries often slyly equate illusion with delusion, the masking of some straightforward and somehow unperformed meaning, presenting Indonesian society as pervasively self-deluded.

21. In nationalistic discourse dating from Sukarno, *kesatuan* and *persatuan* are often paired and translated into English respectively as "oneness" and "unity." However, the difference is more tonal than semantic. *Kesatuan* could just as accurately be translated "unity."

22. Theweleit 1989, 79.

23. *Wayang* shadow puppetry, besides being an ancient, popular form of theatre in Sumatra, Java, and Bali, is a ubiquitous source of imagery for Indonesian culture. *KPSN* makes many more uses of *wayang* imagery than I have taken the time to trace. The play is set in the kingdom of "Astina," derived from "Astinam," home

of the Pandawa and Kurawa brothers of the Mahabharata. Max Lane points to numerous other elements referencing *wayang*, some evident to the spectators, others not: characters, such as the wise king and the wicked queen and her buffoonish retainers, reference to the foreign nations as *tanah sabrang*, home of *raksasa*, both referring to the *sabrangan* scenes depicting ogre kingdoms, etc.

24. Rendra 1979, 77.

25. Suharto was far less creative in this regard than Sukarno who hardly ever made a public statement without reference to *wayang*.

26. To my knowledge, the truth about the 1978 bombing has never come to light, but the playing out of Rendra's tribulations resembled that of many dissidents before and after. Some crisis event acts as justification for rounding up those dangerous to the state and subjecting them to prolonged surveillance, blacklisting, and other persecutions without bringing them to a formal trial. As Max Lane tells it, official charges were actually dropped on October 15 of the same year, but all potential sponsors, including Taman Ismail Marzuki, were pressured to maintain a de facto ban.

27. Williams 1985, 15, 22, 109.

28. Sutan Takdir Alisjahbana (1908–1989) tirelessly defended the desirability of Western influence and modernization in Indonesia since the 1920s. In each successive generation from the pre-war nationalists to Angkatan '45 (the revolutionary generation) to Angkatan '66 (the New Order generation), Alisjahbana re-emerged to argue for modern answers to the challenge of the moment. Although never an apologist for the central government per se, his views epitomize the school of artistic thought in Indonesia which, in coinciding with the developmental goals of early nationalism, did not overtly challenge the official development agenda of the postcolonial state.

29. Hooker 1993, 2.

30. Pane 1974. The similarity in subject, character, and action between this play and Gerhart Hauptmann's *The Weavers* (1892) is striking. Pane's importance as an innovator of Indonesian dramatic realism also bears comparison to Hauptmann's role in German naturalism.

31. Bengkel's *mini-kata* productions invoked *kampong* spatiality from their improvisatory ensemble mode of creation to their depictions of the negotiations between individual expression and collective culture.

32. D.S. 1997, 31.

33. See Kayam 1981.

34. There is no reason to see this ideological position as simply imposed by the New Order government. The New Order artists were predominantly those who had spoken out in the early 1960s, and had signed the *Manifesto Kebudayaan* (Cultural Manifesto) in 1963, a declaration of artists' rights to creative independence from the communist agenda. LEKRA responded to *Manikebu* by censoring all signatories. As I have mentioned, Rendra was exceptional as a prominent poet who did not sign *Manikebu*.

35. Rendra himself made significant contributions in this latter field, presenting historic adaptations of *Oidipus* (1969), *Antigone* (1974), *Hamlet* (1970), *Macbeth* (1970), and *Menunggu Godot* (1969), using various regional Indonesian performance conventions.

36. Yusra 1994, 32.

37. I am judging from records collected in the Jakarta Arts Council archives.

Also see reviews published in *Suara Pembaruan*: "Pentas Rendra Tertantang Lebih Dahsyat Dulu Atau Sekarang?" 25 September 1998; and "Drama 'Kisah Perjuangan Suku Naga' Rendra Memang 'Badung,'" 30 September 1998.

38. Critics complained that it seemed that even the most abstract dance pieces took on a superficial Reformasi "theme," denouncing the oppressive military regime. Many of these critics challenged artists to make use of their fledgling artistic freedom to develop unprecedented idioms. They dismissed these polemical diatribes as transitional, hopefully on the way to something wholly original. The general opinion towards Reformasi art at the end of 1998 was "Belum," "Not yet."

39. These were not, however, the only spaces for theatre in Jakarta post–1996. The German Goethe Institut and the Dutch Erasmus Huis Institut both have spaces that have hosted theatrical performances and installations. Of even greater significance, the well-funded *Galeri Utan Kayu* has several performance spaces that allow small installation performances. These spaces certainly offer alternatives to the two big prosceniums, but represent the style of Western experimental performance spaces.

40. Butet Kertarejasa, one of the celebrity personalities of post–Suharto *teater* regulars, elicits uproarious laughter in his *Lidah Pingsan* (Paralyzed Tongue) monologues, when he impersonates Habibie affirming that he is the same as Suharto. *"Pak Harto itu professor saya!"* (He is my professor!)

41. The cripplingly brief production calendar is a holdover of Suharto-era restrictions yet to be overturned. It is generally thought that no production would be allowed to run for more than a few performances, so that no production could gather enough momentum to incite a popular movement.

42. Adi Sosono 1998.

43. For example, the extraordinary 1999 election laws, whereby the proportions of popular votes for the 35 participating political parties translated directly into the number of representatives in parliament, is arguably more democratic than the congressional election system in the United States.

Works Cited

"Adi Sosono Kunjungi Bengkel W.S. Rendra, Jadikan Koperasi Lembaga Terpercaya." *Suara Pembaruan*, 10 November 1998.

Anderson, Benedict R. O'G. *Imagined Communities: Reflections on the Origin and Spread of Nationalism*. London: Verso, 1983.

Aspinall, Edward. *Student Dissent in Indonesia in the 1980s*. Clayton, Vic., Australia: Centre of Southeast Asian Studies, Monash University, 1993.

Budiman, Arief. "Portrait of a Young Indonesian Looking at His Surroundings." *Internationales Asienforum* 4.1 (1973): 76–88.

"Catatan Akhir Tahun Seni Tari, Krisis Dan Gerakan Reformasi Warnai Tema-Tema Tarian." *Republika*, 31 December 1998.

Crouch, Harold. "The 15th January Affair in Indonesia." *Dyason House Papers: Australia, Asia and the World*. Ed. Australian Institute of International Affairs. Victorian Branch, 1–6. Melbourne: Australian Institute of International Affairs Victorian Branch, 1974.

"Drama 'Kisah Perjuangan Suku Naga' Rendra Memang 'Badung.'" *Suara Pembaruan*, 30 September 1998.

Ernawati, Sesilia Nuke. "Karena Angin Reformasi, Seniman Bingung Dan Penikmat Seni Masuk Angin?" *Suara Pembaruan*, 30 August 1998.

Geertz, Clifford. *Negara: The Theatre State in Nineteenth-Century Bali*. Princeton, N.J.: Princeton University Press, 1980.

H., A.I. "Catatan Teater 1998." *Republika*, 4 January 1999.

Hooker, Virginia Matheson. *Culture and Society in New Order Indonesia, South-East Asian Social Science Monographs*. Kuala Lumpur, New York: Oxford University Press, 1993.

Jansen, Christel. "A Poet and His Plumage." *Index on Censorship* 6 (1992): 15.

Kayam, Umar. "Sang Lenong." *Seni, Tradisi, Masyarakat: Karangan-Karangan* 118–28. Jakarta: Penerbit Sinar Harapan, 1981.

Pakis, Dewi. Personal Interview. 20 June 1999.

Panâe, Sanusi. *Manusia Baru*. Jakarta: Pustaka Jaya, 1974.

"Pentas Rendra Tertantang Lebih Dasyat Dulu Atau Sekarang." *Suara Pembaruan*, 25 September 1998.

Rendra, W.S. "Alternatif Dari Parangtritis." *Mempertimbangkan Tradisi: Kumpulan Karangan* 24–28. Jakarta: Gramedia, 1983a.

_____. *Ballada Orang2 Tertjinta*. Djakarta: Pembangunan, 1957.

_____. *Disebabkan Oleh Angin*. Cet. 1. ed. *Seri Pustaka Puisi*. Jakarta: Pustaka Jaya, 1993.

_____. *Empat Kumpulan Sajak*. Cet. 6. ed. *Seri Pustaka Puisi*. Jakarta: Pustaka Jaya, 1990.

_____. "From the Mysteries of Nature to Structural Analysis." *Prisma* 29 (1983b): 44–49.

_____. *Kisah Perjuangan Suku Naga*. Yogya: Produksi Bengkel Teater, 1975.

_____. *The Mastodon and the Condors*. Calcutta: Pr. Lal, 1981.

_____. *Mempertimbangkan Tradisi: Kumpulan Karangan*. Jakarta: Gramedia, 1983c.

_____. "Pertemuan Teater 1982 Di Tim." In *Mempertimbangkan Tradisi: Kumpulan. Karangan* 45–58. Jakarta: Gramedia, 1983d.

_____. *Potret Pembangunan Dalam Puisi*. Jakarta: Lembaga Studi Pembangunan, 1980.

_____. *The Struggle of the Naga Tribe: A Play*. St. Lucia, Queensland: University of Queensland Press, 1979.

_____. *Tentang Bermain Drama: Catatan Elementer Bagi Calon Pemain*. Jakarta: Pustaka Jaya, 1976.

Rendra, W.S., interviewed by Walter Isaac Cohen. "An Untimely Art: An Interview with W.S. Rendra." *Newsletter of the Institute for International Studies*. Leiden, Netherlands: University of Leiden, 1999.

Rendra, W.S., interviewed by Wing Kardjo. "Potret W.S. Rendra Dalam Wawancara." *Budaya Jaya* 1 (1968): 288.

S.D. "Kampung Naga: A Unique Cultural Preserve in West Java." *Image of Indonesia* 3.12 (1997): 31.

Saunders, Joseph, and Human Rights Watch (Organization). *Academic Freedom in Indonesia: Dismantling Soeharto-Era Barriers*. New York: Human Rights Watch, 1998.

Theweleit, Klaus. *Male Fantasies, Theory and History of Literature*. Vols. 22–23. Minneapolis: University of Minnesota Press, 1987.

Toda, Dami N. "Teater Baru Indonesia." *Hamba-Hamba Kebudayaan* 34–40. Jakarta: Penerbit Sinar Harapan, 1984.

van Dijk, Cees. "The Hariman Siregar Trial." *Review of Malayan and Indonesian Affairs* 9.1(1975): 1–33.

Wijaya, Putu. "Kalau Hati Nurani Sudah Tak Punya." *Suara Pembaruan*, 27 December 1998.

Williams, Raymond. *Keywords: A Vocabulary of Culture and Society.* Rev. ed. New York: Oxford University Press, 1985.

Winet, Evan Darwin. "Interpolating American Method Acting in 1950s Indonesia." *Journal of Dramatic Theory and Criticism* 18.1 (2003): 87–104.

Yusra, Abrar. "Berdirinya Pusat Kesenian Jakarta." *25 Tahun Pusat Kesenian Jakarta, Taman Ismail Marzuki* 32. Ed. Pramana Padmodarmaya. Jakarta: Yayasan Kesenian Jakarta, 1994.

Robert Lepage:
Product of Québec?

Karen Fricker

On April 15, 2003, the Parti Québécois, founded in 1968 to bring independence to Québec, was voted out of provincial leadership for the first time in nine years. The defeat, according to the Toronto newspaper *The Globe and Mail* in April 2003, struck "a devastating blow to the sovereignty option and [placed] status quo federalism in Québec on its strongest footing in decades." In his concession speech, however, the leader of the Parti Québécois, Bernard Landry, pledged continued resistance: "We will start right now and I assure you that in the next election the Parti Québécois will be the party of change.... It is my deep conviction, and I say it again in English, Québec is a nation.... And I hope our compatriots in the rest of Canada will understand that Québec is not just a province."[1]

The separatist platform rests on an understanding of Québec as a distinct nation and continues to do so even though official political recognition as a state has evaded the province over forty years of active struggle and two referenda on sovereignty. Whether the constituent elements of Québec nationhood are territory, ethnicity, or language has been the focus of active and ongoing debate, with no option ever agreed on as wholly satisfactory. This debate has raged over four decades of rapid modernization within Québec and in the larger context of globalization. Québec has struggled to assert its nationhood at the same time as new groupings, systems, and frameworks are challenging the nation as primary organizational social units. Not surprisingly, Québec nationalists respond to these challenges by asserting the enduring importance of nation: "Globalization notwithstanding, everyone has to be a citizen of somewhere before being a citizen of the world, which is why the nation still provides a necessary horizon."[2] These are the first lines of *Vive Québec!*, a volume of essays reprinted from a 1999 series in which the "openly sovereigntist"[3] Montreal newspaper *Le Devoir* attempted to "take stock very calmly of the Québec nation, its challenges, its priorities, and its demands."[4] The nineteen essayists' diagnoses of Québec's problems cover a wide gamut. Independence is no longer a viable option because too many oppose it, says Charles Taylor; independence is the *only* option, counters Gérard Bouchard. National sovereignty should be shared between two associate states, Québec and Canada, with special rights for self-government given to aboriginals, argues Gilles Bourque; Québec is a differentiated culture within Canada, itself made up of three distinct worlds: francophone, anglophone, and aboriginal, says Jocelyn Létourneau. Contributors argue variously that the problem is economic, that it is political, and that it is cultural.[5]

While the essayists in *Vive Québec!* disagree on many levels on what defines Québec and Quebeckness, they are nearly all united in their (sometimes implicit) assumption that nationhood relies upon the possession of a unique and definable culture. The concept of nationhood as being constituted through cultural uniqueness is a historically specific one, reflective of a modern Western definition of identity. As Eva Mackey argues,

> ...nationalist views of culture and history are tied to processes of modernity and to Western liberal notions of personhood, in particular the Enlightenment concept of individual sovereignty and autonomy..., having a differentiated, bounded, and defined identity comes to be an essential feature of "normal personhood" or normal nationhood, as constituted in a modern Western framework.[6]

Taken together, however, the very diversity of the arguments within *Vive Québec!* and the passion with which their proponents make them, offer a challenge to this modernist, essentialist equation of nationhood with the possession of a "differentiated, bounded, and defined identity." A more contemporary approach, informed by an understanding of identity as dialogic, ongoing, and contingent rather than absolute, locates Québec within, rather than outside or above, the discussion of its existence. Discourse about what constitutes Québec is not just evidence of the vitality of the fight for Québec nationhood: it is constitutive of that nationhood. Frank Davey has argued that, in the face of globalization, Canada's national status continues to exist through and within the very debate about that status: "The only means that Canadians have of defending themselves against multinational capitalism [is] participating in the arguments of a nation that is being continually discursively produced and reproduced from political contestation."[7] This argument can usefully be extended to the Québec situation. Legally, Québec is a province within Canada; it is only through the imagination and belief of some of its citizenry that it "exists" as a nation at all. Landry's defiant election-night assertion, "I say it again ... Québec is a nation," underlines the status of Québec nationhood as a discursive production, a production that is by its nature ongoing.

The status of all contemporary nations as dialogic constructions, as "more fiction than fact,"[8] is the topic of extensive scholarly discussion across a number of fields. Political scientist Richard Handler has argued that "...the search for an integral identity, or the attempt to formulate an undeniable interpretation of the true national culture, can never succeed — and hence must be repeated indefinitely";[9] literary theorist Homi Bhabha, for his part, celebrates the "production of the nation as narration."[10]

It is important not to overplay, however, the demise of the nation-state and the excitement of free-flowing, post-national, global identities. Even as corporate multinationals and supra-national alliances have grown in power and influence, the nation-state has not yet been supplanted as the primary political and organizational site of contemporary society, and nationalism remains a potent ideology which delineates, unifies, motivates, and excludes. The notion of a free-flowing, performative, evolutionary national culture may sound attractive and liberating in the abstract, but both at official levels and for citizens on the ground, such performativity can be experienced as instability, insecurity, and threat; as Bhabha notes, "the political unity of a nation consists in a continual displacement of the anxiety of its irredeemably plural modern space."[11]

That anxiety is heightened in stateless nations, such as Québec, which have, as noted, only the uniqueness of their national culture to rest on as proof of their existence. While, to a certain extent, official Québec and the Quebeckers themselves have developed sophisticated strategies, which absorb and exploit the evolutionary, discursive qualities of their culture, we also see the vulnerability of the national idea of Québec, when attention is too closely drawn to the nation's porousness and indeterminacy — as with the extreme and controversial measures taken in the 1970s to copper-fasten French as the only official language of the province in the face of increased immigration and linguistic diversification.[12]

Along with language, another of the foundational principles of the Québec nation-building project is internationalism. The Québec government has promoted an international definition of the nation from its earliest days, positing that interaction with "legitimate" nations would enhance the legitimacy of its own image. As Michael Keating has argued, "[a]n active external affairs policy not only projects Québec in the world, it also serves the interests of nation-building at home by defining national interests in relation to the outside and raising the prestige of the Québec state by placing it in the company of sovereign nations."[13] This internationalization has been a marked success, and Québec is now an enthusiastic participant in economic globalization: between 1992 and 2000, exports from Québec to the US increased by 140 percent, making it the USA's eighth-largest trading partner, and exports from Québec to the world have increased 80 percent during that time period, compared to 18 percent for Canada overall.[14] As Guy Lachapelle and Stéphane Paquin have argued, Québec's global economic success has advanced the cause for sovereignty, by helping convince Quebeckers and others that there is a "decrease in risks associated with Québec independence,"[15] because Québec has become less dependent on the Canadian domestic market. But this drive towards internationalization inevitably sends Québec into situations in which the fragility of its national status is exposed. Paradoxically, placing the nation in the international arena, while helping legitimize the nation, also exposes the inherent elusiveness and porousness of the idea of Québec. Awareness of this problematic has driven the Québec government to spearhead a drive towards an international treaty on cultural diversity, which would allow governments to continue to subsidize cultural products even though such subsidies conflict with the rules of the World Trade Organization. This campaign took two major steps forward in 2003 with the signing of a Franco-Québécois alliance on cultural diversity, and the launch of a new cultural diversity initiative by UNESCO, which Québec has promoted as the ideal supra-national organization to safeguard the individuality of national cultures.[16]

In this paper I will discuss the work of Québec theatre artist Robert Lepage to demonstrate the complexity of the relationship between cultural production, internationalism, and Québec nationhood. It is my argument that Lepage, and other internationally successful Québec artists, play a key role in the formation and dissemination of the Québec nation, and as such are inextricably caught up in the ambiguities and contradictions surrounding contemporary nationhood. Aggressively marketed by the nation as "products of Québec," Québécois artists are more accurately described as among the nation's most potent producers. I agree with Erin Hurley that the cultural productions, and the performing arts in particular, actively help make the national idea material, by "grounding it in an emotional and experiential reality."[17]

Lepage is in many ways the consummate Québec internationalist: all of his original works have travel as a theme, and depict Quebeckers in contact with other cultures. And, from almost the earliest days of his career, Lepage's work has itself traveled: with the aid of funding from local, provincial, and federal sources, Lepage's productions have toured around Québec,

Canada, and, increasingly, the world. Lepage's career is now itself a global oeuvre, with productions backed by dozens of international founders as well as Canadian government sources, and touring to numerous foreign venues. Lepage has called touring internationally "un propos nationaliste";[18] in turn, his success is held up by critical commentators and the Québec government as a shining example of the international viability of the nation itself, and Lepage is celebrated as a leading cultural ambassador. In November 2003, Lepage was awarded the Prix du Québec, the highest honor given by the government to figures from the sciences and the arts, for "having delivered his visionary artistic sensibility to stages the world over."[19] Commentators frame Lepage, both through his self-identified characters and the overall arc of his career, as the model Quebecker, mapping onto his successful personal trajectory the course of the nation towards international agency. His moves are closely watched and he is sharply criticized when he is seen to be betraying or surpassing the nation, while at the same time his early works have become sentimental national classics which, at the level of popular discourse, seem to stand outside or above criticism.

Before turning to the specifics of Lepage's career, I'd like to turn the clock back forty years to underline the extent to which culture and internationalism were fundamental tenets of Québec's nationalist movement. In 1961, the newly elected Liberal Party created the Ministère des Affaires Culturelles, only ten years after the formation of its federal equivalent, the Canada Council. This new ministry adhered closely to the vision of the 1956 Tremblay Commission Report, which "gave ideological and statistical support to provincial autonomy and to the idea that the Québec government was the primary defender of a threatened culture."[20] The Tremblay Report and the election of the Liberals spurred on the national consolidation process, which was to become the Quiet Revolution and which constituted, in the words of Michelle Gagnon and Martin Allor, "nothing less than the production of the Cultural field both as the legitimating agency of government and as an emergent regime of social power..."[21] The state was to support actively not only the creation of cultural products, but the promotion of those products outside the province: the new Arts Council, an arm of the Ministère des Affaires Culturelles, was created, according to then Prime Minister Jean Lesage, to "...try to stimulate artistic expressions which bear a seal, a sign, a trademark, which calls the world's attention to them as products of Québec."[22]

Just what such a seal, sign, or trademark of Quebeckness might be remains undefined in the document. There is no essential Quebeckness, no set of signifiers that can be isolated to sum it up. "Québécois" thus becomes an ever-expanding catchall for anything cultural that emanates from the province, and the more that cultural emanation is capable of "calling the world's attention" to itself, the more it is celebrated, at official levels, as representative of the nation. We see the circularity of this thinking indicated in the eclectic group of artists whose names are currently listed as proof of the vibrancy of Québec's culture on the nation's official website: a selection which includes cultural workers as various as Denys Arcand, the Cirque du Soleil, Leonard Cohen, Céline Dion, Marc-André Hamelin, and Robert Lepage.[23] Together these artists help their province send a potent message, the current official slogan of the Ministère de la Culture et Communications: "Québec, a culture that travels the world."

Lepage, a native of the provincial capital, graduated from the Conservatoire de Théâtre in 1978, and began his career staging small-scale productions with Conservatoire classmates in Québec's small theatres and cafés, before joining the existing company Théâtre Repère. He quickly became one of the company's leading lights, securing his growing reputation with the huge success of *La Trilogie des dragons*, a collaborative creation with Repère artists that was developed over a period of several years and in its final version was six hours long. Originally produced in Québec, the production was spotted and lionized by a London critic at the 1986 Toronto World Stage Festival and subsequently booked into many major festivals and venues; it ended up touring for over six years to fourteen countries.

The ambitious narrative of *La Trilogie des dragons*, that runs from 1910 to the 1980s, traces the interwoven lives and families of two girls from Québec City, Jeanne and Françoise, a Chinese immigrant laundryman, an Englishman who arrives in Québec to open a shoe store, and a Japanese geisha deserted by her American lover during World War II. The production was celebrated by local critics and audiences for the visual inventiveness and emotional power of its staging, the engagement and persuasiveness of its actor-authors, and its messages about Québec culture and its place in the world. It was performed in French and English, with a smattering of Chinese, and even when it was performed in English-speaking provinces and countries, wide swathes of dialogue spoken in colloquial Québécois were not translated. This was perceived by Québec critics, as well as by Lepage himself, to be a nationalist gesture that reminded anglophone audiences of the linguistic disadvantage that Quebeckers feel they hold within Canada. Several Québec critics celebrated the production as an expansion of the communicative, representative, and cultural possibilities of theatre, and read the misunderstood and linguistically marginalized Chinese characters as standing in for the position of Québec within Canada. The mingling of cultural references in the production and its depiction of internationally-minded Québec characters was read as sending a message about the nation itself, representing the voice of a new generation of Quebeckers, who, building on the foundational work of Quiet Revolution artists and intellectuals, were able to look outward beyond the province and what had become an oppressive discourse about national identity. "The political message is implicit," wrote Québec critic Jeanne Bovet of *La Trilogie*, "Québec's place in the world can only be insured by a strong sense of identity coupled with open mindedness towards other cultures."[24] That the production was a major international success became part of Québec's internationalizing process: both internally and externally, it sent the message that Québec held an important place in the world. That it was taken as representative of Québec when it toured was resoundingly obvious, when an entire audience walked out on a 1989 performance of the production in Manitoba as a protest against Québec separatism.[25]

Moreover, domestically, not all the feedback that Lepage and his collaborators received for *La Trilogie* was positive. A counter-discourse developed which derided the production as opportunistically *fédéraliste*, as having exploited Canadian and international content to make it more appealing to audiences outside the province, an allegation that has been repeated against Lepage throughout his career. Lepage responded to these criticisms in a 1987 interview with Carole Frèchette in *Cahiers de Théâtre Jeu*:

> FRÈCHETTE: You have been criticized for having made, with La Trilogie, a "festival show," pan–Canadian, completely in the federalist spirit. What do you think about that?
>
> LEPAGE: They made those criticisms in Montreal. There's never a question of federalism in Toronto. I have the impression, on the contrary, that this show is very nationalist. Putting Québec protagonists on stage who defend a nationalist idea is perhaps not the best way to promote nationalism. I think it is interesting to stage Québec artists who are required to exile themselves in Vancouver. But I am not selling that idea. I'm just saying that this is what has to be done: I am required to tour in the West and in the United States in order to get to the next level. For me, that's a nationalist proposition.[26]

The fictional Québec artist, who finds it necessary to exile himself in Vancouver, is the *Trilogie* character Pierre la Montagne, a recurrent character throughout Lepage's *oeuvre* and an acknowledged stand-in for Lepage himself, as Lepage played the role in the *Trilogie*'s original incarnations. In this quotation, Lepage blurs the distinction between his own situation and that of his character: he portrays the fact that he tours his work outside of Québec not as a choice but as inevitability and obligation. His views on internationalism dovetail closely with those of official Québec policy in a manner that seems self-serving: if touring internationally makes him a good nationalist, "getting to the next level" in his career makes him an even better one. The more internationally successful the Quebecker, he seems to argue, the better it is for Québec.

By that standard, the next decade saw Lepage as a very good Quebecker indeed. Propelled by the domestic and international success of *La Trilogie* and his first solo show, *Vinci*, Lepage's career, and his productions became increasingly ambitious and increasingly international. His next major production was *Les Plaques tectoniques*, a "bicontinental work in progress,"[27] created and performed by Québécois and Scots actors, funded by the European Economic Community (now the EU) to be performed as part of the festivities in Glasgow, 1990 Cultural Capital of Europe. The production, in various stages of development, eventually toured to six countries over three years (1988–90) and piloted the form of internationally financed, developmentally traveling production, which would become the standard for Lepage's work. Set in Venice, Montreal, and New York, *Les Plaques* traced the stories of three Québécois friends in search of romantic and personal fulfillment, against the backdrop of the real-life stories of Chopin and Georges Sand.

Les Sept branches de la rivière Ota set the bar of internationalism even higher, and marked the moment when Lepage's work became fully integrated into the international arts festival network. Throughout the late 1980s and 1990s, Lepage acquired a small network of producers, in Québec City, Toronto, London, and Paris, who developed a financing scheme for his work, not unlike that used in the film industry: co-producers and presenters buy into the shows before they are created, in return for a program credit and a run of the production in their venue. In the case of *Rivière Ota*, as soon as Lepage had broadly conceived an epic collaborative production about the city of Hiroshima, his producers began to sell the production to potential partners and presenters.[28] Some 23 co-producers eventually came on board, and over the span of its five-year life, the production had 28 short runs in thirteen countries. As with *La Trilogie* and *Les Plaques tectoniques,* the work was developed in a series of versions, in this case four versions of three, five, seven, and eight hours long; each version built on the next, with the company regrouping after each tour to rework and expand material based on audience and critical feedback, as well as their own new insights and ideas. While many aspects of the production changed greatly in its development, its basic through-line remained the same: the connection of three tragedies of the twentieth century — the Holocaust, the atom bomb, and AIDS — through the stories of several generations of people connected by bloodline, love, and circumstance. The production's set represented a house in Hiroshima whose owners became the center of the narrative, with all the characters in the production's many fictional settings — New York, Amsterdam, the Terezin concentration camp outside Prague, and Osaka — connecting to the story of that house and that family.

The pattern of increased internationalism in the financing and touring of these productions was mirrored in their fictional settings. *La Trilogie* was set almost totally in Canadian locations — Québec City, Toronto, and Vancouver — with a brief episode in wartime Japan; significantly, while several of its characters aspire to travel to the Far East in its final section, they never actually get there: the plane carrying the shoe salesman Crawford to Hong Kong, the city of his birth, crashes into the sea, and while it is thematically important that Pierre la Montagne decides to travel to China to study painting, that fictional voyage has not begun at the play's end. *Les Plaques* locates two of its three primary Québécois characters as expatriates, who nonetheless retain close ties to the homeland: the art student Madeline wanders in Europe, looking for inspiration but preoccupied by her unrequited love for her art teacher back in Montreal, while the object of her affections, the transvestite Jacques/Jennifer (played by Lepage), relocates herself in Manhattan, and supports herself by broadcasting reports about American culture on Radio Canada. By contrast, in most of its versions, *Rivière Ota* featured relatively few Québécois characters — only two out of the ten primary characters — and never set fictional foot on Canadian soil.

In turn, critical discourse about Lepage has moved on from viewing his productions as evidence of Québec's readiness to enter the international sphere to evidence of its active place within that sphere; recent commentators celebrate the staging of the negotiations between cultures and languages as an indication of Québec's full-blown participation in globalization. "More than providing a mapping of hyphenated ethnic identities," wrote Sonia Poirer in 1996, "the Québec-informed cultural innovations of Lepage negotiate the discourses of nationalism, sovereignty, métissage, and alterity within globalized processes of transcultural commodification and communication, and proffer the making of new Quebeckers, the forging of a larger imaginary in which to situate the fin-de-siècle Quebecker subject."[29] Sherry Simon, for her part, classes Lepage's productions as embodying a "transnational culture," which "propose[s] a vision of 'cosmopolitan globalism' as a dialogue among differences" and identifies Lepage as "an exemplar of the transnational intellectual,"[30] a figure familiar from the globalization theories of Ulf Hannerz.

But the transition from internationalist *nationaliste* to transnational intellectual has emphatically not decoupled Lepage from his home territory; on the contrary he has affirmed his commitment to Québec in the most material way possible. In the 1980s and early 1990s, at the same time he was creating these increasingly globalized productions, he was also working as a director for hire at high-profile theatres and venues around the world. While he remained nominally based in Québec, the hectic pace of this traveling wore on him, and in 1994 he declared his intention to ground himself more firmly in his native city with the formation of a new production company, Ex Machina, and the renovation of La Caserne Dalhousie, a former fire station which opened in 1997 as a state-of-the-art multi-arts creation facility. Lepage framed these developments as an affirmation of his connection to, and need for, Québec:

> The meetings and exchanges I have abroad enrich my work and the work of my company, work that remains profoundly Québécois. This is what has motivated me to return to the province of Québec and more precisely to Québec City, where I grew up and which inspires me much like the Plateau area in Montreal inspires the playwright Michel Tremblay. It's from Québec that I want to make contact with the rest of the world.[31]

A.S. Dundjerovich, author of two books on Lepage's work, claims that one of Lepage's reasons for relocating to Québec was in fact a direct criticism from Michel Tremblay, who said that Lepage's work was "not relevant to Québécois culture, but concerned with international festival trends."[32]

A related argument has been forwarded by scholars Erin Hurley and Jennifer Harvie, who criticized what they saw as the strategic internationalism of Lepage's work with Ex Machina in their article "States of Play: Locating Québec in the Performances of Robert Lepage, Ex Machina, and the Cirque du Soleil." Lepage's work for Ex Machina, Harvie and Hurley argue, is created "primarily for export,"[33] the Caserne was built without a public performance space, and Lepage has said that Ex Machina's *raison d'être* is to "export our shows."[34] Indeed Québec audience's access to much of the company's work in the 1990s was limited: of the 28 short runs of *Rivière Ota*, only two took place in the province of Québec,[35] and only one the twenty runs of their subsequent production, *La Géométrie des miracles*, was staged in Québec.[36] For Harvie and Hurley, internationally ambitious artists like Lepage and Cirque du Soleil "exploit" the Québec nation for funding to establish their practice, and then "repeatedly evacuate the specific, if shifting, nationhood of Québec" by creating and touring work that is vaguely internationalist in theme and setting.[37]

The larger point that I am making, however, is that the "specific, shifting nationhood of Québec" is *already* void, or perhaps overstuffed: the province's aggressively internationalist cultural policies and the inherent undefinability of the idea of nation have worked together to create the amorphous, infinitely expandable and exploitable concept that is Québec. While Harvie and Hurley defend the Québec nation against its exploitation by its cultural workers, this is "exploitation" which Québec has invited and does not appear to feel the need to defend itself against. Harvie and Hurley question the ethics of Ex Machina taking considerable subsidy from the Québec government and then rarely performing their work in the province itself. On the other hand, the number of domestic performances required of a subsidized company is written into its grant: that is, while commentators may question how well Ex Machina is serving its home audience, underserving is being carried out with the nation's approval at the official level.

The anxiety about the responsibility of Québec artists to the nation is shared by the Québec media, as it was resoundingly indicated in 2001, when Lepage's barring of several Québec critics from a press conference spiraled into a Canada-wide debate over Lepage's relationship to the Québec nation. The press conference had been planned by the Montreal-based Festival de Théâtre des Ameriques to publicize upcoming performances of Lepage's one-man show *La Face cachée de la lune.* When the critics to whom he had refused entry started to raise a public fuss, Lepage simply cancelled the conference, saying to several media outlets that he did not need the press to sell his shows, and underlined that artists must be responsible to themselves and their vision. The media reacted with further indignation at what they saw as an arrogant dismissal of the investment that the Québec government, and by extension the Québec taxpayer, had made to his career: "Monsieur Lepage isn't accountable to anyone? That's a lie. Nothing is more false. Monsieur Lepage is nothing *but* accountable because he is subsidized to the bone."[38] In *La Presse*, Nathalie Petrowski took things a step further by likening Lepage's behavior to that of "Maurice Duplessis ... or some other black king reigning over a banana republic."[39] The reference is to a now-infamous incident in which the then–Premier Duplessis, in the midst of the Hydro Québec scandals of the late 1950s, had a journalist from *Le Devoir*, the newspaper at the forefront of uncovering the scandals, forcibly removed from a press conference. This prompted André Laurendau, a prominent *Le Devoir* writer, to forward a theory likening Duplessis to a neo-colonial Negro King, a *roi nègre*, who answered to big business rather than the interests of the people.

Clearly "L'affaire Lepage," as it was dubbed in the press, escalated to remarkable levels of rhetoric and emotion. Lepage banned journalists from a press conference and continued to engage publicly with the issues that arose. But it does seem extraordinary that a journalist would go so far as to compare the behavior of an artist, usually championed as a valued national asset, to that of a politician associated with corruption and pre–Quiet Revolution conservatism and oppression, and would do so using controversial and outdated metaphors eliding Quebeckness and blackness. The scandal overall is a measure of how charged are issues of personal responsibility to the nation in the Québec context, particularly when international stars like Lepage are involved, fame and success are seen as bringing with them a responsibility to be humble and loyal to the old soil. For the record, Michel Bernatchez, Ex Machina's producing director, maintains that much of this controversy was based on a misquotation of Lepage, who according to Bernatchez never said he was not responsible to the nation, but rather to the media,[40] a point Ex Machina underlined in April 2001 by unfurling a banner down the side of La Caserne reading: "Les artistes sont libres et n'ont de comptes à rendre à la 'médiocrité.'"[41]

Early on, Lepage and his collaborators defended their aggressive pursuit of touring as a natural expression of their interests and personal and national identities, and as a necessity because of the limits of their local audience base. Québec is a provincial capital with a population of 650,000 and a much less developed arts infrastructure than the cultural center of Montreal; touring around the province and beyond was a necessary step for their work to be seen by a substantial audience. For Ex Machina today, touring is a fiscal necessity. Lepage's productions are expensive, and his vision has by now well outgrown the Québec government's ability to fund it. According to Bernatchez, Ex Machina's budgets are the largest of any theatre company in Québec ($3–5 million Canadian),[42] but only 15–25 percent of those budgets come from government sources, lower than the Canadian standard of 45–55 percent dependence on government funding. In Bernatchez's view, the company is chronically underfunded by the government. The rest of the company's costs — some 70 percent of their total annual turnaround — are met by non–Québec sources, in the form of co-production funds and performance fees. In Jennifer Harvie and Erin Hurley's view, this diversification of Ex Machina's income sources is having two related effects: it diminishes "Québec's potential ideological claims on Ex Machina," as the company "migrat[es] in pursuit of ever greater and wider sources of funding and ever more elite contexts of production," and it encourages the company towards a creative practice that is "homogenous and unified," in order to appeal to a "unified production context," that of the international theatre festival circuit.[43]

It is true that we have seen in Lepage's work a gradual move away from specific Québec references, characters, and settings to a more internationalized milieu. But this progression was presaged in the international impulses and outward looking ethos of even his earliest work, and official and critical discourse within Québec has ably absorbed and appropriated Lepage's increasing globality as a reflection of the nation's international viability. This

is not to idealize Lepage's output, or his current milieu, as unproblemati-
cally international: much has been written of the use of the Orient as "other"
in Lepage's productions,[44] and of the relationship of this Orientalism to the
tourist gaze promoted by the circulation of works in the international festival circuit.[45] The current of "exploitation" between Lepage and Québec runs
both ways. Lepage's decision to base himself in Québec, arguments such as
Harvie and Hurley's, and "L'affaire Lepage" fracas, are all various indications
of the tensions and anxieties that accompany attempts to negotiate the global
on local terms.

I will now discuss in more detail two of Lepage's most recent stage productions, both of which are currently on international tour: the aforementioned solo show *La Face cachée de la lune,* and a revival of *La Trilogie des
dragons,* which premiered in Montreal at the Festival de Théâtre des
Ameriques (FTA) in May 2003. Taken together they seem to indicate a move
back towards more specifically Québec content and a renewed commitment
to the presentation of Lepage's work within the province. With *La Face
cachée,* Lepage seems to have hit a workable balance between the local and
the global; the production is physically set primarily in Québec City and
returns to one of Lepage's favored personal themes, one that had been less
apparent in his more recent work: the attempts of a Québec artist to find
his place in the world. Arguably his most personal show since *Vinci* in 1987,
it is also his biggest critical and audience success since the original production of *La Trilogie des dragons.* Over three years it has played in 49 separate
runs in 21 countries on five continents, and its touring plans continue.[46] Of
those 49 runs only three were in Québec, but it is significant that one of these
was a sold-out, extended seven-week run at the Théâtre du Nouveau Monde
in Montreal in the summer of 2003, featuring Yves Jacques, Lepage's replacement in the show's solo role. Local press responded positively to the extended
presence of a major Lepage production in Montreal, particularly as it coincided with the premiere of the revived *Trilogie* in the FTA. The latter was
the third in as many new Lepage productions to be presented in Montreal
in co-production with a local festival. *Zulu Time* was presented as part of
the Festival International de Jazz de Montreal in June-July 2002, and *The
Busker's Opera* had its world premiere in February 2004 in Montreal.[47]

The revival of *La Trilogie* was marketed by the FTA and Ex Machina
as a major cultural event: the return of a foundational, and now legendary,
production, "une oeuvre qui a changé la face de théâtre au Québec," in the
words of FTA director Marie-Hélène Falcon.[48] The press echoed and reinforced this interpretation, discussing the production in preview and review
articles as a central text, not just of Québec theatre, but of contemporary
Québec nationhood, and using it as an opportunity to reminisce nostalgi-

cally about the production's first incarnation, as in Luc Boulanger's preview piece for *Voir*, not unsymbolically titled "Je me souviens."[49] The production was described in press releases and interviews as an opportunity for a new generation of Quebeckers to experience *La Trilogie*, as performers of the new production featured an all-new cast, including several young Québécois and Québec-based actors. This assertion was accepted apparently without question by critics and all the reviews were highly positive: the production was a major success, selling out nine performances in the 600-seat performance space at the Usine d'Alstom and receiving standing ovations after each performance.[50]

The revival of *La Trilogie* generated a highly uniform discourse of nostalgia and positive nation-building, in which the production was framed as an experiential pedagogical tool, wherein a new generation could be edified by their contact with a living monument from the nation's recent cultural past. What is curious here is the lack of interest of commentators in a potential counter-discourse, which Lepage and his collaborators themselves attempted to generate in the run-up to the Montreal premiere. The project description by the Festival and Ex Machina foregrounds the original production's "naive" representation of the East and describes the revival as an attempt to redress and update this point of view:

> The naive, intrigued tone of his original mounting of the first *Trilogie* as a gaze focussed on an imaginary China reminiscent of North American Chinatowns of the 1930s no longer exists. For the last fifteen years, Lepage has incorporated into several productions his understanding of an Eastern universe explored again and again, an Orient with which he is intimately familiar. He is thus presenting a revised and updated *Trilogie des dragons*, one that includes Asian artists...[51]

Throughout his career, Lepage has created his work through a developmental process, changing and adding material to subsequent versions as his perceptions and those of his collaborators change, and often incorporating the insights and critiques of reviewers. His comments about the revived *Trilogie* reflect this approach: he is at pains to present this new production not as a straight revival but as a re-creation, a fresh look at the material with an awareness of the commentary that has developed since on the treatment of the Orient in this and other productions. It is highly debatable, however, whether the revisions to the *Trilogie* solved as many representational problems as it created new ones. Jennifer Harvie has argued that the naive and objectified portraits of Asian characters in the original *Trilogie* were framed in a larger critique of the Québec viewpoint itself: "Rather than betraying the racism of the production, [these representations] portray the racism of its main characters, problematizing it by highlighting its naiveté, crudity, and extent, and emphasizing its change over time."[52] As Harvie and Christie Carson have argued, the perception of the *Trilogie*'s cultural depictions changed across cultures: British critics, for example, tended to take the original *Trilogie*'s depiction of Oriental and British characters as cliché-ridden and limited, whereas to commentators within Québec these depictions resonated as self-conscious and self-critical.[53]

Fifteen years later, the cultural specificity of the original *Trilogie* is even more pronounced: the production represents a way of looking at culture that, it could be argued, is itself now part of the past. But just what stance the revival is taking towards the original material is not yet clear: was it an attempt to update its representations, to offer a current Québécois point of view on the world? Or was it an attempt to historicize its past viewpoint, to look back fondly or perhaps critically on the way that a certain group of internationally ambitious Québec artists, and by extension perhaps a whole generation of young Quebeckers, saw the world? The casting of apparently Asian and/or Eurasian actors in the Asian roles, and indeed an "authentic" Briton in the role of the Englishman, indicates a desire to bring the production's representational practices up to date. But because very little of the production's actual content has changed from the original version, this casting seems literal and appears to sanction what the production is otherwise at pains to point out as externalized, distant impressions of otherness. By contrast, the collaborators chose to keep the production's last section set in 1985, the original production's real time, rather than updating it to today. With this gesture the audience is kept at a remove from the material and encouraged to see it as a historical rather than current commentary.

The contradictory impulses apparently at play in the *Trilogie* revival — the desire to update outdated representations of cultural otherness and the attempt to freeze the production as a representation of the past — are a further indication of the anxiety that pervades the creation and circulation of Lepage's work as both a national and international product. Is *La Trilogie des dragons* a prized monument of Québec's international cultural viability, or is it a site for the recording of Québec's ongoing discussion on national identity? That local audiences and commentators were clearly eager to construct it as the former seems a gesture of pride, but could also be read as one of insecurity: *La Trilogie* is a life raft on which the unstable Québec nation clings as it negotiates the rapid waters of globalization without its national status secured by law. However, the story of this *Trilogie* is very much ongoing, as its touring life has only recently begun again. Ex Machina is continuing to book international touring dates for the production, and it seems likely that there will be changes along the way. It will be interesting to see how current international audiences respond to this historic production, and how those responses will in turn feed into the further development of *La Trilogie des dragons*.

Notes

1. Jeff Gray and Allison Lawlor, "Landry's future in doubt," *The Globe and Mail*, 14 April 2003.
2. Michael Venne, ed. *Vive Québec! New Thinking and Approaches to the Québec Nation* (Toronto: James Lorimer & Company, 2001) 1.
3. Venne 6.
4. Venne 5.
5. The latter three arguments are made by Gilles Gagné, Mark Chevrier, and Claude Bariteau.
6. Eva Mackey, *The House of Difference: Cultural Politics and National Identity in Canada* (London: Routledge, 1999) 11.
7. Frank Davey, *Post-National Arguments: The Politics of the Anglo-Canadian Novel since 1967* (Toronto: University of Toronto Press, 1993) 24.
8. Erin Hurley, "Céline Dion and the Production of National Feeling" (unpublished conference paper, 2004) 1.
9. Richard Handler, *Nationalism and the Politics of Culture in Québec* (Madison: University of Wisconsin Press, 1988) 130.
10. Homi Bhabha, *The Location of Culture* (London: Routledge, 1994) 178.
11. Bhabha 177.
12. Further discussion of Québec language laws and Canadian multiculturalism can be found in Handler 1988; Michael Keating, *Nations against the State: the New Politics of Nationalism in Québec, Catalonia, and Scotland* (London: Palgrave, 1990); and Mackey 1999.
13. Keating 125.
14. "Globalization and Cultural Diversity: What does Québec Want?" Address by the Québec Minister of International Relations, Louise Beaudoin, at Harvard University, 7 February 2000. www.mri.gouv.qc.ca/english/ministere/speeches/2000/discours_20000207_an.html
15. Guy Lachapelle and Stéphane Paquin, "Québec's International Strategies: Mastering Globalization and New Possibilities of Governance," (conference paper, Queen's University, Ontario, 2003) 14.
16. www.mcc.gouv.qc.ca/international/diversite-culturelle/eng/review2003.html
17. Hurley 4.
18. In Carole Frèchette, "'L'arte è un veicolo,' entretien avec Robert Lepage," *Cahiers de Théâtre Jeu* 42 (1988): 118.
19. "pour avoir transporté sur les scènes du monde entier sa sensibilité d'artiste visionnaire," http://www.ledevoir.com/2003/11/19/40952.html?318
20. John Dickinson and Brian Young, *A Short History of Québec* (Montreal, McGill-Queen's University Press, 2003) 296.
21. Michelle Gagnon, and Martin Allor, "Québec," in *Public 14* (1996):8. Qtd. in Erin Manning, *Ephemeral Territories: Representing Nation, Home and Identity in Canada* (Minneapolis: University of Minnesota Press, 2003) 127.

22. Qtd. in Handler 105–6, emphasis in original.

23. "Culture Québec, a culture that travels the world," http://www.mcc.gouv. qc.ca/publications/culture_Québec_eng.pdf

24. Jeanne Bovet, "Identity and Universality: Multilingualism in Robert Lepage's Theater," *Theater sans frontières: Essays on the Dramatic Universe of Robert Lepage*, Joseph I. Donohoe Jr. and Jane M. Koustas, eds. (East Lansing: Michigan State University Press, 2000) 18.

25. Jill MacDougall, *Performing Identities on the Stages of Québec*, Ph.D. Dissertation (New York University Department of Performance Studies, 1993) 292.

26.

> FRÈCHETTE: On t'a reproché d'avoir fait, avec *La trilogie des dragons*, un "show-festival," pan-canadien, tout à fait dans l'esprit *fédéraliste*. Qu'en penses-tu?
>
> LEPAGE: C'est à Montréal qu'on nous a fait ces reproches. Il n' a jamais été question de *fédéralisme* à Toronto. J'ai l'impression, au contraire, que ce spectacle est très nationaliste. Montrer des protagonists québécois qui défendent une idée nationaliste n'est peut-être plus la meilleure façon de témoigner du nationalisme. Il est davantage intéressant, je crois, de montrer des artistes québécois obligés de s'exiler à Vancouver. Mais je ne *vends* pas cette idée-la. Je veux simplement dire que c'est ce qu'il faut faire: je suis obligé de faire les tournées dans l'Ouest et aux Etats-Unis pour pouvoir accéder à un autre palier. Pour moi, ça, c'est un propos nationaliste. Frèchette 117–118, translation mine.

27. MacDougall 213.

28. Specific information about the creative and production history of *Les Sept branches de la rivière Ota* is the product of my first-hand observation of the production's development and performances between 1994–1997. I have written more extensively about the development and touring of *Rivière Ota* in "Tourism, the Festival Marketplace, and Robert Lepage's *The Seven Streams of the River Ota*," *Contemporary Theatre Review* 13.4(2003): 79–93.

29. Sonia Poirer, *Beyond Nationalism: Re-envisioning Québec*, MA Thesis, (University of Toronto, Department of Education, 1996) 111.

30. Herry Simon, "Robert Lepage and the Languages of Spectacle," in Donohoe and Koustas, 215, 227.

31. Rémy Charest, *Robert Lepage: Connecting Flights* (London: Methuen, 1997) 50.

32. A.S. Dundjerovich, *Theatricality of Robert Lepage: A Study of his Transformative Mise-en-Scène*, Ph.D. Thesis (Royal Holloway, University of London, Department of Drama and Theatre Studies, 1999) 149.

33. Jennifer Harvie and Erin Hurley, "States of Play: Locating Québec in the Performances of Robert Lepage, Ex Machina, and the Cirque du Soleil," *Theatre Journal* 51 (1999):306.

34. Charest 114, qtd. in Harvie and Hurley 306.

35. Fricker 87.

36. www.exmachina.qu.ca/ENGLISH/ex.asp?page=GeoDiffus

37. Harvie and Hurley 314.

38. Monsieur Lepage n'a de comptes à rendre à personne? C'est une leurre. Rien n'est plus faux," wrote Franco Nuovo in *Le Journal de Montréal*. "Monsieur Lepage n'a *que* des comptes à rendre parce que Monsieur Lepage est subventionné jusqu'a

l'os." Franco Nuovo, "Qui paie le banquet?" *Le Journal de Montréal*, 5 April 2001, emphases in original.

39. "Maurice Duplessis ... [ou un] autre roi nègre régnant sur une république des bananes." Nathalie Petrowski, "Ses meilleurs ennemis," *La Presse*, 3 April 2001.

40. Michel Bernatchez, personal interview, Montreal, 13 July 2002.

41. "Artists are free and aren't accountable to 'mediocrity.'" "*Le Devoir*, "Robert Lepage critique la 'médiocrité,'" 26 April 2001.

42. See Bernatchez.

43. Harvie and Hurley 309.

44. See Dundjerovich; Barbara Godard, "Between Performative and Performance: Translation and Theatre in the Canadian/Québec Context," *Modern Drama* 43 (Fall 2000): 327–352; Jennifer Harvie, "Transnationalism, Orientalism, and Cultural Tourism: *La Trilogie des dragons* and *The Seven Streams of the River Ota*," in Donohoe and Koustas 109–125; Poirer; Sherry Simon, *Le Trafic des langues: traduction et culture dans la littérature québécoise* (Montreal: Boréal, 1994).

45. See Fricker.

46. www.exmachina.qc.ca/ENGLISH/ex.asp?page=Lune

47. www.exmachina.qc.ca

48. "A work which changed the face of theatre in Québec," Jean St.-Hilaire, "Acte de transmission," *Le Soleil*, 22 May 2003, translation mine.

49. Luc Boulanger, "Je me souviens," *Voir*, 15–21 May 2003. "Je me souviens," or "I remember," is the Québec provincial motto.

50. Solange Levesque's review in *Le Devoir* is representative of the critical response: "Cette première grande oeuvre collective de Robert Lepage et de Repère ne devait pas tomber dans l'oubli ou devenir un souvenir fétiche. La nouvelle production permettra aux jeunes générations de découvrir le spectacle qui a contribué à faire connaître la dramaturgie québécoise sur les cinq continents et, par la même occasion, de se familiariser avec le Québec et certains événements majeurs de l'histoire du monde au siècle dernier." Solange Lévesque, "Hereux retour des dragons," *Le Devoir*, 27 May 2003.

51. Le regard naïf et intrigué qui a guidé la création de la première *Trilogie* et celui posé sur une Chine exportée dans les *chinatowns* nord-américains des années '30s n'existe plus. Depuis 15 ans, Lepage a intégré dans plusieurs productions sa comprehension d'une orientalité explorée à répétition, et plus intimement connue. Il propose donc aujourd'hui une *Trilogie des dragons* "revue," qui implique des collaborateurs asiatiques... "*La Trilogie des Dragons*: L'Orient, au fil des temps," press release, Festival de Théâtre des Ameriques, 2003. Translation by the FTA.

52. Harvie 114.

53. Christie Carson, "From *The Dragon's Trilogy* to *The Seven Streams of the River Ota*: The Intercultural Experiments of Robert Lepage," in Donohoe and Koustas 43–77; also see Harvie.

Works Cited

Bernatchez, Michel. Personal interview, Montreal, 13 July 2002.

Bhabha, Homi. *The Location of Culture*. London: Routledge, 1994.

Boulanger, Luc. "Je me souviens." *Voir*, 15–21 May 2003.

Charest, Rémy. *Robert Lepage: Connnecting Flights*. London: Methuen, 1997.

Davey, Frank. *Le Devoir.* "Robert Lepage critique la 'médiocrité'". 26 April 2001.
_____. *Post-National Arguments: The Politics of the Anglo-Canadian Novel since 1967.* Toronto: University of Toronto Press, 1993.
Dickinson, John, and Brian Young. *A Short History of Québec.* Montreal: McGill-Queen's University Press, 2003.
Donohoe Jr., Joseph I., and Jane M. Koustas, eds. *Theater sans frontières: Essays on the Dramatic Universe of Robert Lepage.* East Lansing: Michigan State University Press, 2000.
Dundjerovich, A.S. *Theatricality of Robert Lepage: A Study of his Transformative Mise-en-Scène.* Ph.D. Thesis, Royal Holloway, University of London, Department of Drama and Theatre Studies, 1999.
Frèchette, Carole. "'L'arte è un veicolo,' entretien avec Robert Lepage." *Cahiers de Théâtre Jeu* 42 (1988).
Fricker, Karen. "Tourism, the Festival Marketplace, and Robert Lepage's *The Seven Streams of the River Ota.*" *Contemporary Theatre Review* 13.4 (2003).
Godard, Barbara. "Between Performative and Performance: Translation and Theatre in the Canadian/Québec Context." *Modern Drama* 43 (Fall 2000).
Gray, Jeff, and Allison Lawlor. "Landry's future in doubt." *The Globe and Mail,* 14 April 2003.
Handler, Richard. *Nationalism and the Politics of Culture in Québec.* Madison: University of Wisconsin Press, 1988.
Harvie, Jennifer, and Erin Hurley. "States of Play: Locating Québec in the Performances of Robert Lepage, Ex Machina, and the Cirque du Soleil." *Theatre Journal* 51 (1999).
Hurley, Erin. "Céline Dion and the Production of National Feeling." Unpublished conference paper, 2004.
Keating, Michael. *Nations against the State: the New Politics of Nationalism in Québec, Catalonia, and Scotland.* London: Palgrave, 1990.
Lachapelle, Guy, and Stéphane Paquin. "Québec's International Strategies: Mastering Globalization and New Possibilities of Governance." Conference paper, Queen's University, Ontario, 2003.
Lévesque, Solange. "Hereux retour des dragons." *Le Devoir,* 27 May 2003.
MacDougall, Jill. *Performing Identities on the Stages of Québec.* Ph.D. Dissertation, New York University, Department of Performance Studies, 1993.
Mackey, Eva. *The House of Difference: Cultural Politics and National Identity in Canada.* London: Routledge, 1999.
Manning, Erin. *Ephemeral Territories: Representing Nation, Home and Identity in Canada.* Minneapolis: University of Minnesota Press, 2003.
Nuovo, Franco. "Qui paie le banquet?" *Le Journal de Montréal,* 5 April 2001.
Petrowski, Nathalie. "Ses meilleurs ennemis." *La Presse,* 3 April 2001.
Poirer, Sonia. *Beyond Nationalism: Re-envisioning Québec.* M.A. Thesis, University of Toronto, Department of Education, 1996.
St. Hilaire, Jean. "Acte de transmission." *Le Soleil,* 22 May 2003.
Simon, Sherry. *Le Trafic des langues: traduction et culture dans la littérature Québécoise.* Montreal: Boréal, 1994.
Venne, Michael, ed. *Vive Québec! New Thinking and Approaches to the Québec Nation.* Toronto: James Lorimer & Company, 2001.
www.exmachina.qu.ca.
www.ledevoir.com.

Staging the Nation on the Ruins of the Past: An Investigation of Mexican Archeological Performance

Patricia Ybarra

On September 23, 1975, in Tlaxcala, Mexico, a farmer looking for a stash of valuable relics stumbled upon a mural near his home village of San Miguel de Milagro, in the Southwest part of Tlaxcala State. Soon after, excavations began that uncovered extensive murals, including a polychrome panorama of a battle between jaguar and eagles warriors. Dated at 650–900 C.E., Cacaxtla was the oldest Pre-Columbian site excavated in Tlaxcala, and the most physically impressive. Cacaxtla's importance was recognized quickly. In 1978, President Portillo gave 1.5 million pesos to the National Institute of Anthropology and History (INAH) for exploration; at the same time, the Tlaxcalan governor underscored the ruins' importance for local tourism and Tlaxcala's historical patrimony.[1]

The attention given to Cacaxtla as a site of cultural heritage and tourism is not surprising. Tlaxcala is the smallest of Mexico's thirty-four states and one of its least economically productive. Its citizens largely support themselves through small-scale farming and manufacturing work, particularly textile production. While not reaching the levels of poverty found in indigenous areas in the south and the shantytowns surrounding Mexico City, Tlaxcala's lack of resources has made the nation's recent economic woes hard to bear. Together with the fall of the peso in 1982, the nationalization of the banks which followed, and the 1994 passage of NAFTA have left many Mexicans and much of Mexico in financial disaster.[2] Like leaders in many other areas of the country, Tlaxcala's leaders have often looked toward revenue from cultural tourism to rectify this problem. To do so, the Tlaxcaltecans have had to rely primarily upon their colonial past rather than bank on their indigenous past or the area's natural attributes, Tlaxcala's lack of monumental Pre-Columbian architecture precluding these options. Cacaxtla provided Tlaxcala with the opportunity to shift that emphasis.

The coincidence of Cacaxtla's development, a burgeoning local history project, economic crises, and a large scale critique of both cultural nationalism and the Mexican archeological establishment's role in that nationalism made for a dynamic process of knowledge production around the site. As the development of the site continued, investigations were published that provided local historians and historiographers with the information to rewrite Tlaxcalan history, for its own sake and for that of the tourism industry.[3] Performance had an important role in the process; Cacaxtla appeared in state-sponsored theatrical performances beginning in 1992. In this paper, I analyze how knowledge production and dissemination in performances about and at Cacaxtla-Xochitecatl demonstrate the complicated negotiation between national, local, and indigenous identity that contemporary archeological sites enact within state-sponsored performances. Excavated between 1975 and 1997 in an area outside of the scope of its major Maya and Aztec ritual centers, Cacaxtla-Xochitecatl is an ideal site to investigate how contemporary changes in state archeological policies and politico-cultural rhetoric played out in the development of local cultural tourism. Particularly arresting is how performances of archeological ruins came to articulate indigenous and/or local identity in respect to national identity, in relationship to the educational and governmental decentralization that emerged in the 1980s. By analyzing how these performances create meaning theatrically — by inhabiting space, juxtaposing textual and stage actions, and orchestrating various media such as dance, music, and narrative, I will expose the trajectory that the *productions of* identity have taken in recent years. This investigation will show that performance plays an important role in both the popular interpretation of archeological monuments and in re-articulating national and local identities under the thumb of hemispheric Neoliberal capitalism. Ultimately, my analysis of performances about and at Cacaxtla reveal that the historiographical and cultural specificity upon which these projects depended were ultimately less sustainable in the practice of knowledge production than the homogenizing discourses they initially sought to interrogate.

Performing Archeology in Mexico: A History

In Mexico, relationships between emergent identity projects based on pre–Columbian indigenous heritages and state-sponsored archeological developments are intimate, transformative, and ultimately performative. Archeology has played an important role in the process of Mexican national identity construction from the late nineteenth century to the present day. In the nineteenth century, archeological ruins were used to provide "vivid testimony of the existence of and achievements of the ancient civilizations of central and southern Mexico."⁴ Following its revolution (1910–1917), the Mexican State attempted to re-construct national identity as a mixture of indigenous and Spanish heritages which placed the glory of indigenous cultures in the past so as to advocate their integration and/or elimination as a key step in the progress of the Mexican nation. "Father of Mexican Anthropology" Manuel Gamio, the biggest advocate of these views, used the Teotihuacán excavations in the 1920s to make this claim, contrasting the achievement to which its monumental ruins attested with the lack of success displayed by the area's poor *campesino* residents. Dissemination of images associated with or discovered at these sites, largely Aztec, Olmec, and Mayan also provided a visual iconography for the state: Mexican muralists used them in both state-sponsored and privately funded works. By the 1930s, President Lazaro Cárdenas used these ruins more explicitly to attract tourists to Mexico, eventually institutionalizing their protection by the creation of INAH, the National Institute of Anthropology and History. Instead of providing an allegory for a course of cultural development, or national iconography, under Cárdenas, archeological ruins were turned into commodities, whose protection by INAH simultaneously made them into objects of cultural patrimony and legitimized highly centralized governance of that patrimony. Governmental support of archeological excavation continued throughout the early 1960s, when both the Street of the Dead at Teotihuacán and the National Museum of Anthropology were opened to the public. Since then, money for archeological projects has declined despite a brief surge following the 1978 discovery of the Ruins of the Templo Mayor in Mexico City's central plaza.

While the role of archeological ruins in Mexican State formation was changed drastically over the course of the twentieth century, archeological excavations have consistently served as important sites of ideological and discursive dissent. This has been especially true since 1968, when critics positioned the excavations, interpretations, and displays of pre–Columbian sites, as examples *par excellence* of governmental practices, which sold national culture to tourists, while ignoring the demands, needs, and local histories of its own people.[5] These practices were usually referred to as *indigenista* archeology, because of their place in the larger national project that sought to integrate and/or destroy indigenous cultures in order to solidify a larger national culture.[6] Even when investigators' purposes were more salutary to indigenous groups, their rhetorical strategies often compromised the autonomy and obfuscated the specific economic conditions of indigenous people; the results of their work did not benefit living indigenous persons, as this was not their main goal.

Ultimately, the government was accused of using archeology to legitimize, rather than critique state power; many public intellectuals asked for these activities to end. Today, primarily because of the power of these critiques, the business of archeology has shifted. The government has uncovered more non-centrally located sites. Archeologists' research has been used to critique as well as support discourse about Mesoamerican civilizations that formed the bedrock of national identity and legitimized centralized state power. And researchers have complicated rather than simplified the relationship of the Indian past to the Indian present. In combination with the educational and governmental decentralization of Mexico's recent past (including the federalization of the Secretariat of Public Education, which placed the creation of historical materials in the hands of local historians), these innovations have allowed these sites to multiply.[7] The opportunities given to diverse people to articulate their agendas through archeological remains allowed various responses, many of which were not related to political dissent.

Performances have been just as diverse. Sometimes they legitimized fantasies of Mesoamerican spirituality, as in the case of equinox celebrations at Mayan sites in the Yucatan.[8] And, at others, they critiqued the government that supported the archeological industry itself, as when *concheros* dancers outside the Templo Mayor protested policies affecting indigenous people in Chiapas during the 1990s.[9] Despite the wide range of possibilities reflected in these performances, each of them share one trait: they write archeological ruins into their narratives so as to make a claim about the relationship between the indigenous past and particular Mexican presents. *Concheros* performers use the representational gestures of a highly recognizable indigenous past to point to the disparity in the representation of contemporary indigenous citizens. Equinox celebrations as Mesoamerican pyramids attempt to erase the boundary between indigenous and Gregorian calendars so as to make Mayan cosmologies present for contemporary New Age subjects. Although the Cacaxtla performances use aspects of both of these types of performances, its closest relationship is to state-sponsored performances from the early twentieth century.

Looking back to Manuel Gamio and the performances at *Teatro Sintético*, staged at an open-air theatre near his excavations at Teotihuacán, reveals the Cacaxtla-Xochitecatl performances' dramaturgical heritage. One of *Teatro Sintético*'s first programs consisted of "a choreographic representation of native industries, a rhythmic pantomime of daily tasks in saddlery and blacksmithing, and a mime about the life of slavery lived by Indians on cane plantations in the state of Morelos."[10] Combined with theatrical architecture that replicated glyphs of the indigenous past[11] and the presence of contemporary actors, the day's events narrated the whole of Mexican history as articulated by the new government. The performance displayed the glories of the past (the space), the horrors of the colonial period (the play on slavery), and the possibilities of proletarian industry (the labor pantomimes). Acquainted with Teotihuacán by design, and a modern community by location, the theatre and its performances created a link between past and present that validated the actions of the Revolution, its cultural policies, and its vision for the future of its citizens. The performances at the theatre were an analogue for Gamio's positioning of Teotihuacán as an allegory for the nation in which the glories of past indigenous cultures served as a model for their future. At the same time, this juxtaposition suggested that the "degeneracy" of current indigenous cultures stemmed from historical movements from the conquest forward that ignored the noble values of the Indian past.[12] The success of the project is revealed by the fact that the state, under the auspices of the Secretariat of Public Education, took over the site only a year later.[13]

Representing indigeneity as the root of contemporary Mexican culture was one of the main goals of these performances. Representation of indigenous cultures, much less contemporary indigenous people, was particular and limited. During the 1930s and 1940s performances that replicated or were inspired by these archeological performances either privileged the display of Aztec or Maya cultures (which had become examples *par excellence* of indigenous character and culture)[14] or a general "indigenous" culture that was constructed from the "best" qualities of numerous autonomous cultures. These performances were dependent upon contemporary actors temporarily embodying their indigenous ancestors and effectively inscribing a connection to a glorious past that was nonetheless gone, except in spirit. This methodology had two primary effects: it estranged the struggles of contemporary indigenous people from their pasts and it excluded the representation of many indigenous and local groups by privileging only Aztec and Mayan heritages. Interestingly, however, in as much as the creators of the Tlaxcalan history pageants felt they were working against the erasure of local identities that these nationalist spectacles had produced, the dramaturgy of the *Celebración de la Salida de los Cuatrocientos Familias* and the Cacaxtla-

Xochitecatl celebrations were largely dependent on nationalistic performances and their rhetoric. This dependence increased as the demands made by Neo-liberal economic policy increased the pressure on the local and regional elite to market their local cultures for financial gain. The intersection of these pressures with developments within the Tlaxcalan educational and historical communities formed the paradoxes inherent in both the use of the history of Cacaxtla in local history production and within state-sponsored performances.

Cacaxtla and the Archeology of Knowledge

Tlaxcalan identity has a very particular intersection with both local and national identities. Plainly, the historical indigenous Tlaxcaltecans (and modern Tlaxcaala residents) have a reputation in Mexico as traitors because they joined Cortés in battles against the glorious Aztecs. Thus, while the indigenous past worked to create a positive identity for the nation as a whole, for the Tlaxcaltecans, the indigenous past worked to alienate them from those same historical narratives. As a result, Tlaxcalan identity has often had an antagonistic relationship to Mexican identity within national narratives. Even when this myth is put aside, the relationship of indigenous identity to Tlaxcalan identity is complicated because the state's residents are largely *mestizo* and working class, indigenous identity thus playing a smaller role in contemporary Tlaxcala than in some other regions of the country. Nonetheless, Tlaxcaltecan identity is still a part of Tlaxcalan social fabric. As Luis Reyes explains:

> In Tlaxcala, there is no word to express ethnicity, which is interesting, but that does not mean that there is no consciousness of ethnic belonging (adscripción) or that there are no ethnic or racial distinctions. A concrete example is this pueblo, Tepeapulco. Here people use the Nahua language in everyday life, although there is no word to designate Indian and non–Indian. However, here no one accepts being called *indio* or *mestizo*. They only accept the word Tlaxcalteca (the name for the region, not the ethnic group). But people here use the word *indio* for peasants who sell their labor.[15]

Thus, in Tlaxcala, indigenous identity is often compounded with local, regional, and ultimately historical identity (hence the use of the derogatory word *indio* to describe "sellouts") in a way that diverges from more orthodox Mexican understandings of ethnicity.[16] Tlaxcala's historiographical and touristic disenfranchisement was a palpable reality despite educational efforts to rewrite Tlaxcalan history and revitalize cultural tourism. Cacaxtla's discovery promised not only to attract potential tourists, but also to rectify the errors of the Tlaxcalan indigenous past.

While colonial chronicles, such as Diego Muñoz Camargo's *Historia de Tlaxcala*, acknowledged its existence, both Cacaxtla's history and that of its inhabitants, the Olmeca-Xicalancas, were usually a footnote to Tlaxcalan history.[17] Tlaxcalan indigenous heritage was linked primarily to pre–Conquest Teochichimeca history. The only excavated archeological site in the state, Xicohtencatl's palace in Tizatlan, was dated at about 1350, and despite being dug in 1927 by Alfonso Caso himself, it was small, neglected, and under-funded. Cacaxtla, on the other hand, was a giant complex with impressive murals. Despite economic woes, Cacaxtla was opened to the public quickly. By 1986, officials covered its murals to prevent damage to its façades. Researchers from around the world wrote about the site. In addition to the systemization of technical data, investigators found Teotihuacáno, Olmec, and Mayan influences in the murals, which had rarely been associated with Tlaxcala. They interpreted this data to mean that Cacaxtla might have been a site where various groups met, but not that it was a site where the various groups became a unitary culture. Instead, most archeological explanations referred to Cacaxtla as a possible trading site, a popular stop for travelers moving from the coasts to the central basin, or a self-conscious use of imagery by its Olmeca-Xicalanca settlers to display their allegiances with other groups.[18] Despite the fact that most scholars analyzed the iconography in the murals with an index based on locating its particular indigenous origins, neither these scholars nor the Mexican government made large-scale claims about its findings, underscoring monolithic understandings of indigenous history. Cacaxtla was not placed in a national narrative as Teotihuacán had been. Its role as a site of national patrimony then depended on the fact that Cacaxtla's development and maintenance was controlled by the federally con-trolled INAH, but not on its inclusion into a cultural national narrative, designed primarily to promote national tourism.

Interestingly, however, while the 1970s and 1980s marked a period when nationalistic archeology and its dependence on tourism were under attack, in Tlaxcala, it was a period that saw a resurgence of interest in popular local and regional history. Under the administration of Governor Tulio Hernán-dez (1981–1986), textbooks written about Tlaxcalan history by local histo-rians were introduced for the first time.[19] Alongside the refurbishment of the colonial city center and the creation of a state hymn and motto, educational decentralization gave more opportunities to Tlaxcaltecans to know Tlax-calan history than ever before. After Hernández's governorship ended, schol-arly publications on Tlaxcalan history continued along this path, including those published about Cacaxtla. All of these scholarly products came to foment the use of Tlaxcala's historiography as a source of cultural tourism. The interdependency of these two trends aside, their combination changed the *loci* where archeological discoveries were transformed into historiography and cultural rhetoric. As the state's only substantial pre–Columbian archeological site, Cacaxtla was certain to become part of a system of commerce to the economically troubled state. How the site was positioned to achieve this goal was less straightforward, however, having involved both a discursive re-alignment of local history and identity and a re-conception of archeology within performance.

In 1992, soon after published scholarly sources about the site were available, Cacaxtla became a part of the *Salida de los Cuatrocientos Familias*— an historical re-enactment that celebrated the 1591 colonization of the Northern Borderlands by Tlaxcalan Christianized Indians since 1981. Authored by Desiderio Hernández Xochitiotzin and State Secretariat of Public Education functionary Jamie Flores, the pageant was meant to re-engage local history by critiquing the traitor myth and providing its audience with a synthetic history of the area long occluded by official state histories. Held at La Señora de las Nieves Church from where colonizers first left, this yearly event created linkages between past and present Tlaxcaltecans, encouraging local pride. This re-enactment expanded throughout the 1980s to include scenes from the history of Tlaxcala from before the Spanish Conquest to the 1591 event.[20] This festival centered on Tlaxcala City's history and on showcasing its archeological remains. The 1992 addition of information about Cacaxtla in the *Salida* signaled that it was ready to become part of an accepted popular narrative of Tlaxcalan history and that it was gaining equal footing with Tlaxcala City's colonial architecture as a potential tourist site.

Cacaxtla's representation in the *Salida* was centered on one of the murals in particular that featured a large battle, which was enacted by the performers within the representation. The program of the celebration now consisted of four parts: Cacaxtla, the foundation of the *cuatro señorios*, the encounter with the Spanish, and the 1591 exit.[21] This program change both showcased information about the archeological site, and generally expanded the amount of information about indigenous Tlaxacaltecans in the representation. In addition, historiographically, the incorporation of Cacaxtla into the performance altered the genealogy of Tlaxcalan identity by linking it not only to the Teochichimecas who had immigrated there in the twelfth century, but also to the Olmeca-Xicalancas, who inhabited the area from 600 to 900 C.E.. This innovation moved the "birthplace" of the Tlaxcaltecans from the land upon which the *cuatro señorios* were founded in Tlaxcala City to Cacaxtla. The script of the 1994 celebration, for example, claimed that "Cacaxtla was the place, in its environs, where our culture was born, there was the dawn;

there was where the stories of the times were tied together."[22] By extension, the Tlaxcaltecans' descent from this place "where our culture was born" entitled them to this glorious past, the script of the performance *presenting* their past once again by stating that the murals unite "yesterday with our own time."[23] The inclusion of the re-enactment of the events in the Cacaxtla murals into the celebration of the four hundred families, then, not only expanded the range of Tlaxcalan history presented there but, through the enactment of the murals, materialized the aforementioned imagining of the connection between past and present. The performance of the figures in the mural by the celebration's participants led them to embody this newly disseminated history, both creating and performing a new Tlaxcalan identity drawn from the histories of the Mayans, Olmecs, and Teotihuacános. The inclusion of the murals' Jaguar Man and Scorpion man into the *Salida* extended this identity project to include new religious cosmologies as well as a new history, making the mythical world of these groups their own as well.

Mirroring earlier representational practices in the development of the *Salida*, the transition between the Cacaxtla portion of the representation and the section that represented the founding of the four *señorios* that constituted Conquest-era Tlaxcala City naturalized this addition.[24] By occluding the evidence of historiographical revision that the information about Cacaxtla initiated, the performance made these events a part of a seamless narrative of Tlaxcalan history. By 1996, Xochitecatl, a ritual complex uncovered in 1994, containing three pyramids — the pyramid of the flowers, the pyramid of the serpent, and the spiral pyramid — was also a part of this history, providing more information about Tlaxcalan "roots."[25] Since the site was older than Cacaxtla (it was dated at 100–400 C.E.), its incorporation strengthened the *Salida*'s new narrative by creating an unbroken through line for Tlaxcalan identity and history from "prehistory" to the present. For example, the 1994 event began with an exaltation of the areas volcanoes — Itzacíhuatl, Popocatépetl, and Matlacueyetl — which existed at a time before "history was written" and ended with the present incarnations of the colonization over the course of the performance. The reconstruction of this narrative not only confirmed the existence of "Tlaxcalan" history from early in the Common Era to the present, but also indicated that the roots of this history were not dependent on Judeo-Christian or Western understandings of time or civilization.[26] Consequently, the sections devoted to Xochitecatl and Cacaxtla were renamed, called variously "moments that create the base of Tlaxcalan culture," "the roots," and "the foundations."[27] Ideologically, the emphasis on older indigenous civilizations rectified the "problem" with Tlaxcalan indigenous identity — that it had always been defined by complicity with the Spanish conquerors, and animosity against the Aztecs.

While the articulation of identity was profoundly local, the presentation's dramaturgy mimicked pageants that emerged from within the very totalizing archeological and historiographical narratives that its localness critiqued. A close look at the *Salida* reveals how its authors incorporated these pageants' performance methodologies even as they rejected the *grands récits* of Aztec — and Mayan — centered indigenous histories the pageants represented. Like the actors in early twentieth-century pageants, who enacted their Aztec ancestors so as to embody their noble nationalistic spirits in the modern world, the *Salida* actors embodied the figures in the Cacaxtla battle murals to the same end. Juxtaposed with the students' representation of themselves as colonial Tlaxcaltecans in the *Salida*, their participation in the mural battle made them descendants of the figures in the battle, without addressing the complicated relationship between the participants' historical and contemporary economic, social, and ethnic identities. As most of the indigenous people in Tlaxcala lived in the Eastern part of the state and did not attend or participate in the representation, the assumption of indigenous identity was usually by *mestizo* Tlaxcala City residents who had a complex and often distant relationship to the indigenous past. Since no connections were made between contemporary indigenous people and the groups that inhabited Cacaxtla, the combination of these factors performed an ideological obfuscation that served up a very simplified version of Tlaxcalan history, despite its placement in a local and, one might argue, resistant, historical narrative.

As these performances developed, the Cacaxtla role as a part of a continuous historical narrative diminished. Instead, the text of the Cacaxtla section began to re-inscribe the valorization of Aztec/Teotihucano, Mayan, and Olmec cultures ahistorically. The *Salida* stressed the importance of the features of these "major" indigenous cultures' incorporation into a singular Tlaxcalan indigenous consciousness, rather than underscoring these groups' role in specific local historical events.[28] Using scholarship that postulated Mayan, Olmec, and Teotihuacáno influences as indicative of historical political configurations, the *Salida*'s authors claimed instead that all of these cultures were the foundation of "Tlaxcalan" identity. The resulting homogenization reduced Cacaxtla to metaphorical status — even while situating it within a Tlaxcalan historical time line. By 1994, the *Salida* named Cacaxtla as a "point of confluence," where "the wisdom of the Maya," "the profundity of the Teotihuacáno," and "the strength of the Olmec" were mixed.[29] Going on, the presentation claimed it was "where the bird man, the jaguar man and the spider man speak to us of a world that will never return, but is present."[30] The combination of these discourses suggested the embodiment of the spirit of indigenous residents within the archeological site and its environs themselves. This choice precluded the possibility that today's indigenous residents have access to that spiritual power in their present as opposed to the past. The contemporary carriers of indigenous nobility are the ruins, not Tlaxcalan residents. The performance script, then, reproduces Gamio's "lost civilization" despite coming some 70 years later. This reproduction suggests the longevity of nationalistic rhetoric in performance even when used within the context of local history production.

Ultimately, the *Salida* reinforced the message that it was better to feature what was understandable as "indigenous" in the national sphere than to represent Cacaxtla's complexity in order to make it a worthy tourist site. While a certain amount of simplification is necessary in such a commercial venture, the absolute obfuscation of the scholarly conclusions used to create the *Salida* indicates that the presentation's authors fell back on a self-conscious use of *indigenist* discourse to meet their aims. The performance's positioning of the battle mural as evidence of a timeless struggle — "man against man, triumph and defeat, life and death, good and bad" — made claims for the universality of Cacaxtla and indigenous history more generally.[31] This rhetoric replicated early twentieth-century tactics that made Indian cultures examples *par excellence* of "universal" cosmic culture. Although far removed from the New Age ceremonies at Maya temples Quetzil Castañeda describes at Chichén Itza, the assumptions behind them are similar. Both maneuvers compromise the cultural and historical specificity of the indigenous cultural artifacts at hand to sell a generic form of indigenous cosmology and culture. The fact that these tactics were successful in Tlaxcala, a site where local historians and the populace in general were aware of the power that universalizing narratives had to manipulate and erase local histories, is curious. Ultimately, I believe, it points to the possibility that although universalizing national conquest and post-conquest narratives had been chipped away in the course of the Tlaxcalan local history movement, the narrative of universal indigenous history as the base of Mexican culture was both harder and less convenient to revise, re-write, or even reconsider, especially within a local tourism industry.

On a more material level, the visual representation of the Cacaxtla murals within the *Salida* exemplified the emergent touristic value of placing the murals within the performance. It was not only because it was the most active "scene" from either of the existing murals, but also because it was simply the most visually impressive and best restored part of the murals. The enactment of the mural at La Señora de las Nieves Church, near Tlaxcala City, a location far enough away to contain potential tourists who may not have ventured to see the murals previously, attests to this aim.[32] As such, the Cacaxtla portion of the performance evoked indigenous culture as much as it authenticated or re-wrote local history. The question of historical narrative within these performances is not a small one. In fact, it is the relationship of the performances to historical narrative that marks the transformation of the use of archeological ruins within theatrical representation. The staging of the murals in costumes against a painted backdrop contrasted, then, with the *Salida's* use of La Señora de las Nieves church. Since the church was neither a tourist destination nor an active place of worship, largely because of its state of disrepair, unlike the murals, its significance was drawn entirely from its placement within a Tlaxcalan historical narrative.[33] The importance of the Cacaxtla portion of the *Salida* increased over the years of Jose Antonio Álvarez Lima's term (1993–1999). When performances move to the actual Cacaxtla-Xochitecatl site, the need for historical narrative disappears. While this shift certainly has a very simple relationship to Cacaxtla-Xochitecatl's physical presence, it also serves to mark the salability of nationalistic *indigenista* tropes, and their accompanying dramaturgy, whose relationship to historical narrative is distant, if not entirely absent.

Performances and Anniversary Celebrations at Cacaxtla-Xochitecatl

Events related to the anniversary of the discovery of Cacaxtla occurred throughout the 1980s. These events were usually planned in September, around the time of the discovery of the murals. They typically featured academic conferences about the site and the publication of these studies in book and pamphlet forms. These conferences served not only to disseminate information, but also to advocate future funding for excavations at Cacaxtla-Xochitecatl. By 1990, however, these conferences were more explicitly designed as commemorations. The celebration that year was a weeklong program that included the exhibition of painting introduced by Desiderio Hernández Xochitiotzin and dance performances by the group Ometcotl Calpulli.[34] The publicity around this celebration was not only to bring attention to the site at this time, but to advertise a larger conference planned for the 500-year celebration in 1992 of Columbus' arrival, which would feature art historians from around the globe.[35] In 1994, officials added a half-marathon and a performance of the Cacaxtla murals to the commemorative celebration.[36] This performance was very similar to the one presented within the *Salida* and occurred in front of a reproduction of the murals. The following year, the program did not include this re-enactment, although indigenous dances were performed at the base of the archeological site.[37] By 1997, however, a larger scale performance that featured a 700-person cast celebrating the ceremony of the New Flame, occurred on the site itself, coinciding with the first exhibition of the Xochitecatl.[38] Governor Jose Antonio Álvarez Lima (1993–1999) initiated new investments in Cacaxtla, largely because of the excavation of Xochitecatl, a ritual center just steps away from Cacaxtla. Combined with the interests of his wife, Veronica Rascón de Lima who functioned as an arts patron within the state, Lima's investment in Cacaxtla-Xochitecatl increased the site's role within state-sponsored performances.

The Cacaxtla-Xochitecatl anniversary celebrations' evolution indicates a growing investment in cultural performance there, but also a particular development in the events' content and form. In the beginning, these anniversary celebrations were concerned primarily with disseminating historical information about the site. As time went on, the celebrations incorporated more evocative and spectacular presentations. They also worked more closely to the site. The dance performances at the base of the pyramid, while unrelated to the history of Cacaxtla-Xochitecatl, used the performance to highlight the importance and grandeur of its environs. Together with the half-marathon, the dance presentations marked Cacaxtla Xochitecatl as a part of the Tlaxcalan historical landscape. Marathons and half marathons were often used to authorize spaces by drawing attention to them by traversing them, by bringing spectators along to authorize the site. Dance performances functioned similarly, often as auxiliary activities for many state-supported historical and civic celebrations that were used to foment cultural unity and pride. Placing the Cacaxtla-Xochitecatl performances within the frame of celebratory orthodoxy that the *Salida* came to embody effectively placed Cacaxtla on the map, literally and figuratively. Interestingly, however, what all of these celebrations shared was a disconnection between the academic conferences about Cacaxtla and the performances there. This "gulf" between these parts of the celebrations became greater over the years, pointing to a movement away from using the performances as a direct means of information dissemination toward using them to glorify the beauty of the archeological ruins themselves. Rather than analyzing the diachronic trajectory of these celebrations, however, I will analyze the process of producing the 1997 New Flame Ceremony to explore this development, and to suggest the implications these changes have for the relationship between archeology and performance as a whole.

The 1997 Cacaxtla-Xochitecatl commemoration celebrated not only the nineteenth anniversary of the discovery of Cacaxtla, but the third anniversary of the Xochitecatl's excavation. The latter settlement was an impressive site, on par with many others in the nation that attracted substantial amounts of tourism. The November 1997 celebration, sponsored by SEP, INAH, and the Secretary of Tourism set out to make this fact known to the public at large. Its organizers used the coincidence of the anniversary of Cacaxtla's discovery and St. Miguel's saint day and the site's physical proximity of the annual pilgrimage to St. Miguel de Milagro to create a larger audience for their own celebration.[39] Although there were many events associated with the anniversary, the centerpiece of the performance was the closing ceremony for the month's events: the Ceremony of the New Flame.

The spectacle staged at the Cacaxtla-Xochitecatl site was similar to the *Salida*. This is not surprising considering Xochitiotzin and Jamie Flores were also its authors. The narrative of the performance centered on the Ceremony of the New Flame, a ritual associated with the Aztec calendar. As it is generally understood, the event occurred when an alignment in the calendar made the five extra days of an Aztec year occur at the end of a 52 year cycle (somewhat equivalent to a century's end in the Gregorian calendar). It is generally acknowledged, from information contained in various codices, that the aforementioned calendar position coincides with a particular placement of the Pleiades constellation in the sky. To its observers this alignment indicated a time when the sun and the earth were vulnerable to destruction. To prevent this occurrence, all fires, private and public, were extinguished until the period passed. After this period was over, flames would be relit. This action was "the Ceremony of the New Flame."[40] The Ceremony of the New Flame is usually associated with Nahua and Aztec people, having been found in the Bourbon codex, although it could also be linked to various central Mexican groups. In recent years, it has also been attributed to a specific site, Xochicalco, where a stone was found that described the ceremony.[41] The last recorded celebration of the New Flame by indigenous groups is estimated at about 1507 C.E..[42] In recent years, however, this ceremony has been re-staged for various purposes, without regard for calendar or astronomy, drawing its significance from its "celebratoriness" in itself. The New Flame Ceremony was used as part of events as divergent as Easter mass and the Pan-American games. The ubiquity of this ritual performance outside of Tlaxcala speaks to its use in Tlaxcala, specifically at the Cacaxtla-Xochitecatl site. Although it is not impossible that the ceremony could have occurred there, there is no evidence that it did. This celebration then focused instead on making the site "indigenous" by association with the widely recognizable Ceremony of the New Flame, rather than providing evidence that the Ceremony of the New Flame had a particular relationship to Tlaxcala-Xochitecatl itself. At the same time, the celebration also lent itself to another project: the showcasing of the Cacaxtla-Xochitecatl in itself. The Ceremony of the New Flame, because of its dependence on dramatic lighting changes, worked to illuminate the space itself. The celebration reveals the interdependence of these operations.

The ceremony began with the illumination of the space with lamplight and the establishment of the pyramids of Xochitecatl as holy places, a site where indigenous rituals were enacted.[43] Shortly thereafter, the lights were extinguished and a prayer-like evocation was addressed to the site. Then a group of female dancers were sent to the spiral pyramid in order to dance around the sacred flame, which was soon lit. After the flame was lit atop the spiral pyramid, it was carried to the ground level. Once the dance was over, the torch was taken up to the Pyramid of Flowers accompanied by music. The performance continued with a longer paean to the area without music, a dance to Xochitecatl, the illumination of both pyramids with fluorescent lights, and a patriotic speech which linked the battle in the mural to the brave nature of the people, underscored with indigenous instrumentation.[44] The ceremony concluded with another blackout.

As suggested by this brief narration, the actions in this performance served mostly to show off the archeological features of the site. The different forms of lighting and traversal of the pyramids by the actors underscored the site's size and its excellent preservation. In addition, the action of carrying the torch from one pyramid to another narrated the space connecting its different parts and making it into a coherent site that could be consumed as a singular object. The placement of this light show within another performance, the Ceremony of the New Flame, framed the extinguishing and re-lighting of the space as an indigenous narrative, performing a double evocation of past and present grandeur; this operation "sanctified" the actions of the event, obfuscating the very material economic purposes behind it, that is, showing of the archeological site so that it would become a tourism site.[45] Thus, the relevance of the New Flame to Tlaxcalan history was subsumed by its function as a performance that alluded to an indigenous past and, more practically, to the illumination of the archeological site itself, which had not been lit previously.

Within the context of the performance, Xochitiotzin's script, despite its historiographic agendas, also worked toward this goal. His attempt to link Cacaxtla-Xochitecatl to astronomical re-alignments connected to the New Flame Ceremony in early drafts of the script were eliminated in the final one.[46] In contrast with the *Salida*, then, this performance concentrated less on re-writing local history or disseminating aspects of it that could be linked to traits of other Mesoamerican cultures than on making Xochitecatl-Cacaxtla a site of cultural patrimony by the fact of re-enacting a "recognizable" indigenous ritual there. At this time, it was the juxtaposition of the performance of the New Flame Ceremony and the exhibition of the site that made Cacaxtla comprehensible as important to Mesoamerican culture, and thus worth viewing and investing in. The use of the Ceremony of the New

Flame became a validating, if not authenticating, gesture in itself. More plainly, the ceremony performed there gave the archeological site meaning through its existence *alone*. Thus, the archeological ruins in Tlaxcala changed their purpose in the 1997 ceremony. They were used neither as historical evidence upon which a narrative was based nor as a representation of Tlaxcala's articulation of Mexican identity. Instead, they played the lead role, the subject of the performance itself, with Cacaxtla-Xochitecatl's relevance to history or identity serving only as background noise. Performance follows suit, gaining relevance from the very act of being juxtaposed with archeology, instead of from the chronological interrogations or representational assertions it makes. Historical narration, then, has been replaced by juxtaposition, Xochitiotzin's efforts non-withstanding.

Today, celebrations of the excavation of Cacaxtla-Xochitecatl continue. Scholarly conferences around the events are usually a part of the program. Nevertheless, the 2000 script of the Cacaxtla-Xochitecatl anniversary celebration shows that these performances have continued to move away from historical specificity and toward pure display. While the 2000 celebration did place the development of Xochitecatl on a timeline, information about the presence of different cultures at Cacaxtla — namely the Mixteca, Chochoppopoloca, and the Nahuatl — represented the harmoniousness of men, their cultures, and their gods.[47] The juxtaposition of this text with projections of the archeological ruins brings the point home. The presence of artifacts used for ceremonies of water and fertility gods was also used to link the Tlaxcaltecans to well-recognized indigenous gods. Evoking Cacaxtla's subtitle as "the place where the rain dies," the script transitioned to the Ceremony of the New Flame. After this dance extravaganza and light show, the celebration ended with a paean to the *communitas* created by the ceremony, followed by the acknowledgement of state officials and the grandeur of Cacaxtla-Xochitecatl.[48] The 1997 and 2000 Cacaxtla celebrations, like the *Salida*, depended on the dramaturgy of nationalist performances. Their structures recalled the Aztec spectacles of the 1930s and 1940s, whose grandeur came from the staging of exotic rituals, such as symbolic sacrifices in large-scale productions.[49] The sheer mass of bodies was an important part of the performance, because it created a spectacle that displayed, rather than explained, indigenous cultures. The Cacaxtla celebrations replicated these 1930s and 1940s performances, both in their emphasis on spectacle and in their *indigenista* subject matter and rhetoric. Considering the growing emphasis on archeological site tourism in both periods, this parallel is not surprising.

Despite substantial investment on the part of the celebration's organizers, since Governor Lima left office, finances have sometimes curtailed the staging of the Ceremony of the New Flame, the elaborate 2000 celebration being the exception rather than the rule. A celebration planned for 2001 was scaled back;[50] the 2003 *Salida* cut the section on Cacaxtla entirely. Although the latter development was instituted largely out of concern for the *Salida's* performance time, the fact that Cacaxtla's role in representation was not viewed as efficacious enough to insure its inclusion indicates a change. Whether these changes occurred despite or because of a stagnating local cultural tourism industry is difficult to determine. It is equally difficult to decide whether or not the lag in tourism at the ruins themselves is the result of Cacaxtla's lack of a place within a nationalistic cultural narrative or is simply a subsidiary effect of global economics. What *is* certain is that today, tourism at Cacaxtla-Xochitecatl is still largely regional. Tourist buses only run to the city from Central Tlaxcala City once a week; buses from Puebla and Mexico City are infrequent. Control of the archeological site is also in turmoil, and funding for it is inconsistent: the state's financial problems have often curtailed general maintenance of the sites themselves.[51] This may be a national problem as much as it is a regional one. Recent studies indicate that almost half of INAH-protected sites are not adequately maintained.[52] There seems to be little possibility that this situation will change in the near future.

In the long term, what we learn from performances about and at Cacaxtla-Xochitecatl is that their use of archeology has developed in such a way that they work primarily by re-articulating national indigenous *grands récits* at the local level, despite their emergence as part of a local history movement whose purpose was to challenges those very narratives. Ironically, this trajectory points to the fact that the assumptions behind nationalistic archeological practices, criticized so bitterly from 1968 to the present, are still a large part of Mexico's rhetorical baggage even as these practices have been modified. Neither the reformulation of the anthropological project, Mexican cultural nationalism, nor the structural demise of the central nation state, then, has eliminated the efficacy of nationalistic dramaturgies of identity. The emphasis on the reification and dissemination of the tropes of nationalist cultural identity for consumerist rather than nationalist use points to the fact that their effectiveness remains despite their distance from a role in manufacturing consent with the Mexican government. If nothing else, the longevity of these tropes, despite their distance from their originating national projects, demonstrates that the very structures within which it was possible to articulate alternate identities not only allowed for but would ultimately be made dependent on nationalist dramaturgies in order to be made comprehensible.

Materially, the economic crises of recent years have only exacerbated these problems. In the lacunae created from the collapse of many centralized structures, local and regional actors, particularly those participating in tourism, have had to recreate nationalist ideologies to compete within the context of hemispheric neoliberal capitalism. In this respect, performative re-constructions of national culture, at least in Mexico, may have a more bright and varied future than its creators ever imagined, despite the rather modest goals they end up achieving.

Notes

1. "Pavimientan el Camino a la Zona Arqueológia," *El Sol de Tlaxcala*, (Tlaxcala) 3 September 1977: 1, "Fructífera Visita del Presidente JLP," *El Sol de Tlaxcala* (Tlaxcala) 10 September 1978: 1+. The history of tourism in Tlaxcala can be traced in state bulletins from 1978 to the present including Beatriz Paredes Rangel, *Government Informe 1989* (Mexico: Gobierno de Tlaxcala, 1989) 48–55, Tulio Hernández Gomez, *Gov. Informe de 1983* (Mexico: Gobierno de Tlaxcala, 1983), Hernández Gomez, *Gov. Informe de 1984* (Mexico: Gobierno de Tlaxcala, 1984), Hernández Gomez, *Gov. Informe de 1985* (Mexico: Gobierno de Tlaxcala, 1985) 37–38, Hernández Gomez, *Gov. Informe de 1986* (Mexico: Gobierno de Tlaxcala, 1986) 152–156, Emilio Sanchez Piedras, *Informe Municipio 1977–1979* (Mexico: Gobierno de Tlaxcala, 1980) 12–23, José Álvarez Lima, *Primer Informe de Gobierno 1993* (Mexico: Gobierno de Tlaxc ala, 1994) 31–32, 63–65, Paredes Rangel, *Plan Estatal de Desarolo, Raíz y Compromiso 1987–1993* (Mexico: Gobierno de Tlaxcala, 1993) 54–55, 135–146, and Álvarez Lima, *Plan Estatal de Desarollo, Gob del Estado de Tlax 1993–1999* (Mexico: Gobierno de Tlaxcala 1999) 68–71, 93–98.

2. Briefly speaking, the petropolitics in the 1970s and early 1980s and the collapse of the peso in 1982 fomented a feeling of distrust in the national government, and the dissemination of discourse suggested that the values of the Mexican Revolution were no longer driving governmental policy, and that the country was now under the rule of a few technocrats and oil barons. Combined with the end of ISI and the disempowerment of state supported institutions as the bedrock of nationally articulated modernity, many Mexican thinkers declared a crisis in revolutionary nationalism, including Roger Bartra and Claudio Lomnitz, amongst many others. While these men have different views on the causes and effects of this collapse, they all claim that this period was one of "crisis" even when national rhetoric and discourse still relied on slogans from the nationalist period (1940–1982). These analyses are contained in Michael C. Meyer and William Sherman, *The Course of Mexican History* (Oxford: Oxford University Press, 1987) 677–691, Ramón Eduardo Ruíz, *The Great Rebellion: Mexico, 1905–1924* (New York: W.W. Norton, 1980), Roger Bartra, *The Cage of Melancholy: Identity and Metamorphosis in the Mexican Character*, trans. Christopher J. Hall (New Brunswick: Rutgers University Press, 1992), Bartra, "Missing Democracy," *Blood, Ink and Culture: Miseries and Splendors of the Post Mexican Condition* (Durham, NC, and London: Duke University Press, 2002) 65–77, Bartra, "The Political Crisis of 1982," *Blood, Ink and Culture* 78–89, Bartra, " The Crisis of Nationalism" *Blood, Ink and Culture* 104–132, and Claudio Lomnitz, "Fissures in Contemporary Mexican Nationalism," *Deep Mexico, Silent Mexico* (Minneapolis: University of Minnesota Press, 2001) 110–122.

3. These works include Garcia Cook, Angel, Beatriz Carrión, and Lorena

Mirambell, eds., *Antología de Cacaxtla*, 1st ed., 2 vols. (D.F.: INAH, 1995), Marta Foncerrada de Molina, ed., *Cacaxtla: La Iconografía de los Olmeca-Xicalanca* (México: Universidad Nacional Autónoma de México, Instituto de Investigaciones Estéticas, 1993), Sonia Lombardo Ruíz et al., *Cacaxtla: El Lugar Donde Muerte la Lluvia en la Tierra* (México: Gobierno del Estado de Tlaxcala, Instituto Nacional de Antropología e Historia, Instituto Tlaxcalteca de Cultura, Consejo Estatal de Cultura Tlaxcala, 1991), and *Cacaxtla: Proyecto de Investigación y Conservación* (Tlaxcala: Consejo Nacional para la Cultura y las Artes, Instituto Nacional de Antropología e Historia, Centro Regional Tlaxcala: Gobierno del Estado de Tlaxcala, Consejo Estatal de Cultura Tlaxcala, 1990).

4. Thomas Patterson, "Archeology, History, Indigenismo, and the State in Peru and Mexico," Peter R. Schmidt and Thomas Patterson, eds., *Making Alternative Histories: the Practice of Archeology and History in Non-Western Settings* (Santa Fe, NM: School of American Reasearch, 1995) 77. This essay also provides the summary of the history of archeology in Mexico. A more thorough critical engagement of Gamio's work, to which I am greatly indebted is found in Claudio Lomnitz, "Bordering on Anthropology: Dialectics of a National Tradition," *Deep Mexico, Silent Mexico: An Anthropology of Nationalism* (Minneapolis: University of Minnesota Press, 2001) 228–262. A thorough history of the development of anthropology in Mexico is contained in Carlos García Mora's fourteen-volume set, *La antropología en Mexico: Panorama histórico* (Mexico: INAH, 1988). Other synthetic histories include Julio César Olivé Negrete and Augusto Urteaga Castro-Pozo, *INAH: Una Historia* (Mexico: INAH, 1988) and Ignacio Bernál, *A History of Mexican Archeology* (London: Thames and Hudson, 1980).

5. Extended studies on post-1968 critiques, the resulting methodologies used by Mexican archeologists, and the changes in their social roles can be found in Claudio Lomnitz, "Descubrimiento y desilusíon de la antropología mexicana," Claudio Lomnitz, *Modernidad Indiana: Nueve ensayos sobre nación y mediación en Mexico* (Mexico: Planeta, 1999) 79–98, José Luis Lorenzo, *La Arqeología y Mexico* (Mexico: INAH, 1998), and Andres Medina, *Recuentos y Figuraciones: Ensayos de Antropología Mexicana* (Mexico: UNAM, 1996), including a critique of the fourteen-volume set mentioned above.

6. Strictly speaking, the definition of *indigenista* (indigenist) archeology is the study of indigenous cultures. In reality, this type of research works to make indigenous cultures into something "other" either for the purpose of subsuming these cultures into Mexican culture as a whole — effectively preserving cultures in order to eliminate them — or setting them apart for tourist consumption. Critics of these projects suggested that anthropologists and archeologists concentrate on how their finding furthered understandings of political and economic systems in which indigenous people participate in so as to better their economic conditions in the country, rather than justifying their poverty through "cultural idiosyncrasies." The foundations of indigenista archeology are found in Manuel Gamio's *Forjando Patria: Pro Nacionalismo* (Mexico: Porrúa, 1916). Modern analysis is contained in works mentioned in the notes above.

7. "La politica educativa del sexenio 76–82 impulsó la decentralización educativa," *Sintesis Tlaxcala* (24 Jun 2003) Universitarios 5. Gutíerrez 93, explains the implementation of the State offices of the Secretariat of Public Education.

8. Quetzil E. Castañeda, *In the Museum of Maya Culture: Touring Chichén Itza* (Minneapolis: University of Minnesota Press, 1996).

9. Nancy Ruyter, "Ancient Images: The Pre-Cortésian in 20th Century Dance Performance," *Gestos 21* (April 1996): 145–155.

10. Rudolfo Usigli, *Mexico in the Theatre*, trans. and Intr. Wilder P. Scott (University of Mississippi Press, Romance Monographs, 1976) 124 and Adam Versényi, *Theatre in Latin America: Religion, Politics, and Culture from Cortés to the 1980s* (Cambridge University Press, 1993) 99.

11. A picture of this theatre is in Usigli, between pages 128 and 129.

12. Lomnitz, *Deep Mexico, Silent Mexico* 250.

13. Versényi 99. Although the site, as constructed by Rafael Saavedra, was approved by the Secretary of Agriculture and Economic Development, it was not formally taken over by the state until a year later.

14. The dominance of Aztec culture as a source of national glorification is duly noted by Guillermo Bonfil Batalla, *Mexico Profundo* (Austin: University of Texas Press 1996) 113. He also mentions the use of Maya and Aztec motifs in architectural design to create indigenity, mirroring the use of the features of the theatre at San Juan Teotihuacán. This movement met its heyday in the period between 1920 and 1940, fetures associated with Aztec classical culture finding their way into various national symbols such as the Mexican flag. Even after this period, the Aztec dominates the national imagination. For example, the renowned National Anthropology Museum, despite its desire to include artifacts of the various indigenous groups from each part of Mexico, still "centralizes" Aztecs through its architecture, by placing the exhibit of the Aztecs in a central and elevated location in the museum. For more on this see Nestor Garcia Canclini, "The Future of the Past," *Hybrid Cultures* (Minneapolis: University of Minnesota Press, 1995).

15. Qtd. in Natividád Gutíerrez, *Nationalist Myths and Ethnic Identities: Indigenous Intellectuals and the Mexican State* (Lincoln: University of Nebraska Press, 1999) 52. I have kept the author's quotation of Reyes' use of the word "ethnic" here, although I have chosen to use "indigenous group identity" in an attempt to translate the word *etnica*, because "ethnic" has a different history and usage in the U.S. than in Mexico.

16. The use of the term *indio* as a derogatory term has a complicated history in the 20th century. The issue is too large to handle here in detail, but usually it is used to designate "cultural inferiority" of the named groups. Thus, it is not an ethnic distinction. A more thorough treatment of this issue is found in Judith Friendlander, *Being Indian in Hueyapan: A Study of Forced Identity in Contemporary Mexico* (New York: St. Martin's Press, 1975) 71–100.

17. Román Piña Chan, *Cacaxtla: Fuentes Historicas y Pinturas* (Mexico: Fondo de Cultura Económica, 1998) lists all historical sources that mention Cacaxtla or the Olmeca-Xicalanca settlements in Tlaxcala.

18. The last contention is explored in depth by Debora Nagao in "Proclamación pública en el arte de Cacaxtla y Xochicalco," *Antología de Cacaxtla*, first ed., vol. 2 (D.F.: INAH, 1995) 270–330.

19. Desiderio Hernández Xochitiotzin. Personal interview on 17 July 2003.

20. I discuss this pageant at length in "Re-imagining Identity and Re-centering History in Tlaxcalan Performance," *Theatre Journal* 55.4 (December 2003): 633–655.

21. Program, *La gran jornada Tlaxcalteca del Siglo XVI 1992*, Personal Collection Desiderio Hernández Xochitiotzin, Tlaxcala, Mexico.

22. Secretary of Public Education, "Guia de Jornada Tlaxcalteca del Siglo XVI 1994," Collection of SEP Tlaxcala, Tlaxcala, Mexico, 2.

23. SEP, " Guia de Jornada Tlaxcalteca del Siglo XVI 1994" 2.

24. The separation of the scenes was bridged by a dance, which, by default, displayed indigenous Tlaxcalan culture by creating a narrative rather than a disjuncture between the two events.

25. Program, *Salida de los 400 familias 1996*, Personal Collection Desiderio Hernández Xochitiotzin, Tlaxcala, Mexico.

26. SEP, "Guia de Jornada Tlaxcalteca del Siglo XVI 1994" 1.

27. As found in the programs and scripts for the *Salida* in 1994, 1996, and 1998 respectively.

28. By major traditions, I mean the Toltecs, Teotihucano, Maya, Aztecs, and Olmecs. All but the last were associated primarily with monumental architecture, and thus were accorded the status of important civilization, as archeological grandeur came to signal the existence of "great civilizations." As Batalla explains, the Olmecs came to be considered, for lack of a better term, an Ur-race, as they began to create sedentary town settlements as early as 2300 B.C.E., thus being designated progenitor of all of the other great civilizations.

29. Secretary of Public Education, "Guia de 1994" 2.

30. Secretary of Public Education, "Guia de 1994" 3.

31. Secretary of Public Education, "Guia de 1994" 3.

32. Descriptions of the scenery and photos of it are found in newspaper articles of the event from 1992 to the present, Fotos, *Salida* 1992, *El Sol de Tlaxcala* (8 July 1992):1A. "La Gran Jornada del Siglo XVI," *El Sol de Tlaxcala* (Tlaxcala, Mexico) (3 July 1993): 4A+, Angelica Terova Tepatzi, "En Escena La Gran Jornada Tlaxcalteca del S. XVI, Colonizadora del Norte de Páis," *El Sol de Tlaxcala* (Tlaxcala, Mexico) (8 July 1996): 1C+, and Foto, *La Salida*, 1998, *El Sol de Tlaxcala* (Tlaxcala, Mexico) (5 de July 1998): 1A.

33. The Church is sufficiently damaged so it is never used for worship. Despite its "significance," it is not a part of any historical tour that I am aware of, or protected by any governmental preservation group. Most of the year the site is abandoned.

34. "Nuevos Hallazgos en la Zona de Cacaxtla," *El Sol de Tlaxcala* (Tlaxcala, Mexico) (7 September 1990): 1A+.

35. Adriana Díaz Manrique, "Evento Universal con Historiadores de Arte," *El Sol de Tlaxcala* (Tlaxcala, Mexico) (14 September 1990): 1+.

36. "XIX Aniversario del Descubrimiento de Cacaxtla: Cacaxtla, Magica y Cultura," *El Sol de Tlaxcala* (Tlaxcala, Mexico) (15 September 1994): A1+.

37. "Invitación a Colaborar en los festejos de Cacaxtla," *El Sol de Tlaxcala* (Tlaxcala, Mexico) (5 September 1995):2A, Constanza A. Guarneros, "Emotivo Festival Socio Cultural en Cacaxtla" *El Sol de Tlaxcala* (Tlaxcala, Mexico) (11 September 1995): C1.

38. "Hoy, Luces y Musica en Cacaxtla-Xochitecatl," *El Sol de Tlaxcala* (Tlaxcala, Mexico) (8 November1997): D1.

39. The celebration was carefully timed. As the San Miguel festival was a reterritorialization of the indigenous festivities in the area anyway, the institution of a ceremony that honored the site, which inspired these non–Christian rituals, rematerialized the indigenous history of the area, which served its organizers' desire to bring attention to the site itself. Although the event was not framed as entirely touristic, a perusal of SEP, *Anteproyecto de los eventos para conmemorar el 22 Aniversario del Descubrimiento de la Zona Arq. de Cacaxtla y el 3 de Xochitecatl* (Mexico:

Collection SEP, 1997) suggests how carefully orchestrated the event was to coincide with other cultural events that brought tourists to Tlaxcala. The objectives of the event were related as both "cultural" and "recreational."

40. Descriptions of this ceremony are contained in Mark J. Dworkin, *Mayas Aztecs and Incas* (Toronto: McClelland and Stewart, 1990) 85–86, Meyer and Sherman, *The Course of Mexican History* 70–71, Carlos Saenz, *El Fuego Nuevo* (Mexico: INAH, 1967), and Robert Townsend, *The Aztecs* (London: Thames and Hudson, 1992) 130–132.

41. This is the subject of Saenz's work, particularly 11–15, 28–35.

42. Saenz 19.

43. Secretary of Public Education, "Guión del Espectaculo de nocturno de Luz y sonido en la zona arqueologica de Xochitecatl 1997" (Collection SEPE Tlaxcala, Tlaxcala, Mexico) 2–3. The script for the event talks about feminine rituals because of the popular association of the site with a water goddess. Xochitiotzin's narration also plays on Christian forms, as his speech to Xochitecatl has the form of a Christian prayer.

44. SEP, "Guión del Espectaculo de 1997" 5. Although it could be assumed he is talking about the Tlaxcaltecans, considering the paragraph that follows, the language, I believe, is purposefully vague.

45. Certainly, this process echoes the procedures described by Bourdieu as belonging to the creation of symbolic capital. Nevertheless, I shy away from using Bourdieu directly because of some of the incompatibilities between the colonial and governmental systems his work is based on and those enacted by the Mexican government.

46. Historical information which attempts to connect the New Flame Ceremony to Tlaxcala historiographically is found in both SEP, *Anteproyecto de los eventos para conmemorar el 22 Aniversario del Descubrimiento de la Zona Arq. de Cacaxtla y el 3 de Xochitecatl* and a typescript copy of information about Cacaxtla-Xochitecatl authored by Desiderio Hernández Xochitiotzin (Mexico: Collection SEP, updated), which I discovered in the agency's file on the event. The *Anteproyecto*, probably written by Flores, among others, quotes Xochitiotzin alongside other investigations. Despite the research in these files that links the site very specifically to the event, however tenuously, they were absent from the script and event as I have been able to recover it.

47. Secretaria de Educación Publica del Estado, Tlaxcala, Guión del evento Cacaxtla con Motivo del XXV Aniversario de su Descubrimiento (Mexico: SEP, 2000) 6.

48. SEP Tlaxcala, Guión del XXV Aniversario de su Descubrimiento 6.

49. An example *par excellence* of this type of performance was *Sacrificio Gladitorio*, a play about Aztec sacrifice that was combined with an "exhibition of Aztec culture" that included 3000 participants. Here, ethnographic display replaced classical indigenous design features, but worked to the same end: establishing a connection between past indigenous cultures and the present. In addition, mass participation in the event suggested that the embodiment of Aztec identity was possible for a wide array of Mexicans, not limited to the spectacle's participants. This form of embodiment of indigenous identity became a major feature of many later *teatro de masas* productions. These performances are described in Versényi 101.

50. "Sin celebraciones el aniversario de Cacaxtla, mejor propondremos un plan de trabajo: Sabino Yano," *El Sol de Tlaxcala* (Tlaxcala, Mexico) (14 August 2001): D1+.

51. "No alcanza el dinero para adquirir predios de zonas arquelógicas: INAH," *El Sol de Tlaxcala* (Tlaxcala, Mexico) (22 April 2002): D1+.
52. "Sin celebraciones" D1+.

Works Cited

"XIX Aniversario del Descubrimiento de Cacaxtla: Cacaxtla, Magica y Cultura." *El Sol de Tlaxcala* (Tlaxcala, Mexico) 15 September 1994: A1+.
Álvarez Lima, Jose. *Plan Estatal de Desarollo, Gobeirno del Estado de Tlax 1993–1999.* Mexico: Gobierno de Tlaxcala, 1999.
_____. *Primer Informe de Gobierno 1993.* Mexico: Gobierno de Tlaxcala, 1994.
Bartra, Roger. *Blood, Ink and Culture: Miseries and Splendors of the Post Mexican Condition.* Durham, North Carolina, and London: Duke University Press, 2002.
_____. *The Cage of Melancholy: Identity and Metamorphosis in the Mexican Character.* Trans. Christopher J. Hall. New Brunswick: Rutgers University Press, 1992.
Bernál, Ignacio. *A History of Mexican Archeology.* London: Thames and Hudson, 1980.
Bonfil Batalla, Guillermo. *Mexico Profundo.* Austin: University of Texas Press, 1996.
Cacaxtla: Proyecto de Investigación y Conservación. Tlaxcala, Mexico: Consejo Nacional para la Cultura y las Artes, Instituto Nacional de Antropología e Historia, Centro Regional Tlaxcala: Gobierno del Estado de Tlaxcala, Consejo Estatal de Cultura Tlaxcala, 1990.
Castañeda, Quetzil E. *In the Museum of Maya Culture: Touring Chichén Itza.* Minneapolis: University of Minnesota Press, 1996.
Diaz Manrique, Adriana. "Evento Universal con Historiadores de Arte." *El Sol de Tlaxcala* (Tlaxcala, Mexico) 14 September 1990: 1+.
Dworkin, Mark J. *Mayas Aztecs and Incas.* Toronto: McClelland and Stewart, 1990.
Marta Foncerrada de Molina, ed. *Cacaxtla: La Iconografía de los Olmeca-Xicalanca.* México: Universidad Nacional Autónoma de México, Instituto de Investigaciones Estéticas, 1993.
Friedlander, Judith. *Being Indian in Hueyapan: A Study of Forced Identity in Contemporary Mexico.* New York: St. Martin's Press, 1975.
"Fructífera Visita del Presidente JLP." *El Sol de Tlaxcala* (Tlaxcala) 10 September 1978: 1+.
Gamio, Manuel. *Forjando Patria: Pro Nacionalismo.* Mexico: Porrúa, 1916.
Garcia Canclini, Nestor. *Hybrid Cultures.* Minneapolis: University of Minnesota Press, 1995.
Garcia Cook, Angel, Beatriz Carrión, and Lorena Mirambell, eds. *Antología de Cacaxtla,* first ed. 2 vols. Mexico City: INAH, 1995.
García Mora, Carlos. *La antropología en Mexico: Panorama histórico.* 14 vols. Mexico City: INAH, 1988.
"La Gran Jornada del Siglo XVI." *El Sol de Tlaxcala* (Tlaxcala, Mexico) 13 July 1993:4A+.
La gran jornada Tlaxcalteca del Siglo XVI 1992. Program. Personal Collection of Desiderio Hernández Xochitiotzin, Tlaxcala, Mexico.
La gran jornada Tlaxcalteca del Siglo XVI 1994. Program. Personal Collection of Desiderio Hernández Xochitiotzin, Tlaxcala, Mexico.

La gran jornada Tlaxcalteca del Siglo XVI 1998. Program. Personal Collection of Desiderio Hernández Xochitiotzin, Tlaxcala, Mexico.

Guarneros, Constanza A. "Emotivo Festival Socio Cultural en Cacaxtla." *El Sol de Tlaxcala* (Tlaxcala, Mexico) 11 September 1995: C1.

"Guión del Espectaculo de nocturno de Luz y sonido en la zona arqueologica de Xochitecatl 1997." Collection SEP Tlaxcala, 1997.

Gutíerrez, Natividád. *Nationalist Myths and Ethnic Identities: Indigenous Intellectuals and the Mexican State*. Lincoln: University of Nebraska Press, 1999.

Hernández Gomez, Tulio. *Gov. Informe de 1983*. Mexico: Gobierno de Tlaxcala, 1983.

_____. *Gov. Informe de 1984*. Mexico: Gobierno de Tlaxcala, 1984.

_____. *Gov. Informe de 1985*. Mexico: Gobierno de Tlaxcala, 1985.

_____. *Gov. Informe de 1986*. Mexico: Gobierno de Tlaxcala, 1986.

Hernández Xochitiotzin, Desiderio. Notes on Cacaxtla-Xochitecatl, undated. Tlaxcala, Mexico: Collection SEP Tlaxcala.

_____. Personal interview. 17 July 2003.

"Hoy, Luces y Musica en Cacaxtla-Xochitecatl." *El Sol de Tlaxcala*, Tlaxcala, Mexico (8 November 1997):D1.

Invitación a Colaborar en los festejos de Cacaxtla." *El Sol de Tlaxcala*, Tlaxcala, Mexico (5 September 1995):2A.

Lombardo Ruíz, Sonia, et al. *Cacaxtla: El Lugar Donde Muerte la Lluvia en la Tierra*. México: Gobierno del Estado de Tlaxcala , Instituto Nacional de Antropologíae Historia, Instituto Tlaxcalteca de Cultura, Consejo Estatal de Cultura Tlaxcala, 1991.

Lomnitz, Claudio. *Deep Mexico, Silent Mexico*. Minneapolis: University of Minnesota Press, 2001.

_____. *Modernidad Indiana: Nueve ensayos sobre nación y mediación en Mexico*. Mexico City: Planeta, 1999.

Lorenzo, José Luís. *La Arqueología y Mexico*. Mexico City: INAH, 1998.

Medina, Andres. *Recuentos y Figuraciones: Ensayos de Antropología Mexicana*. Mexico City: UNAM, 1996.

Meyer, Michael C., and William Sherman. *The Course of Mexican History*. Oxford: Oxford University Press, 1987.

Nagao, Debora. "Proclamación pública en el arte de Cacaxtla y Xochicalco." *Antología de Cacaxtla*, first ed. Vol. 2. Mexico City: INAH, 1995. 270–330.

"No alcanza el dinero para adquirir predios de zonas arquelógicas: INAH." *El Sol de Tlaxcala*, Tlaxcala, Mexico) (22 April 2002): D1+.

"Nuevos Hallazgos en la Zona de Cacaxtla." *El Sol de Tlaxcala*, Tlaxcala, Mexico (7 September 1990): 1A+.

Paredes Rangel, Beatriz. *Government Informe 1989*. Mexico: Gobierno de Tlaxcala, 1989.

_____. *Plan Estatal de Desarollo, Raíz y Compromiso 1987–1993*. Mexico: Gobierno de Tlaxcala, 1993.

Patterson, Thomas. "Archeology, History, Indigenismo, and the State in Peru and Mexico." *Making Alternative Histories: the Practice of Archeology and History in Non-Western Settings*. Eds. Peter R. Schmidt and Thomas Patterson. Santa Fe, New Mexico: School of American Reasearch, 1995. 69–86.

"Pavimientan el Camino a la Zona Arqueológia." *El Sol de Tlaxcala* (Tlaxcala) 3 September 1977: 1.

Photo Salida 1992. *El Sol de Tlaxcala*. 8 July 1992: 1A.

Photo Salida 1998. *El Sol de Tlaxcala*. 5 de July 1998: 1A.

Piña Chan, Román. *Cacaxtla: Fuentes Historicas y Pinturas*. Mexico City: Fondo de Cultura Económica, 1998.

"La politica educativa del sexenio 76–82 impulsó la decentralización educativa." *Sintesis Tlaxcala*, Tlaxcala, Mexico (24 June 2003):Universitarios 5.

Ruíz, Ramón Eduardo. *The Great Rebellion: Mexico, 1905–1924*. New York: W.W. Norton, 1980.

Ruyter, Nancy. "Ancient Images: The Pre-Cortésian in 20th Century Dance Performance." *Gestos* 21 (April 1996): 145–155.

Saenz, Carlos. *El Fuego Nuevo*. Mexico City: INAH, 1967.

Salida de los 400 familias 1996. Program. Personal Collection of Desiderio Hernández Xochitiotzin, Tlaxcala, Mexico.

Sanchez Piedras, Emilio. *Informe Municipio 1977–1979*. Mexico: Gobierno de Tlaxcala, 1980.

Secretaria de Educación Publica del Estado, Tlaxcala. *Anteproyecto de los eventos para conmemorar el 22 Aniversario del Descubrimiento de la Zona Arq. de Cacaxtla y el 3 de Xochitecatl*. Mexico: Collection of SEP Tlaxcala, 1997.

_____. *Guia de Jornada Tlaxcalteca del Siglo XVI 1994*. Collection of SEP Tlaxcala, Tlaxcala, Mexico, 1994.

_____. *Guión del evento Cacaxtla con Motivo del XXV Aniversario de su Descubrimiento*. Mexico: SEP, 2000.

"Sin celebraciones el aniversario de Cacaxtla, mejor propondremos un plan de trabajo: Sabino Yano." *El Sol de Tlaxcala* (Tlaxcala, Mexico) 14 August 2001: D1+.

Terova Tepatzi, Angelica. "En Escena 'La Gran Jornada Tlaxcalteca del S. XVI,' Colonizadora del Norte de Páis." *El Sol de Tlaxcala* (Tlaxcala, Mexico) 8 July 1996): 1C+

Townsend, Robert. *The Aztecs*. London: Thames and Hudson, 1992.

Usigli, Rudolfo. *Mexico in the Theatre*. Trans. Wilder P. Scott. University of Mississippi Press, Romance Monographs, 1976.

Versényi, Adam. *Theatre in Latin America: Religion, Politics, and Culture from Cortés to the 1980s*. Cambridge: Cambridge University Press, 1993.

Ybarra, Patricia. "Re-imagining Identity and Re-centering History in Performance." *Theatre Journal* 55.4 (December 2003): 633–655.

The Corpse of Algerian Identity: Achour Ouamara's *La Défunte* (The Deceased)

Susan Haedicke

Pale red lights come up slowly as Hebrew music (a religious chant sung a cappella or accompanied by a string instrument) plays in the background. In the dim light, a dreary make-shift morgue is visible. It is empty except for a casket placed perpendicular to the back wall. Olivier leans against the wall to one side of the casket and stares straight ahead; Domino, on the other side, dozes, resting his head in his hands on the lid of the coffin. It seems as though they have been in these positions for some time, but this stationary tableau is soon disturbed as Olivier shakes Domino: "Domino, wake up, it's not time to take a snooze." Domino sits up, rubs his eyes, and yawns. "The smell of this dead body knocks me out," he explains. Domino removes the lid of the coffin as Olivier leafs through a notebook that we later learn contains the writings of the dead woman. The two men are investigating not the cause of her death, which is obvious — torture and dismemberment — but the identities both of the corpse and of her executioner by detecting his modus operandi. They plunge into the task noting all the lacerations and indignities performed on her body. "Can't you see that she suffered an unimaginable agony? Look! Look at her well, my friend," instructs Domino (Ouamara 99).[1]

But what is the audience to make of the bizarre opening moments of Algerian playwright, Achour Ouamara's surrealistic play, *La Défunte* (The Deceased)? Are these two grotesque officials, leaning over the coffin from

211

opposite sides, their heads touching and their hands moving pieces around in the casket, to be taken seriously? Certainly, the situation depicted in this play is deadly serious and one that reflects the horrific events that took place in Algeria in the 1990s. The spiral of violence that swept over Algeria in this troubled decade represents one of history's most savage and incomprehensible civil wars as torture, mutilations, kidnappings, disappearances, and assassinations, often committed in front of family and friends, terrorized the population. This civil war claimed over 100,000 lives between 1990 and 1999 according to the estimates of the government of Abdelaziz Bouteflika, Algeria's president since 1999, although some scholars insist that over 120,000 were killed.[2] However the Algerian civil war is so poorly documented, so shrouded in obscurity, that historian Benjamin Stora calls it the "invisible war." He identifies this strategy of invisibility as a form of erasure: "Can a war that is not seen even exist?" he asks (Stora, *La Guerre* 8).[3] During the 1990s, the Algerian government denied access to foreign journalists and photographers and confiscated evidence of the brutalities. This suppression of information is just beginning to ease. "Ten Years of Algeria in Images," an exhibition in Paris in the fall of 2002, had as its centerpiece the "censorship wall," a wall with photographs revealing the atrocities of the 1990s that were blocked from distribution by the Algerian government until the summer of 2002.

Now many Algerians, writers and politicians alike, insist that the only way to move forward is to expose the culture of violence that swept over their homeland with such ferocity in the 1990s and to unravel the intertwined allegiances and opposing goals.[4] Algerian playwright Slimane Benaïssa in the introduction to his play, *Les Fils de l'amertume* (Sons of Bitterness), a play which looks at causes and consequences of Islamic extremism, catalogs the many risks attached to writing about Algeria in the last decade of the twentieth century and ends his list with "But the most terrible risk is to remain silent."[5] Those who refused to remain silent during this period took great personal risks as Algerian authors, journalists, educators, and intellectuals, especially French-speaking ones, were repeatedly targeted for assassination, since they were perceived as traitors and corrupting influences from within and thus considered legitimate targets for elimination. The years 1993 and 1994 alone, saw the murders of novelist Tahar Djaout, poet Youssef Sebti, psychologist and author Mahfoud Beucebci, sociologist M'Hamed Boukhobza, playwright Abdelkader Alloula (murdered in Paris), the former Minister of Higher Education, Djilali Liabès, a member of the National Advisory Council, Ladi Flici, the director of the Advanced School of Fine Arts, Ahmed Asselah, the president of the Algerian League of Human Rights, Youcef Fathallah, and rai singer Cheb Hasni: just a few of the most well-known names among the many killed. Between 1993 and 1996, fifty-seven journalists were murdered and five disappeared.[6] Tahar Djaout in *The Last Summer of Reason*, his final novel found among his papers soon after his assassination on May 26, 1993 and published posthumously, bears witness in his text and his death to the assaults against the power of words waged by religious fanatics. The novel's main character Boulem Yekker, the bookstore owner, conducts a solitary protest against the extremists who charge art and literature with heresy. He explains:

> They understand the danger in words, all the words they cannot manage to domesticate and anesthetize. For words, put end to end, bring doubt and change. Words above all must not conceive of the utopia of another form of truth, of unsuspected paths, of another place of thought. You do not easily part with utopia; it is an acid that cuts holes in the opacity of dogma [Djaout 143–4].

It was not until 1995 that an official document acknowledged the atrocities. The Sant'Egidio Platform, adopted by most of the warring political parties, outlined strategies for political reform and an end to the violence and marked a major step in admitting the horror:

> Today, the Algerian people live in a climate of terror never equaled, aggravated by intolerable social and economic conditions. In this faceless war, arrests, disappearances, assassinations, systematic torture, mutilation and reprisals have become the daily lot of Algerian women and men.... The risks of the civil war are real, threatening the physical integrity of the people, the unity of the country, and national sovereignty [Pierre 59].

In *The Deceased*, Achour Ouamara, anticipating the extreme violence and barbarity of the 1990s, rejects documentary reportage as the best way to expose this culture of atrocity. Rather he transforms an all-too-real situation into a grotesque absurdity that alternates between tabloid sensationalism and a carnivalesque form of humor. These braided strands that comprise his complex dramaturgical strategy enable him to dramatize the unthinkable nature of the events in graphic detail, at the same time as he shifts the focus from the gruesome situation of an examination of a dismembered corpse to the representation of her body, both as the site of and the symbol for the violent unrest experienced by the nation. Her mutilated body metaphorically represents Algeria, and her individual story, fragmented and struggling to be heard, parallels that of the terrified population. This brutally murdered body, never actually seen by the audience, functions as a subversive critique of the tactics of the warring factions. Ouamara, however, does not connect the world of the play to the actual world by having the former simply reflect the latter. Rather, he creates a strategy of nesting the play's world in the actual world. Embedded in the fictional actions of the play are actual events which occurred in Algeria, as the play offers a sequence of unveilings through realistic as well as symbolic images that reveal the confiscation and distortion of the nation by political forces, which resulted in the horrors of the 1990s.

In addition, the play makes references to historical events outside the Algerian context. Each of the five acts, for example, opens with music associated with populations from around the world who have experienced some form of genocide: Hebrew music is heard before Acts I and V; Bosnian music begins Act II; African music (eliciting associations with Rwanda) is heard in Act III; and Arabic (Algerian) music opens Act IV. But the destruction of a nation is not the final word of *The Deceased*. Instead, the play offers the possibility of a better future embedded within the traumatic present. For Ouamara, that future is an Algerian identity freed from the unrelenting terror caused by the impasse that paralyzed the nation in the 1990s. The play symbolically claims that even an act of extreme violence imprinted on the body of the victim (either the character represented by the invisible mutilated corpse or the actual nation of Algeria) cannot silence it or make it invisible. The dead woman's presence gains strength throughout the play as the investigators read her writings aloud so that, in the final surreal scene, her spirit — now visible on stage (embodied by an actress) — wrests power from her tormentors. So too, suggests Ouamara, will Algeria — now visible on the world stage, as writers speak out and reverse the process of erasure of the nation's history — wrest power from the internal forces, which have been so destructive. The body of the dead woman as she regenerates herself represents the struggle of the Algerian nation.

To understand the trauma of Algeria that Ouamara surrealistically depicts, it is necessary to place it within the context of the complicated colonial and postcolonial relationship between Algeria and France.[7] The French military arrived on Algerian soil in 1830. Almost from the beginning, the relationship between Algeria and France developed along a different path than that between France and her other colonies in the Maghreb, Morocco, and Tunisia. The mission in Algeria was not to colonize the country, but to absorb it. French colonial rule not only replaced indigenous languages and cultures with French models, it also designated Algeria as an overseas department and administered it as part of France. The policy, which strove to make Algeria a continuation of France on the other side of the Mediterranean, is vividly portrayed in the image evoked by one of the characters in Mohamed Kacimi's play *1962*, performed at Ariane Mnouchkine's Théâtre du Soleil in 2001. Gharib, recollecting his school days in Algeria, impersonates his teacher in the French school who reminds the Algerian pupils that "The Mediterranean crosses France as the Seine crosses Paris" (Kacimi 16).[8] As a result of this complete subjugation of the Algerian people, the bloody and violent War of Independence (1954–62) with its tangled allegiances, its frequent terrorist acts, and its habitual use of torture as a way to infiltrate the ranks of the revolutionaries left a legacy of hatred and terror that seemed to condemn the new nation to dictatorial rule. The revolutionary party, the FLN (National Liberation Front), that assumed leadership of the new nation, soon resorted to a repressive single-party rule that held onto power for thirty years. Striving to restore an "Algerian" identity to Algeria, the new government put aggressive Arabization measures in place to erase all traces of the colonial past. But the maimed and distorted policies of independent Algeria, policies that often mimicked the tactics of the French, ignored the country's centuries-old diverse cultural and religious heritage and plunged the nation into political, socio-cultural, and economic chaos.

The corruption, secularization, and frequent use of excessive force of the FLN encouraged the disaffected people, especially the young, to turn to the only viable ideology, Islam, as represented by the opposition movement of the Islamic Salvation Front (FIS). By the mid–1980s, small opposition groups began to accuse the FLN of "confiscating" the revolution by favoring French speakers over Arabic speakers and neglecting traditional Islamic values. This accusation was somewhat surprising since the FLN had pushed for a strict Arabization policy, a major Islamic demand. At the same time, the economy began to falter with the drop in oil prices and the rapidly increasing national debt, and the boundaries between economic grievances and cultural and political protests began to blur. In the first serious challenge to the FLN in October 1988, young men in jeans were joined by older bearded Islamic militants to protest the removal of government subsidies for basic necessities. The FLN called in security forces to end the protest, and several hundred people were killed. For the next few years, from 1989 to 1991, the government tried to respond to popular demands with Constitutional reform, freedom of the press, and authorization of new political parties. The FIS emerged as the strongest of the new parties, and in the 1990 local elections gained control of most of the major towns. The newly elected officials began Islamic reforms in education and dress immediately. A character in *Such a Great Hope, or the New Song of a Lost Country* (1994), Noureddine Aba's polemical play about Algeria in the 1990s, explains the appeal of the FIS: "When the people supported them in the past, the Islamists hadn't yet killed anyone. They supported them because they were denouncing the depravity and corruption of the State Party and promising to punish all FLN leaders who were responsible" (Aba 338).

When, in mid–1991, the FIS won a large number of seats in the National Assembly in the first round of balloting, the military stepped in to prevent the second round of balloting, which would clearly place the power in the hands of the Islamic party. President Chadli Benjedid was replaced by Mohamed Boudiaf. Boudiaf pledged to eradicate the FIS, which was dissolved by the Algiers Administrative Court in March 1992, and to end government corruption. Nevertheless in reality, the same political/military party in control since independence gained power. The apparent shift to a multiparty system was shown to be a sham. It did not take long for Islamic militants, who claimed that they represented the Algerian people who had been cheated and disempowered, to resort to violence to bring down the regime. In June 1992, Boudiaf was assassinated, which, of course, led to a tighter crackdown by the military forces. Several Islamist factions with varying goals and methods continued the struggle against what they felt was an illegitimate government, but that conflict soon expanded to oppose those who questioned Islamic law and traditions. The situation rapidly degenerated. One of the characters in *Such a Great Hope* presents us with the extreme nature of the situation: "the day of the assassins has come. From now on, they and they alone will speak! The corpses are piling up: after the police, the soldiers, and the military, now they're shooting down doctors, poets, journalists, they're cutting the throats of psychiatrists, professors, sociologists" (Aba 337). But this seemingly obvious conflict between state-sponsored security forces and Islamic extremists does not tell the whole truth as fragments of the story that are beginning to surface through the work of journalists, historians, and artists reveal: the opposing sides at times had similar goals. Even the 1995 Sant'Egidio Platform admitted to the formation of government-sponsored militias "in the midst of the population," and Luis Martinez, in *The Algerian Civil War, 1990–1998*, argues that a simple analysis of a bipolar conflict is inadequate and that only "a war-oriented *imaginaire* or world view" that regards "violence as a method of accumulation of wealth and prestige" (Martinez 9, 7) makes the conflict comprehensible. A war-oriented *imaginaire* also supports the idea that the violence of the 1990s was an intensification of brutalities that had existed for years rather than a new phenomenon.

Ouamara, in *The Deceased*, thrusts the audience into the center of this labyrinthine conflict as the lights come up on the bare investigating room inhabited by two government officials, Olivier and Domino, and a corpse. As the investigators begin their task of piecing together the mutilated body parts of the dead woman, in order to discover her identity, as well as the identity of the torturer, the audience never sees the body, but the descriptions as the men move the pieces around in the coffin are very vivid:

Admire the color of her skin, at least what's left of it. It's as clear as spring water. Didn't she receive bludgeoning from all sorts of blunt instruments! Look at her eyes, Domino, this poached egg, the other one sliced by scissors, ripped out for having seen too much, cried too much. The blade embraced her mouth enlivened with lipstick. The incisors still have a trace of lichen on them, the ears, oh, the ears; I'm coming to that…. The eyelashes ripped out, the hair sauced with brownish blood that is still smoking. The whole face is ripped up. Out of it is coming the fury of thousands of years as if she had seen all the horrors of the world since the big bang. God must have cried as he took her soul. I'll tell you, the agony must have been long so that she had time to measure the perversity of her offenders [Ouamara 99, 106].

Into this gruesome setting, however, Ouamara interjects a gallows humor to shift the focus away from the reality of the events, to turn the horror of the situation on its head. After detailed descriptions of the state of the body parts by the men, their hands in the coffin, moving these mutilated pieces around, it is with relief that the spectator laughs at Olivier's remark that the reassembled body does not look very pretty since "sewing is not our strong point" (Ouamara 101). This comment occurring early in the play, alerts the audience to the multiple embedded layers signaled by humor. The incongruous comment hints at a search for feminine beauty in a tortured corpse, but behind that ridiculous image is a more serious endorsement of traditional gender roles: the men should not be responsible for domestic tasks, like sewing. In fact, it is possible to see that Olivier and Domino unconsciously place the blame for the mutilation on the corpse herself since she, as the only woman in the scene and in her current state, is forcing the men to perform tasks for which they are ill-suited.

This emphasis on the gruesome details, whether in the form of tabloid sensationalism or humor, enables the absent body to gain an uncanny presence, a technique that, as Gilbert and Tompkins note, takes place in a wide range of post-colonial plays: "the absent body generates an 'ironic' presence…, the absent body occupies dramatic, if not always actual, space. It follows, then, that the audience experiences absence as a palpable, 'embodied' presence, a paradox … absence can be extremely unsettling for the viewer" (Gilbert 230). This disturbing presence is certainly exploited in *The Deceased* as the assault on the spectator's ear intensifies, when the investigators turn what must be the torso or the head. The spectator begins to *see* the tortured body of the dead woman. This invisible body certainly acts as the site of the horror done to her individual body but, at the same time, as an emblem for the atrocities committed in the 1990s, as well as those committed in the Algerian War of Independence, and probably clandestinely since 1962.

Ouamara, in a later scene, establishes that connection between the corpse and the terrorist acts more blatantly through a strategy Stora calls "the unveiling of successive truths" (Stora, *La Guerre Invisible* 13). Ouamara develops a dramaturgical strategy where the world of the play becomes transparent revealing references to the actual world embedded within it. Olivier instructs Domino, "Look at our corpse. Who killed her? Nothing, really nothing, could prepare her for such an atrocious death. Blood lacks an odor in such times of panic where the end justifies the means" (Ouamara 118). His question of who killed their corpse rapidly shifts to other victims — Ruth, cut down in front of the tomato stall, emptied of her blood, a baby in a cradle sliced from chin to anus, or the young child Wanda desperately trying to reattach her mother's head. Behind the victims are those who benefit from the culture of death — from those who make money off of death (grave diggers and makers of shrouds, coffins, and weapons) to the ungrateful beggar who strangles the host who fed him (Ouamara 118). Behind the profiteers are the people so numbed and terrified that they turn away and, in so doing, collude with the violence. The scene blurs the borders between fiction and reality. Diana Taylor, writing about Argentina's "dirty war" calls this "self-blinding of the population — 'percepticide'" (Taylor 123). She argues that "the triumph of the atrocity was that it forced people to look away — a gesture that undid their sense of personal and communal cohesion even as it seemed to bracket them from their volatile surroundings. Spectacles of violence rendered the population silent, deaf, and blind" (Taylor 122–3). Abuse of power at its most violent is embodied in this invisible body of the corpse, and the spectator becomes the unwitting witness to the political events, as the visible world of the dreary room fades to transparency, exposing the acts of atrocity and the climate of fear and dispassion that allows the violence to continue.

Ouamara does not just expose the acts of violence: he challenges the audience to recognize that guilt is not quite so easy to assign since terrorists "are no rare commodities. All you need to do is knock on the neighbor's door" (Ouamara 114). We are all responsible not just for the things we cause, he seems to say, but also for the things we allow to happen, and thus he accuses those who choose not to act or pretend not to contribute to the atrocities. His play dramatizes the devastating results of Taylor's "percepticide," a cultivated blindness which allows people "to deny what they saw and, by turning away, collude with the violence around them" (Taylor 123).

Ouamara, as he gradually reveals the identity of the executioner, highlights that the murderer is in our midst. As Olivier and Domino detail the wounds, they marvel at the skill of the torturer who was able to inflict unbearable agony and yet keep the victim alive for days. Domino remarks that the "art" of the corpse's lacerations reminds him of the official government manuals he studied in school on the ways to slay traitors. He explains:

> It was recommended to first ask yourself about the victim. You don't kill a calf like you kill a chicken. A police officer, a journalist, a poet, a woman, a child, a foreigner, each one has to suffer the fatal blow according to his or her own rank, race, speech, writings. It's not just any part of the body that you have to attack, but its guilty part.... What do you do with a blaspheming mouth? With a bejeweled neck? With a hand that writes the unspeakable? With an unveiled head? With the curve of an uncovered leg? That's how the weapon is chosen. The sharp knife offers the advantage of costing less, of gleaming with each sharpening, of pressing down on the flesh, of taking in that hollow moan that makes the act of killing sacred. The victim who is given the death blow finally comes to repent in his last breath, in that last sputter that separates the body from the soul.... It is written that each sacrifice is unique, original, that the type of victim, the choice of weapon, and the typography of the place are inseparable, that castration is the best remedy against a future enemy. You have to attack the foe in exactly what it loves or cherishes. When dealing with women, aim for the ovaries. Ravish at the point of the deepest evil, exactly where the devil is hiding, where infidelity is seated, exactly where the damned race begins [Ouamara 106–7].

He even asks Olivier if their corpse doesn't look like the work described in his "unforgettable manual." So it should not be surprising when we learn by the end of the play that Olivier is the skilled torturer, especially since earlier in the play, Olivier has argued that "you and I could be executioners.... Guilt is an affair of the conscience" (Ouamara 114). Why Olivier brutally killed and dismembered this woman is never explained, but clearly it was not for the purpose of intelligence-gathering. Rather, it seems to fall into the category of what Henry Shue calls "terroristic torture," where the goal is not to extract information (Shue 124–34), but to present an unmistakable show of power so others refrain from similar to discredit those in power. Olivier's ability to inflict extreme agony so skillfully on another and to decide when she will die sets him up as omnipotent. In addition, perhaps his avid reading aloud of her tirades, which condemn the regime he stands for, represents his strategy to convince Domino of the justice of his punishment of the rebellious, even traitorous, woman. More important than the reason why the woman is tortured, however, is the fact that Olivier's motivation is omitted. Through that omission, Ouamara highlights that the characters seen on stage are not the object of the play, just the tools to focus the attention on the dead woman.

Nevertheless, the story of the dead woman, which is never completely revealed, is not the real focus of the play either, and neither is her emblematic representation of the atrocities committed in Algeria, even though descriptions of her corpse graphically depict that brutality. Instead, Ouamara again relies on the strategy of "unveiling of successive truths" to identify the dead woman as Algeria. This metaphor of Algeria as a woman is certainly not unique to Ouamara: Kateb Yacine represented Algeria as a beautiful, albeit unattainable young woman (the hope of independence) in the character of Nedjma who first appears in the novel bearing her name and later in the dramatic trilogy, *Le Cercle des Représailles*, where Nedjma continues to define and refine Algerian identity. In Ouamara's play, however, Algeria is no longer the desired woman, but a mutilated corpse who represents the core of Algerian society that has been traumatized by her own people. Just as the dead woman is dismembered by her executioner — a government official, probably in the military, whose role is to protect her — Algeria was torn apart first by the FLN's confiscation of all that the war of independence promised and then by the civil turmoil of the 1990s as internal warring factions sought to destroy one another. The discourse of the body of the dead woman speaks of an Algerian identity mutilated by the misguided and destructive policies of independent Algeria.

Ouamara, however, seeks to go beyond exposing the horrors committed to such an excess and strives to discover the possible future within the wreckage of the past. In spite of the dystopia depicted in the play, his message is one of hope for the nation. Even though maimed by the violence, the dead woman/Algeria refuses to be defeated. She resists silencing and disappearance as she reassembles/reconstructs the disparate pieces of her body and reasserts herself on the (world) stage. Olivier unconsciously points the way to start the healing, as he describes the gathering of all the woman's body parts, and states that without the help of dogs, "we would never have found her. We have sewed her body back together for better or worse so that she is presented to God whole" (Ouamara 101). Perhaps this is an analogy for recent official recognition of the disparate ethnic groups, especially in terms of language, that make up Algeria. The appearance of the spirit of the dead woman in the final scene of the play metaphorically signals a national reincarnation, as evidenced in the actual world by a wide range of ground-breaking political initiatives in Algeria over the last few years, including democratic elections, laws on civil peace granting amnesty to armed Islamists, reforms in the military, international state visits by President Bouteflika, and the naming of Berber as one of the national languages, all of which officially acknowledges the significant non–Arabic population in Algeria.

Several elements in the play point to that interpretation. Olivier and Domino often refer to their superior Locke who ordered the investigation and expects results quickly. The allusion to the philosopher John Locke is firmly established in the scene where the character Locke aggressively enters the morgue and takes over the investigation by announcing that the identities of the victim and the executioner have been determined. John Locke's theory of political obligation assumes that government is a social contract. He argues that government rests on popular consent, not arbitrary power over the welfare and lives of the people, and when government subverts its goals of public welfare for its own gain, rebellion is permissible. Olivier, in particular, and Domino, by association, are government officials who represent a political faction that has abused its power and must be overthrown. The character Locke, on the other hand, stands for resistance to tyranny. From the moment of his brusque entrance with his two body guards, he overthrows the authority of the investigators by claiming knowledge of the identities of the corpse and her killer and by naming them — the dead body is that of Zira (whose name has an uncanny resemblance to *Al Jazeera*, spelled *Jazira* in French) and the torturer is Olivier himself. Olivier, in a final attempt to retain control by discrediting his boss Locke, addresses him as Monsieur Coq. The reference is to the cock, the symbol of France, which attempts to associate Locke with the hated colonial power. Domino quickly corrects Olivier's conscious mistake thus defusing his colleague's not so subtle connection between Locke and France's use of torture during the Algerian War of Independence. Locke immediately accuses Olivier of being the woman's torturer and abruptly orders his arrest. Olivier says nothing more (and his executed corpse replaces the dead woman in the casket in the next scene), so Locke has the final word. Locke, the character, like his namesake, supports the idea that every individual has a right to life and liberty, and those who abuse their political power must be overthrown.

How Ouamara presents his optimistic prediction for a just Algeria, metaphorically through the reassembled body of the dead woman, becomes clearer when one looks at Elaine Scarry's *The Body in Pain: The Making and Unmaking of the World*, in which she analyzes the processes of destruction and creation in terms of the human body. She argues that the "unmaking [of the world] resides in and can thus be represented by two relatively self-contained events, torture and war" (Scarry 177), which reverse, even annihilate, the process of civilization. Both torture and war use physical pain consciously inflicted on another to deprive the victim of his voice and to establish the pain-giver's power. Both convert physical pain into a fiction of power and so have significant political consequences. In fact, Scarry argues, the hurt body in torture and war is inextricable from, and necessary to, the regime's self-defined legitimacy.

Scarry explains that, torture, in particular, intensifies and magnifies physical suffering and, even more significantly, objectifies it by making it visible to others, apart from the sufferer. Thus physical suffering is converted "into the wholly illusory but, to the torturers and the regime they represent, wholly convincing spectacle of power" (Scarry 27). This transformation of one's pain into the power of another occurs with the "renaming" of the infliction of pain as information-gathering, no longer morally reprehensible, but instead justified as necessary for the security of the regime. In addition, torture forces objects and actions to become their inverse. Ordinary objects, hallmarks of civilization like bathtubs, refrigerators, chairs, or soft drink bottles, and even the room itself, its walls, doors, and windows, are converted into weapons — their original function is un-made and rather than providing shelter, sustenance, or comfort, they cause pain and destruction. Physical pain and the disintegration of civilization are inextricably linked in torture: "the de-objectifying of the objects, the unmaking of the made, is a process externalizing the way in which the person's pain causes his world to disintegrate; and, at the same time, the disintegration of the world is here, in the most literal way possible, made painful, made the direct cause of pain" (Scarry 41). Torture is the prelude to the annihilation of language, consciousness, the body, and ultimately civilization. War moves that "decreation" of civilization from a conflict between individuals to one between societies or cultural constructs. According to Scarry,

> In both war and torture, the normal relation between body and voice is deconstructed and replaced by one in which the extremes of the hurt body and anchored verbal assertions (pain and interrogation in torture; casualties and verbal issues in war) are laid edge to edge. In each, a fiction is produced, a fiction that is a projected image of the body: the pain's reality is now the regime's reality; the factualness of corpses is now the factualness of an ideology or territorial self-definition [143].

It is this destruction of the civilized world that Ouamara presents in the opening moments of the play.

For Ouamara, torture is just the starting point as the annihilation of the unknown woman/Algeria becomes the source of rebirth in much the same way that Artaud described the function of both the theatre and the plague. *The Deceased* reverses the deconstructing process of torture and, by extension, the destruction of Algeria through a process of re-construction of both the woman and the nation by making the physical pain visible, not on the torturer's terms, but on the victim's, and by exposing the falseness of the regime's assumption of the rightness of its act. Scarry also asserts that war — the process of torture on a vast scale — is "a huge structure for the derealization of cultural constructs and, simultaneously, for their eventual reconstitution" (Scarry 137). War's destruction of the known world not only allows for, but necessitates a reconstruction of the world, although in a different form, a form which starts with no material presence and so must be created. Scarry breaks the process of creation into two phases: "making-up" (imagining or inventing the idea) and "making-real" (building the material form of the idea). For the audience, *The Deceased* follows this pattern as the presence of the dead woman becomes stronger and more tangible throughout the play until she finally appears in physical form in the final act. This process of reconstruction of the woman/Algeria — the "making-up" and "making-real" — has three distinct stages in this play.

The first stage, part of the "making-up" phase, reverses the decivilizing process of torture in two ways. First, it objectifies the pain which the victim must have felt by speaking it aloud. Scarry argues that pain has no voice since it is just felt, but it also lacks any referential content. It cannot be shared and it cannot be put into words, and so it ultimately destroys language. Nevertheless, argues Scarry, the desire to eliminate pain has necessitated some form of verbal communication, albeit fragmentary and inadequate. The strategy of this verbalization seeks to make the pain "visible" through what Scarry calls the "language of agency" which relies on two metaphors for the pain: the weapon which produces the pain, and the physical damage caused by the weapon on the body. The initial gruesome descriptions in the play move the pain from a private and invisible moment to a very visible, at least in the imagination, picture of the pain: "The bites of a saw on the lower belly indicate that the torture lasted several days. Wait, let me turn her (*he makes the gesture of turning her over*), perhaps you'll be convinced by discovering her scraped neck. And her flayed back? I wonder if she wasn't first washed with some acid" (Ouamara 99). The descriptions, which identify the weapons and the damage they inflict on the body, communicate a reality of the pain, its "presentness," and the graphic details make it visible and audible.

Scarry claims that expressing pain is the necessary prelude to diminishing it, just as Stora asserts that as long as the war remains invisible, it lacks reality and is, therefore, acceptable. To move beyond the violence, one must expose it. One must end "percepticide." The language of agency used in the play's descriptions brutally objectifies pain. Secondly, Ouamara reverses the process of torture by reversing the de-objectification of ordinary objects effectively used in torture to undermine civilization. Scarry points out how ordinary objects become weapons during torture; Ouamara transforms objects associated with death into ordinary domestic objects. He thus overturns torture's transformation of ordinary objects into instruments of torture. The most startling image occurs in Act II, which opens as Domino and Olivier are finishing their lunch. They have turned the coffin into their lunch table, and they sort through the bits of food — "a veritable Cordon Bleu of chopped beef" (Ouamara 103) — with many of the same gestures as they sorted through the body parts in the previous act. The grotesque humor of this image, which establishes clear parallels between the corpse and the meal, intensifies at the same time as it makes a mockery of the horrific act of torture.

The second stage of the corpse's reconstruction, also part of the "making-up" phase of the process of creation, allows the audience to hear her voice. The dead woman's real power comes from her writings. Her refusal to be silenced even by death echoes that of Tahar Djaout's unfinished novel, *The Last Summer of Reason*, where Wole Soyinka writes in the introduction, "This voice from the grave urges itself on our hearing" (Djaout ix). In the play, the dead woman's words begin almost like a witch's spell: "Chirp, declaim, jabber, boast, whine, you will be humbled. Your conceit comes from ideas handed to you. What do you scoundrels know that we don't know of the past? We will put an end to your haughtiness. What conceit that you take yourselves for the salt of the earth, the perfume of the world; what conceit to think for an instant that we will take the blame" (Ouamara 104). Scarry writes that "so long as one is speaking, the self extends out beyond the boundaries of the body, occupies a space much larger than the body" (Scarry 33). It is not surprising then that her presence begins to take over the space as her words fill Olivier's mouth. As Olivier reads her words, he can no longer free himself as she enters his body, and toward the end of the play, Domino accuses him of sounding just like her in his rants on violence: "Calm yourself. You're getting me muddled, you are taking on the voice of the dead woman. To hear you, it's the end of the world" (Ouamara 117). Try as he might, Olivier cannot stop reading: he is convinced that "each sheet [of her writings] is a piece of the puzzle" (Ouamara 120), that each sheet offers a clue to history and to the future. He is taken over by her words.

The woman even enters their dreams causing them to have extraordinary visions. Domino dreams his arms have turned into scythes, which he uses to harvest wheat, although each stalk is topped with a human head. The field is submerged by a red sea of blood which he drinks and drinks. As the blood recedes, *houris* (beautiful young virgins who are the companions of the faithful Muslims in paradise) with a thousand breasts appear. He foresees his own death as a distorted martyrdom, an unanticipated sacrifice for a falsified cause. Olivier's blatantly sexual and violent dream actually includes the dead woman. He dreams that he is transformed into an ass (a potent sexual metaphor) with wings who is flying full-speed toward a mooring post, "un bitte d'enfer capote d'un turban" (Ouamara 113) which, in spoken French, has overt sexual overtones. As he starts to bray, a crowd of his doubles advances on him. Again, the French "queue contre queue" (Ouamara 113) makes obvious sexual references. He tries to escape but lands on the dead woman who is alive and laughing at his plight. She condemns him to inarticulate stuttering, thus destroying his power over language. He, like the person in pain, has been severed from his voice. Her victory is assured. Both men are shaken by their dreams as Domino says, "my God, the dead woman is making us lose our way" (Ouamara 113), and Olivier returns to her writings to find the key. Her words, however, continue to condemn them: "Your bad deeds will return to you one hundred times over. Beware of your offspring. They will pounce on you just as the rapacious eagle does on the chained Prometheus"(Ouamara 114). The legend of Prometheus is a classic story of torture, but here, in *The Deceased*, Ouamara suggests the inverse as the torturer becomes the victim. Olivier soon begins to fulfill the dream he had as he attempts to justify the use of torture, but his impassioned polemic becomes less and less coherent until Domino stops him with "Hollow chatterings, Olivier, you are only spreading confusion and are falsifying the narrative of the deceased.... You drone on making accusations with no proof" (Ouamara 118).

Throughout her writings, the dead woman has used the pronoun "we" as she points out the bravado and hypocrisy of the executioners: "We see your passion for the wound in the care you use to nail the coffins" (Ouamara 121). The implication is that "we" refers to the people of Algeria abused and exploited by the regime and now scared and silent except for an occasional lone voice. But at the end of the play, when the words control Olivier, the pronoun shifts to "I." Is it a coincidence or is Ouamara implying that the people are beginning to speak with one voice that can no longer be silenced even by death:

> I will testify even if my blood runs, even if I lose my life. Let cushions for the slumber of the deaf be made from my body. Let my words be engraved on my shoulder blades, and let what is left of my skin be made into a parchment on which to write them. Make flutes from my bones to sing a requiem. Let the horrors be recorded in the recesses of the soul.... Today, one drinks in the cup of forgetfulness down to the sediment. But I tell you this, the keys to the prison where memory is locked away will be stolen back one day [Ouamara 121–2].

Ouamara implies that just as the dead woman's words eventually impact Olivier's voice and movements, so, too, does the opening up of the past by writers, journalists, and historians take on a life of its own. Restoring history ends the period of national amnesia, which has blocked forward progress.

In the final act, the woman, "made up to look like a ghost," replaces Olivier in his seat by the coffin, and Olivier's corpse has replaced the body parts in the coffin. In this third stage of the reconstruction process, the woman/ Algeria is embodied in the physical presence of the "corpse," pale but whole. The audience *sees* for the first time what was previously invisible in the world of the play by being hidden in the casket or invisible in the actual world by the news blackout lamented by Stora. The "making-up" phase described by Scarry has become the "making-real." Except for the switching of the woman and Olivier, this act begins exactly like Act I with the same setting, lights, and music. Domino is asleep against the coffin, and this time the woman awakens him with the same words used by Olivier earlier: "Domino, wake up, it's not time for a snooze" (Ouamara 124). As he rubs his eyes and yawns, Domino responds to her exactly as he did to Olivier, although in French, his unconscious awareness of the new corpse is signaled by his use of the masculine form for "deceased": "L'odeur de ce défunt m'a assomé" (Ouamara 124) instead of "cette défunte." This replacement of dead "masculine" for revived "feminine" has a direct parallel in contemporary Algerian history. The FLN party was considered the father of independence, but its corruption gave birth to the radical Islamist party, FIS. In French, FIS is a homonym for *fils*, meaning son. For Algeria to move forward, father and son, FLN and FIS, must be put to rest, as the central character in *Such a Great Hope* (written in the height of the conflict in 1994) pleads on his death bed:

> The father and son are one and the same. They're both sensation mongers, smooth talkers avid for power. With the father, you had vain, contemptuous nomenklatura. With the son, you will have pitiless theocracy of the Ayatollahs, equally vain, equally depraved. The father brought you ruin. The son will bring you calamity. The father severed you from the world. The son will cut you off from mankind. The father lynched the dawn, the son will consume your future in fire, along with any chance of your becoming a part of the world at large.... You must take control of your fate, you must assume responsibility for your country.... If you don't, and if you don't do it now, then Algeria will sink into the darkness, like a ship sinking on the high seas, deep under the waters. And your uprising will have been for nothing [Aba 347]!

The people, rather than the corrupted and destructive parties, must represent Algeria and become its future (again pointing to the political theory of John Locke). The appearance of the reconstituted dead woman in Act V signals the revival of the nation where the people are beginning, albeit with very small steps, to have a say in their governance. And in French, the name for the nation of Algeria — *l'Algérie* — is feminine.

Immediately after he awakes, Domino sees that Olivier is in the casket. In a surrealistic moment, Olivier's bloodied dead body sits up and grabs

Domino's sleeve trying to drag him into the coffin as well, refusing to let him escape untouched and guiltless. Domino wriggles out of his shirt leaving it in Olivier's hands and runs to the corner of the room. The woman extricates the shirt and uses it to wipe the blood from the face of the corpse, which she then gently lays back to rest in the coffin. She goes toward the terrified Domino, dresses him in the bloodied shirt, and pats him on the back wishing him good luck, paralleling his own gestures when Olivier was arrested. Although Domino bolts terrified from the room crying "Woe is me! Woe is me!" (Ouamara 125), it is clear that he must take responsibility for the "culture of death" which, as he pointed out earlier in the play, "oozes out of everything. It irrigates daily life, coats all objects, dyes our clothing, bonds friends and provokes enemies" (Ouamara 111). Domino cannot leave his shirt behind. But he is not alone in being forced to accept his complicity with the violent regime since the audience must also take responsibility for the horror, learn to speak out and rid the country of "percepticide." After Domino leaves, the woman turns directly to the audience and with a big smile wishes them good luck as well. She turns her back and waves good-bye over her shoulder, the Hebrew chant increases significantly in volume, and the theatre is plunged into darkness. The woman/Algeria triumphs and warns those who dare to oppose her that they will be destroyed by their own actions.

In writing a play which puts the spotlight on the culture of terror in Algeria, Ouamara offers a strategy of reconstruction for the nation: lifting the veil which has made the civil war "invisible," reclaiming the aspects of Algerian culture confiscated and sabotaged by misguided and power-hungry forces, allowing Algerians to speak out, and embracing the potential of the country's future. Scarry argues that "pain and imagining are the 'framing events' within whose boundaries all other perceptual, somatic, and emotional events occur; thus, between the two extremes can be mapped the whole terrain of the human psyche" (Scarry 165). Imagination thus enables us to move forward, to create an artifact, an idea, a nation out of the wreckage caused by pain, torture, and war. Stora acknowledges the limitations of scholars to provide detailed and accurate records of the events in Algeria, because of continued censorship, and charges the artists to reveal what the journalists and the historians cannot. Ouamara embraces the challenge that expresses his faith that Algeria can reconstruct herself, as does the dead woman from her scattered body parts.

Notes

1. All translations from Ouamara's *La Défunte* are my own.
2. See the histories of Algeria written by Martin Stone and Benjamin Stora.

3. All translations of Stora's *La Guerre Invisible* are my own.

4. Playwrights such as Sophie Amrouche, Slimane Benaïssa, Aziz Chouaki, and Achour Ouamara and novelists such as Tahar Djaout, Assia Djebar, and Khalida Messaoudi are just a few who have looked at the trauma of the 1990s in their works.

5. All translations from Benaïssa's *Les Fils de l'amertume* are my own.

6. See Assia Djebar's *Le Blanc de l'Algérie* in which she creates an homage to the many intellectuals killed by the assassin's bullet.

7. See Le Sueur, Martinez, Naylor, Stone, and Stora.

8. All translations from Kacimi's *1962* are my own.

Works Cited

Aba, Noureddine. *Such a Great Hope, or The New Song of a Lost Country*. Trans. Richard Miller. *Playwrights of Exile: An International Anthology*. New York: Ubu Repertory Theater Publications, 1997.

Artaud, Antonin. "The Theatre and the Plague." *The Theatre and Its Double*. Trans. Mary Caroline Richards. New York: Grove Press Inc., 1958.

Benaïssa, Slimane. *Les Fils de l'amertume*. Carnières-Morlanwelz, Belgium: Lansman, 1997.

Djaout, Tahar. *The Last Summer of Reason*. Trans. Marjolijin de Jager. Foreword by Wole Soyinka. St. Paul, Minnesota: Ruminator Books, 2001.

Garner, Stanton B. *Bodied Spaces: Phenomenology and Performance in Contemporary Drama*. Ithaca: Cornell University Press, 1994.

Gilbert, Helen, and Joanne Tompkins. *Post-Colonial Drama: Theory, Practice, and Politics*. London and New York: Routledge, 1996.

Kacimi, Mohamed. *1962*. Arles: Actes Sud-Papiers, 1998.

Le Sueur, James D. *Uncivil War: Intellectuals and Identity Politics During the Decolonization of Algeria*. Philadelphia: University of Pennsylvania Press, 2001.

Martinez, Luis. *The Algerian Civil War: 1990–1998*. Trans. Jonathan Derrick. New York: Columbia University Press, 2000.

Naylor, Phillip C. *France and Algeria: A History of Decolonization and Transformation*. Gainesville: Florida University Press, 2000.

Orr, John, and Dragan Klaic. *Terrorism and Modern Drama*. Edinburgh: Edinburgh University Press, 1990.

Ouamara, Achour. *La Défunte. Nouveau théâtre algérien*. Paris: Marsa Editions, 2000.

Pierre, Andrew J., and William B. Quandt. *Algerian Crisis: Policy Options for the West*. New York: Carnegie Endowment for International Peace, 1996.

Scarry, Elaine. *The Body in Pain: The Making and Unmaking of the World*. New York: Oxford University Press, 1985.

Shue, Henry. "Torture." *Philosophy and Public Affairs* 7 (Winter 1978): 124–43.

Stone, Martin. *The Agony of Algeria*. New York: Columbia University Press, 1997.

Stora, Benjamin. *Algeria, 1830–2000: A Short History*. Trans. William B. Quandt. Ithaca: Cornell University Press, 2001.

_____. *La Guerre Invisible: Algérie, années 90*. Paris: Presses de Sciences Po, 2001.

Taylor, Diana. *Disappearing Acts: Spectacles of Gender and Nationalism in Argentina's "Dirty War."* Durham: Duke University Press, 1997.

About the Contributors

Natalya Baldyga is completing her doctorate in theatre history at the University of Minnesota–Twin Cities in Minneapolis. Her dissertation reconstructs moments of theatrical representation, traditionally presented as sites of national awakening in eighteenth-century Europe, through an investigation of how the actor's body is used to articulate cultural identity. She plans to continue her research and exploration of discourses of theatre and national identity in eighteenth-century Poland.

Karen Fricker is a Ph.D. candidate at the School of Drama, Trinity College, Dublin, writing about Robert Lepage and globalization. She is the editor of *Irish Theatre Magazine* and writes about the arts for *The Guardian* and *The Irish Times*, among others. Her work on Lepage and on contemporary Irish theatre has been published in book volumes and journals, including *Contemporary Theatre Review*.

Kiki Gounaridou teaches theatre studies at Smith College in Northampton, Massachusetts. Her books include *Euripides and Alcestis: Speculations, Simulations, and Stories of Love in the Athenian Culture*; *Madame La Mort and Other Plays by Rachilde*, and *Euripides' Hecuba: A Translation*. She is the associate editor of *Text and Presentation*, and the guest editor for the 2001 special issue on theatre translation of the translation journal *Metamorphoses*. She has also published numerous articles, book and performance reviews, and encyclopedia entries, and directed for the stage both in Europe and the United States.

Susan Haedicke is a professor of theatre history and performance studies in the Department of Theatre at the University of Maryland, College Park, and directs Inside French Theatre, an annual summer program in France since 1999. Susan Haedicke has published several essays on community-based theatre and co-edited a book, *Performing Democracy: International Perspectives on Community-Based Performance*, in 2001. In addition, she works as a professional dramaturg, most recently in Paris, France.

Scott Magelssen is assistant professor of theatre arts at Augustana College, Rock Island, Illinois, where he teaches theatre history and dramaturgy, advises the student-run experimental theatre group, and occasionally directs. His current research focuses on the performative and historiographic practices employed by outdoor "living history" museums in Europe and the United States.

David Pellegrini received his Ph.D. in theatre and performance studies from the University of Pittsburgh. He has published essays, reviews, and articles, and taught at Indiana University of Pennsylvania, Catholic University, and Eastern Connecticut State University. He has also directed numerous productions and several adaptations of classical and modern texts. His research on the Japanese avant-garde was funded by a grant from the Toshiba Foundation.

Carol Fisher Sorgenfrei is professor of theatre at UCLA, specializing in Japanese and cross-cultural performance. She is the associate editor of *Asian Theater Journal*, and the translator, director, and author of fifteen plays, including *Medea: A Nō Cycle*, based on the Greek myth and the kabuki-flamenco *Blood Wine, Blood Wedding*. Her book *Unspeakable Acts: Terayama Shûji and Postwar Japanese Theater* is forthcoming.

Gary Jay Williams is professor emeritus, Department of Drama, the Catholic University of America, Washington, D.C. His play *Our Moonlight Revels: A Midsummer Night's Dream in the Theatre* won the Theatre Library Association's George Freedley Award in 1998, and he is a former editor of *Theatre Survey*. His essay derives from his book in progress, *Prologue to an American Theatre*.

S.E. Wilmer is a fellow of Trinity College, Dublin, and former director of its School of Drama. His recent books include *Theatre, Society and the Nation: Staging American Identities*, 2002, and an edited volume, *Writing and Rewriting National Theatre Histories*, 2004.

Evan Darwin Winet is assistant professor of theatre at Macalester College in St. Paul, Minnesota. His articles on Indonesian theatre have appeared in *Theatre Symposium* and *The Journal of Dramatic Theory and Criticism*, as well as in the forthcoming anthology *Re/Writing National Theatre Histories*. He is currently translating several plays for a multi-volume anthology of Indonesian drama.

Patricia Ybarra is assistant professor in the Department of Theatre, Dance, and Speech at Brown University in Providence, Rhode Island. She has published articles and reviews in *Theatre Journal, Gestos,* and *Text and Presentation*. Her essay in this volume is part of her manuscript in progress, *Staging Tlaxcala*, which is a performance historiography of Tlaxcala, Mexico. She is also a director and dramaturg.

Index

www.ingramcontent.com/pod-product-compliance
Lightning Source LLC
Chambersburg PA
CBHW031128270326
41929CB00011B/1545